PLAYS

BY

GORDON DAVIOT

I

THE LITTLE DRY THORN

VALERIUS

DICKON

With a Foreword by

SIR JOHN GIELGUD

LONDON : PETER DAVIES

FIRST PUBLISHED 1953

Printed in Great Britain for Peter Davies Ltd
by Richard Clay and Company Ltd
Bungay Suffolk

CONTENTS

FOREWORD BY SIR JOHN GIELGUD
Page ix

THE LITTLE DRY THORN
Page 1

VALERIUS
Page 75

DICKON
Page 155

Application for permission to perform any play in this volume should be made to the Author's Agents:

Pearn, Pollinger and Higham Ltd.,
39-40 Bedford Street, London, W.C.2

PUBLISHER'S NOTE

THESE plays have been printed from typescripts left by the author after her death. A few obvious mistakes have been corrected and an occasional obscurity has been cleared up as well as was possible in the circumstances. It is hoped that they are now presented substantially as they would have been had Gordon Daviot lived to pass the proofs.

Besides the plays in the present volume there are a number of plays on modern themes which will appear in subsequent volumes.

The first Act of *The Little Dry Thorn* was published as a one-act play, under the title *Sara*, in *Leith Sands and Other Short Plays* (Duckworth 1946).

FOREWORD

I FIRST met Gordon Daviot in 1932, when I played the title role in *Richard of Bordeaux*. We were friends until her death last year—1952—and yet I cannot claim ever to have known her very intimately. I directed her play *Queen of Scots* in 1934, and she sent me *The Stars Bow Down* (I think in 1935), which I liked very much except for the last act, but this she was not willing to change. In 1936 she sent me *The Laughing Woman*. This too I greatly liked, but felt the part of Henri Gaudier was too young for me, and the character was subsequently created by the late Stephen Haggard while I was in America. These four plays of hers were the only ones with which I was intimately connected, and I never knew how many more she had written and put away, or whether she had planned others and failed to complete them, or, being dissatisfied, had afterwards destroyed them.

I persuaded Gordon to revise *Richard of Bordeaux* considerably between the time it was originally ' tried out ' (on two Sunday nights in 1932) and its West End production some months later, and, working in Inverness (where she always lived, nursing her father, who was an invalid until his death), she improved the play, by a few brilliant strokes, almost beyond recognition. Later, in attempting similar readjustments to *Queen of Scots*, which we worked on together while I was touring in *Richard*, the results were not equally successful. No doubt I was over-confident and pressed Gordon too hard, and it may be that she felt her original impetus had been spoiled by the re-writing—whatever the reasons, *Queen of Scots* was only a mild success, and I think Gordon felt it had been unluckily treated. Not that we ever openly disagreed, nor did she ever blame me for the comparative failure of the play, but I think she became resolved to trust her own instincts for the future, and not to allow too much interference with her manuscripts from those who sought to bring them to the stage.

Gordon Daviot was a strange character, proud without being arrogant, and obstinate, though not conceited. She was distressed by her inability to write original plots, especially when, on two occasions, she was unfairly accused of plagiarism. On the first occasion she was sued by the author of an historical novel about Richard the Second, but the case was settled out of court. These episodes distressed her greatly and made her over-sensitive—though it was difficult to tell what she really felt, since she did not readily give her confidence, even to her few intimate friends. She would rarely show her manuscripts to managers or actors, and she never read her plays to people. She was seldom to be seen in London. She shunned photographers and publicity of all kinds, and gave no interviews to the Press. I know that all the work she published under the name of Gordon Daviot was particularly dear to her, while her novels and other books, some of them published with great success under the name of Josephine Tey, she would refer to as her ' yearly knitting ', as if they were of little account to her. She made many friends in the theatre, especially among the lesser members of the companies who acted in her plays, and I would often hear how she had kept in touch with them in after years, but I think she had some slight distrust of the leading players, and feared they might become too autocratic and possessive in their friendships. She would sometimes write me long typed letters in her very individual style, but they were usually chatty and inconsequent. She went to the cinema twice a week in Inverness, and preferred to discuss films—their acting and direction—rather than plays, which she very seldom had an opportunity of seeing. I knew that she had worked as a physical-training instructor in a girls' school during her early years, but she never spoke to me of her youth or her ambitions. It was hard to draw her out. Once, motoring in France, I found her name in the visitors' book of a hotel at Chartres where I arrived late one night. But in the morning she had already left, in a coach-party that was touring the cathedral towns. She spoke very bitterly of the first World War, in which I fancy she must have suffered some bereavement, and she was depressed and unhappy when I met her while I was touring in Edinburgh during 1942, though a few days spent with me and Gwen Ffrangcon Davies, to whom she was devoted, seemed to cheer her up, and when we left she appeared to be almost her old self again.

Her sudden death last year was a great surprise and shock to all her friends in London. I learned afterwards that she had known herself to be mortally ill for nearly a year, and had resolutely avoided seeing anyone she knew. This gallant behaviour was typical of her and curiously touching, if a little inhuman too.

I find it difficult to criticise her writing, but I am sure it would please her greatly to know it is now to be given to a generation most of whom have not seen any of her plays acted. Naturally

I find *Richard of Bordeaux* her most successful piece of work, partly because it gave me such wonderful opportunities, and because it was in that play that I won my spurs, both as actor and director. *Richard* brought me confidence as well as success. It was said at the time that Gordon had seen me in Shakespeare's *Richard II* at the Old Vic in 1929, and had me in mind when she wrote her play. I do not know whether this is true or not. At any rate she improved on Shakespeare (from a commercial point of view at any rate) by giving Richard a sense of humour. This attractive quality, allied to a boyish charm in the scenes with his wife, and his gallant behaviour in standing up to the war-mongering nobles, helps to excuse, in Gordon's play, the effeminacy of his character and to condone the essential shallowness of his nature.

In *Dickon*, on the other hand (which I have read in this book for the first time), Gordon does not succeed, to my mind, in making the character of Richard III sufficiently convincing as a hero, and her good Richard does not begin to be an adequate substitute for the thrilling monster of Shakespeare's play. She was evidently obsessed by this idea, for she develops it at considerable length in her novel *A Daughter of Time* (written under the name of Josephine Tey). But here again she writes, rather sadly, that the idea of Richard's innocence is not an original one, and indeed it has been put forward by several other writers before and since.

Similarly in *Queen of Scots*, Gordon tried to refute the accepted popular convention, refusing to depict the *femme fatale* that other writers have suggested in dramatising Mary's story. Nor would she bring herself to make the character wholly sympathetic, the injured heroine and pawn of circumstance, who might have touched an audience by her distresses. She tried to take a middle way, neither praising nor blaming, and, though this treatment might have succeeded in a novel, I do not think she has given sufficiently powerful opportunities in her play for an actress, however brilliant, to carry off with complete success.

The women in the Daviot plays are strongest in their mother-instincts. I do not mean this sentimentally, but in Ann of Bohemia, Sophie Brzewska (in *The Laughing Woman*) and Sara (in *The Little Dry Thorn*), the characters are wives, mistresses and mothers more than they are lovers. I do not think Gordon understood either the intriguer or the harlot in Mary Stuart. Her heroes, too, are men who need to be protected, touching, romantic, boyish. These are the heroes she likes and understands. The villains and her older men are effective by contrast, but they are often sketchily drawn, and sometimes a little overdrawn. They are types rather than characters. On the other hand she is thoroughly at home with her simple people, peasants, servants, plain soldiers and the like. Her 'little scenes', in which such characters give background and colour to the main action, are admirably neat and act delightfully on the stage.

Gordon's plays, along with those of Clifford Bax (especially *The Rose Without a Thorn* and *The Venetian*), and Rudolph Besier's *The Barretts of Wimpole Street*, gave fresh life to the romantic theatre of their day. They were produced at a time when audiences were eager for such entertainment (the revival of Shakespeare's popularity in the West End was to come later). Shaw had led the way, of course, with his *Caesar and Cleopatra* and *Saint Joan*, both written in witty modern prose, but these plays of his are discursive, meaty and controversial. Gordon's plays are comparatively light and delicate. They have great charm, humour and delightful acting parts. They have some of the romantic glamour of the old historical melodramas (*The Scarlet Pimpernel*, *The Only Way*, *The Wandering Jew*), without the pseudo-period dialogue and fustian sentiment which the authors of those plays had inherited from the Victorian and Edwardian theatres.

It is sad to think Gordon will write no more, but I am very proud to be asked to write the Foreword to these plays of hers. We are not so rich in dramatic authors in this country that, when they are as talented and original as Gordon Daviot, we can afford to lose them. The theatre is poorer for an unique talent, and I for a dearly valued friend.

JOHN GIELGUD

September, 1953

CHARACTERS

SARA
HAGAR
LOT
MILCAH
ABRAHAM
LARSA
A WOMAN SERVANT
A MANSERVANT
A HERDSMAN'S SON
ISHMAEL
THE SCRIBE

THE LITTLE DRY THORN

ACT I

SCENE I

A house in Ur, in Mesopotamia, about 2000 B.C.

The house is built round a courtyard, the outer walls being windowless and all the rooms facing into the courtyard. In the room we are looking at two doors in the wall, R., are the only openings both for light and traffic. It is a ground-floor room (there is another storey), and the furnishings, though scanty as befits the climate, are rich.

It is late afternoon, but still very hot. The curtains are drawn across the openings to shut out the heat of the courtyard, and on a couch SARA *lies resting, like everyone else in Ur at this hour.*

She is a very beautiful woman, with intelligent eyes and an ironic mouth, no longer in her first youth, but of a type who will still be beautiful in old age.

One of the curtains is drawn aside, and HAGAR, *her maid, appears in the opening; lithe and graceful and little more than a child.*

SARA (*inquiring*) Hagar? It is not supper-time yet, surely? (*Through a yawn*) The sun is quite high.

HAGAR There is a visitor in the courtyard. The master's nephew.

SARA Lot? What does he want?

HAGAR He wants to speak with you.

SARA With me? Why not with Abraham?

HAGAR The master is not here.

SARA (*sharply*) Is Abraham not in his room?

HAGAR Instead of going to rest after lunch he went out, and he has not come back.

SARA In this heat? What can he be thinking of?

HAGAR In any case, it was for you that Lot asked.

SARA (*suddenly alarmed*) Has something happened? Something that Lot has come to——

HAGAR Oh, no, madam, no; it is not bad news. Lot is quite undisturbed. He is eating sweets from your silver dish.

SARA Lot would eat sweets if his mother were dying. (*She is nevertheless reassured*) Go and tell him that he may come in. (*As an afterthought*) His wife is not with him, is she?

HAGAR No, madam.

SARA Well, let us be thankful for small mercies.

[*Beginning to tidy dress and hair as* HAGAR *leaves.*]

Lot, indeed. With the sun still above the horizon and the town like a cauldron. It can't be to borrow money, or he would have asked for Abraham. And he can't have come to supper, or he would have brought that wife of his. And it can't be—can't be that anything has happened to Abraham. (*Refusing it*) No, it can't. If it were that, he would have rushed in and roused the house and taken charge, as befits a distressed heir. (*To herself in the mirror*) Sara, my dear, you are becoming deplorably bitter. (*Taking another glance*) It is at least comforting that if you are well on the way to being a shrew, you show no signs of becoming a hag. Being one of the best-looking . . . best-looking women in Ur is no small compensation for the daily trials of life, having Lot for a nephew, for instance.

[LOT *appears in the doorway; a good-looking young man with superficial charm and a pervading air of shiftiness.*]

Good-day to you, Lot. What has brought you so early of an evening? There is nothing wrong, I hope?

LOT Aunt Sara. I do apologise for this intrusion. I know it is intolerable of me to curtail your rest on so hot a day. Indeed, nothing would have induced me to such a course, if it had not been that I was so worried.

SARA Worried?

LOT So worried that I could not sleep this afternoon. To be truthful, I have not slept for nights, my mind was so troubled.

SARA Is something wrong with your business again?

LOT *My* business? Oh, no. Everything goes well there, thank the gods. What I am distressed about is my uncle.

SARA Is it that bill he backed for you?

LOT Aunt Sara! Can you never give me credit for a motive that is not personal?

SARA My dear Lot, I do most humbly apologise. But you come to me with your worry, and so I take it to be a personal one.

LOT It is a personal one. But not in that sense. It is about Abraham.

SARA And what worries you about Abraham? (*Her tone is natural, but guarded*)

LOT He is behaving strangely. So strangely that people are beginning to talk.

SARA (*ironically*) What a dreadful thing! And how is he strange?

LOT He seems not to know what is said to him. He passes life-long friends without a bow. If they call to him, he stares through them. Only this morning the Surveyor met him, and stopped to talk about the new drainage scheme they are planning. A big thing it is, and if it went through there would be a lot in it for Abraham. And what do you think Abraham said?

SARA What?

LOT He just stared at the Surveyor and said: 'Bricks. They are made from the mud, and they go back to the mud. What are bricks to build with?' Aunt Sara, do you think he is losing his mind?

SARA I see no signs of it. (*She is guarded and repressive*) He is a little absent-minded lately.

LOT Absent-minded! There is a point where absent-mindedness becomes criminal. Do you know that the King has suggested Abraham as being the ideal person to head the new committee for the improvement of social amenities? Do you know what that means? Do you know who will be on that committee? Representatives of the Court, of the Temple, of the Army, of Big Business, and of the landowners. And who would be the man to keep the balance between them, to play one interest off against another, until the whole city revolved round him, and every last bushel of wheat from the country and every last brick from the kiln was in his gift? Abraham! But if it is whispered that his mind is sick . . .

SARA His mind is not sick!

LOT (*paying no attention*) If they think his judgment no longer of account, there will be no place on that committee for Abraham. It is the chance of a lifetime. Of a thousand lifetimes. And Abraham is likely to throw it away by his odd behaviour.

SARA I don't see why it should be such a worry to *you*, Lot? What Abraham may lose will be his own loss. His oddity harms no one but himself.

LOT (*pouncing*) Then you admit that he is behaving oddly?

SARA (*smoothly*) Oh, yes. It does not need his *nephew* to tell me about my husband. And Abraham is more than my husband, Lot. He is my child too. He has not been well lately. He is absent-minded, and has bouts of rage and impatience. Not at all like himself. But I am hoping that when the cooler weather comes he may regain his old——

LOT By the time the cooler weather comes that place on the

committee will be filled. And unless my uncle controls himself, the place will not be filled by Abraham. That is why I came to see you; when he was not here, I wanted . . .

SARA How did you know he was not at home?

LOT Because he is walking up and down under the trees on the north terrace.

SARA (*relieved*) Well, let us be thankful for the trees, at least.

LOT He has been doing that all the afternoon, while even the hungry pariah dogs slept. So I took the chance of seeing you. I want you to use your influence with him. He is devoted to you; and there is no one in the whole Euphrates valley who has one half your charm and persuasive quality. He will listen to you.

SARA Listen to what?

LOT Tell him that he owes it to his family to be more careful. That there are great successes ahead of him, and that it behoves him to show a little more interest, to make some effort——

SARA For what?

[*As* LOT *pauses, at a loss for her meaning; without emphasis.*]

For what, I ask you? To gain a little fresh honour? He is already well thought of. To be the envy of the town? He has never cared for such things. To buy me a new jewel? I have already more than I can wear. Not a month goes by but he adds to the store. (*With a mixture of irony for the stupidity of man, and tenderness for his childishness*) It is his way of comforting me for having no child; for what reason should I prod my weary husband into——(*She pauses*)

[*The voices of* HAGAR *and another woman can be heard in the courtyard.*]

SARA I think that is your wife's voice.

LOT Yes, it does sound like Milcah.

SARA Did you tell her that you were coming here?

LOT No, I didn't think she would know. It is usually sundown before she wakens these days. She doesn't stand the hot weather well.

SARA (*lightly*) One of these days, Lot, your wife's curiosity will be the death of her.

[MILCAH *appears in the doorway escorted by* HAGAR, *who retires to bring refreshment.* MILCAH *is thin, plain, and plaintive.*]

Good evening, Milcah. Come into the cool and rest. It is not like you to be abroad before the streets are in shadow.

MILCAH I wondered where Lot had gone.

SARA Hagar, a cool drink for Milcah. Lot, I am afraid I offered you nothing. A little wine?

LOT Some whey, please.

MILCAH Why should Lot go rushing out of the house into the heat?

LOT I didn't rush.

MILCAH If I hadn't happened to waken up I should never have known.

SARA Would it have mattered?

MILCAH It matters that one's husband should have secrets from one, surely.

LOT There was no secret.

MILCAH Then why didn't you tell me you were coming here?

LOT It is not a matter of importance that I should visit my uncle's house.

MILCAH Perhaps not. But it is a sufficiently remarkable matter when you do it at an hour when you should be asleep at home.

SARA (*still lightly*) Are you questioning my virtue, Milcah?

MILCAH (*impatient*) Of course not. What I am questioning is Lot's motive. He isn't borrowing money again, is he?

LOT One would think that I was the only person since the Flood to borrow a little ready money.

SARA It was not business that brought your husband through the hot streets, Milcah, my dear. It was sheer altruism, wasn't it, Lot?

LOT (*not very comfortable under* SARA'S *eye*) Of course it was.

SARA He is worried about Abraham.

[*Enter* HAGAR *with drinks.*]

Here is your cold drink, Milcah.

MILCAH And can't he do his worrying under his own roof? (*Taking the drink*) Thank you. I am as worried as he is, but——

SARA You, too?

MILCAH No one likes having a relation who is rapidly becoming the talk of the town.

LOT Oh, Milcah, you exaggerate. She always exaggerates.

MILCAH Indeed I do not. My maid told me only yesterday that her brother's employer—he's a tanner in Eastgate—he told her brother that he had seen Abraham striding up the steps of the Ziggurat, talking to himself and followed by five small boys making fun of him. It's a fine thing when one of the principal citizens of this town——

SARA (*hearing someone come into the courtyard*) Hush!

[THEY *listen.* ABRAHAM'S *voice is heard in conversation with* HAGAR.]

That is Abraham now. Please don't mention these things to him. Whatever has led to his strangeness lately, I am sure that he is unaware of it. So don't suggest—talk of other things. You have come for an evening visit, that is all. Talk of the Surveyor's new scheme. The drainage affair. Anything——

[*Enter* ABRAHAM. *He is considerably older than his wife; unselfconscious and with manners of a charming simplicity. Fairly tall, but small-boned and graceful.*]

ABRAHAM (*in a deep, firm voice that is neither contentious nor unctuous, quite gay, in fact*) Hagar told me that we had guests. I am glad to see you, Lot. And you, Milcah. I hope you are both well. And I hope very much that you have not drunk everything that is cold in the house. (*Raising his voice*) Hagar!

[*As* HAGAR *answers, off, and comes running.*]

Some of that for me. How is business, Lot?

[*It is the usual conventional question.*]

LOT Not too bad for the time of year. Not bad at all.

SARA (*not accusing, but merely rallying*) Whatever time of year it may be for business, it is the wrong time of year to be out of doors in the afternoon.

ABRAHAM (*mildly*) Yes. It was stupid of me. I forgot what time of day it was.

LOT (*unable to contain himself*) You *forgot*?

ABRAHAM (*a little confused by the need of explanation*) Yes . . . I—I was thinking of other things.

MILCAH One would have thought that the sun would have reminded you.

SARA (*sotto voce*) Milcah, *please*!

ABRAHAM Yes, it's odd. I failed to notice the sun. (*As one making up his mind*) To be honest with you, things have been happening to me lately that I don't understand.

LOT You are not worried about business, are you?

ABRAHAM No, not at all. It is not worry which dogs me. It is something much stranger. I am pursued by a Voice.

SARA (*gently*) A voice?

ABRAHAM A Voice that says: What are you doing here? What are you doing with your life in this city, where your days slip by as unremarkable as beads on a string? Is it for this you were born? To live the years round in the beauty and comfort of Ur until you go back to the dust of your beginning? Get up! Get out of this place and see what there is for you elsewhere!

LOT (*half relieved*) But everyone feels like that in Ur at this time of year. There is not a man in the city but suffers from a weariness of the flesh and a desire to be elsewhere.

ABRAHAM You think it is the season that troubles me? I could find it in my heart to wish that it were; that my Voice was merely the breath of the hot wind. If that were so there would be respite to look forward to. As it is, I am pursued by the Voice even in the first cool of the early morning. When the city is at its loveliest, and my own desires can compass nothing more perfect than to be part of that loveliness for the rest of my life, even then the Voice is there, urging me to go.

SARA (*still gently*) To go where, Abraham?

ABRAHAM It doesn't say. All it says is that there is a great destiny for me elsewhere, and that I must leave Ur and follow it.

[*Enter* HAGAR, *with drink.*]

MILCAH But that is absurd. It must be some kind of sickness. Have you consulted the priests?

SARA (*prompting him, as one would a sick person or a child*) Hagar has brought your drink, dear.

[*He takes the cup, and* HAGAR *goes, but he seems unaware of it in his hand.*]

ABRAHAM I don't wonder that you think that. I thought that myself. For a whole winter and a spring I fought the Voice. I planned little ways to trick it. I invented new interests, designed new businesses to fill my life, and said to myself: Now there will be no spare moment for the Voice; I have shut it out; I have defeated it. (*Wearily*) But it was no use. The Voice was everywhere.

SARA Drink, my dear. You are tired.

ABRAHAM Yes, thank you. When the summer came it grew louder. It drowned the humming of the insects. It hammered at me when I walked through the street of the smiths. It talked, talked, talked among the palm leaves. It whispered in the dark as I lay sleepless at night.

LOT That is what is wrong. These sleepless nights. No man sleeps well in this weather; and lack of sleep does queer things to a man. Now, I know a first-class apothecary who can give you a draught that is as nearly a knock-out blow as——

MILCAH You and your apothecaries. I know a woman who will give you a charm for half the money. A quite infallible charm. You tie it round your neck, and turn it over three times, say: 'Thanks be to Nannar for night and sleep and the moon'—and you are asleep.

ABRAHAM It is kind of you to suggest; to want to help. But I shall need neither charm nor apothecary.

LOT But you must have sleep or you will be really ill. And we cannot afford to have you ill.

ABRAHAM (*calmly confident*) I shall sleep tonight.

LOT How do you know?

ABRAHAM Because I have said 'yes' to my destiny.

SARA (*more puzzled than alarmed*) What do you mean, Abraham?

ABRAHAM I would have told you after supper tonight. It happened today when I was walking on the highest terrace of the Ziggurat. In the town, when the Voice pursued me I used to feel trapped. I used to hurry round street corners, and in and out of alleys, trying to escape it. This was Ur, my city, and I didn't want to leave it. But today, from the high terrace, I could see the far distance, like a promise. *That* was where my Voice bade me go, and once I could see it, it was not so frightening. Ur was, after all, only a small thing in a very wide world. And somewhere in that world was the country of my destiny. 'Go out,' the Voice said, 'and when you come into the country you will know it. To your children, and your children's children, I have given that country, and the whole world will be the richer for it.'

MILCAH (*scandalised*) 'I!' Who do you think the Voice is?

ABRAHAM I think it is God. (*He speaks as one having come to a conclusion*)

LOT Which God?

ABRAHAM I don't know. This is the only one that has ever spoken to me.

[*The sentence is unaccented. It is not 'to* me*'; nor even 'ever* spoken'*. There is no emphasis. It is a simple statement.*]

MILCAH It is not the custom of the gods to speak except through a priest. It is much more likely to be a demon.

LOT Milcah is right. It is not likely that a god would advise so strange a course. You had better consult the temple authorities.

ABRAHAM I have no need to consult anyone. (*Emending*) Any authority. (*He has remembered his wife*) Sara. (*He sounds a little uncertain now*) You have said nothing.

SARA What is there for me to say? That I have faith in your Voice? What faith can one have in a Voice whose promises are nonsense?

ABRAHAM Why should they be nonsense?

SARA The country is for your children's children, isn't it? Have you forgotten that you are a childless man?

ABRAHAM (*who has quite genuinely forgotten*) The Voice says that it will be so. And I believe it.

SARA (*in a now-I-think-about-it tone*) It is possible, of course. It was stupid of me not to have seen it. You could put me away and take another wife. A wife who——

ABRAHAM (*angry*) I shall never have any wife but you. If my God gives me a country, he gives it to you too. And it is to your children that he will preserve it.

[*It sounds almost as if he were giving notice to whom it might concern.*]

SARA Are you *bargaining* with your Voice?

ABRAHAM I believe what it says. I believe in my destiny; and I have no destiny apart from you. When I go out from Ur you come with me; and together we shall see the promise come true.

LOT Leave Ur! I think you must be insane. Where would you go?

ABRAHAM I don't know. I have not thought about it yet.

LOT Where do you think there is a country for you to inherit? Every square yard in all the thousand miles from Armenia to the sea, every inch that will grow a blade of grass, is the property of someone.

MILCAH Perhaps he plans to live with the goats among the mountains.

ABRAHAM No. I am no starving prophet. My inheritance is a rich one.

LOT (*pricking up his ears*) Rich?

ABRAHAM I have told you. There is a great future for me

and those belonging to me. Come with me, Lot, and share in it.

LOT And what would I do with my business? Make a gift of it to the priests?

ABRAHAM There is nothing in my Voice which says that we must go out penniless. You could do what I am going to do. One share to the poor, one to the town, one to the temple—they do some good, I think—(*He is not too sure about this, but old habit is too much for him*)—and one in your purse.

MILCAH Do you seriously mean that you are going to drag Sara away from all the people she knows, from all her friends, and the position she has made for herself in society, to go trailing round the world looking for a country that you don't even know the name of?

ABRAHAM I am not dragging Sara anywhere. The promise is for her too. Everything I ever had was Sara's. This is hers too.

MILCAH It is generous of you to give her something she doesn't want.

SARA You mean well, Milcah, but I don't need you to defend me. This is between Abraham and me.

MILCAH Well, we may as well go home and let you have it out with him. It will soon be supper time, anyhow.

LOT I can't believe that you really mean to do this—this absurd thing. I have always looked up to you as a shrewd and far-seeing man. It is incredible——

ABRAHAM And what makes you think I have ceased to be far-seeing?

[*As* LOT *hesitates at that, always afraid he may miss something.*]

A view that embraces the whole earth and its possibilities can hardly be termed parochial. It is you, Lot, whose sight is short. I offer you a principality, but you prefer the security and comfort of a steady income in Ur.

MILCAH (*tartly*) You come home, Lot. You know very well that if you once begin to think you are missing something there is no folly you are not capable of. (*To* ABRAHAM) Have you told anyone of your plans? I mean, is there any reason why we shouldn't tell people?

ABRAHAM Until now I have never mentioned my Voice to anyone. No one, that is, except my father.

SARA (*in the tone of one enlightened*) Ah!

LOT Terah! Don't tell me that you are thinking of taking Terah with you!

ABRAHAM Of course. Why not? Where I go, my father goes.

LOT But the old man is an invalid. Bed-ridden.

ABRAHAM There are such things as litters. I shall never come back to Ur. I could hardly leave my father to be tended by strangers.

MILCAH But Lot and I could take him. That would be better for him than being jolted all over the Euphrates valley.

ABRAHAM I have an idea that Lot may be coming with us.

MILCAH Lot!

LOT Not I. Can you see me arranging my whole life at the bidding of a Voice?

ABRAHAM So far you have had to obey a great many voices. The voice of the priests, interpreting their god according to their fancy or to the needs of the temple. The voice of the King—ever changing as kings come and go. The voice of the law—new and different with each new faculty. A hundred voices; competing, threatening, spelling confusion. I have finished with that. I have one voice to obey, and what I do is between me and my God.

MILCAH (*with decision*) Lot, come home.

SARA (*with the pressing claim of hospitality*) We can give you supper. It is onion soup, and cold meat with cucumber.

MILCAH Thank you, but I know that you want to talk to Abraham. And anyhow, Lot shouldn't have cucumber.

SARA They are just garnish. He doesn't have to eat it.

MILCAH If there are cucumbers there, Lot will eat them.

[*To* SARA, *as the* TWO MEN *take leave of each other.*]

I am sorry that I came so unceremoniously. I didn't know you were in trouble. I was angry because Lot had sneaked out without telling me. Good-night. I shall get my 'charm' woman to give me something to alter Abraham's mind. It is wonderful what she can do with a few bits and pieces. So perhaps all this will blow over. But if it doesn't, remember that we shall be happy to look after old Terah. I like the old man. He was the first to say a kind word to me when I came into this family. And of course Lot is terrified of him; which would be very useful. Are you ready, Lot?

LOT Yes, I'm coming. Good-night, Aunt Sara—and my sympathy.

SARA Good-night to you both. Good-night.

[THEY *go.*]

[*There is a short pause.*]

ABRAHAM She said: 'You will want to talk to Abraham.' (*He waits to hear what she has to say*)

SARA (*avoiding the main point*) Would it not have helped you to tell me about the Voice? Were you so little sure of me?

ABRAHAM If I could not believe, myself, how could I expect belief from you?

SARA It was not belief I meant, but sympathy in your trouble.

ABRAHAM (*quickly*) But you believe now? You believe that my Voice is a true and good thing.

SARA (*slowly*) I believe that you have to leave Ur.

ABRAHAM (*sadly*) You think that I am possessed.

SARA I think you cannot help yourself.

ABRAHAM In other words, I am a madman. And what has sent me mad, do you think?

SARA I don't know. Does it matter?

ABRAHAM Matter?

SARA Mad or sane, you are Abraham, and my husband. And I will go with you out of Ur tomorrow morning if that is what you wish.

ABRAHAM (*wistfully*) I wish you believed.

SARA (*gently reproving*) It is a little greedy of you to want belief *too*.

ABRAHAM (*following his own thought*) If I had told you tonight, as I had planned, when we were alone, you might have believed.

SARA No one who has not heard your Voice for himself could believe, Abraham. You must see that. Did Terah believe when you told him?

ABRAHAM (*seeing her point*) No. No, I suppose he didn't. He just listened. (*Remembering something*) Why did you say 'Ah!' when I said that I had told Terah about the Voice?

SARA Because I knew then why the old man had looked with pity at me when I gave him his broth this morning.

ABRAHAM Pity? Why should he pity you?

SARA Because he knew that I should have no defence against you.

ABRAHAM Defence!

SARA We will follow you out of Ur, Terah and I, because we love you. We have no ear for your Voice, but your way is our way, and your God our God. Come to supper.

CURTAIN

SCENE 2

The Scene is the same.

In the middle of the floor is a leather trunk, and round it are strewn a great collection of garments of all sorts. SARA *is kneeling by the trunk, doing the selecting and packing.* HAGAR *is standing by, sorting and folding.*

SARA Hagar, where is that red frock with the ruching at the neck and the long fringe?

HAGAR You gave it to Basha.

SARA *I* did? Basha who?

HAGAR The herb-woman whose son ran away with the dancing-girl.

SARA I wish I had some control over my impulses. Why did I do that?

HAGAR You said it would be a great comfort to her.

SARA (*ironic*) And was it, do you know? (*She is still busy with the things round her*)

HAGAR Oh, yes. She sold it to the butcher's wife for her daughter's wedding, and went to see her cousin in the country with the money. Her cousin gave her a whole new outfit and lent her enough money to open that new shop in Small Lane.

SARA (*with a faint dash of contempt in her indulgent amusement*) Is there anything in this town that you don't know about, Hagar? Well, I'm glad it did some good, but it's a pity.

HAGAR It is, indeed. I was planning to impress Jabin one day in that frock. When I am looking extra nice he always adds half a shekel to the discount when I pay the bill.

[SARA *pauses to smile up at her maid, busy and unselfconscious, and is about to resume her own activity, when she pauses to look back at the girl, consideringly.*]

SARA (*discovering it for the first time*) You are growing quite beautiful, Hagar. (*Ironic; half to herself*) It's as well for you that I love you.

HAGAR (*missing the point of the latter sentence*) You think I am pretty? (*She stands, the garment she is holding clasped to her, naive and pleased*) Really?

SARA (*unconscious of the girl; slowly*) Very attractive. (*Recollecting herself; going back to her work*) When I think of the skinny brat I bought in the market-place for half the cost of a good meal, I can hardly believe it.

HAGAR Why *did* you buy me?

SARA (*tossing one garment after another at each suggestion*) God knows. Because I like Egyptian women's small bones. Because I wanted a daughter. Because you looked hungry. Because I had nothing to do between breakfast and lunch that day. Because—(*pausing to sit back on her heels and sniff the air loudly*) Go and see what the cook is burning *now*.

[*As* HAGAR *is going*.]

If it is the sauce, tell him he will leave this house tomorrow.

HAGAR He won't care. He knows that we are going to the promised land.

SARA Where?

HAGAR To the land that has been promised to the master.

SARA (*going back to her work*) Oh.

[HAGAR *goes*.]

(*Stares after her, and comes back to the garments on the floor—slowly*) Very beautiful. And young. (*Shaking the thought from her mind, rising and holding up a frock against herself*) I wonder what fashions will be like in the ' promised land '. Quite horrible, I have no doubt. (*She drops the frock, and produces a sandal from the rubbish. She proceeds to look for its mate*)

[*Enter* HAGAR.]

HAGAR It is the sauce. He says he cannot cook because he is ill with grief at parting from us.

SARA The grief is not mutual.

HAGAR His eyes are blind with tears, he says. And Larsa says would it be convenient for you to see him for a moment.

SARA (*holding up the odd sandal*) Where, do you imagine, is the other of this?

HAGAR That is the one the puppy ate.

SARA Oh, yes, I remember. What does Larsa want?

HAGAR He wouldn't dream of telling *me*.

SARA I wish you and Larsa didn't quarrel so much.

HAGAR Oh, we don't *quarrel*. It is just that he despises me and I abominate him.

SARA And I suppose that conduces to a friendly atmosphere.

HAGAR I don't see that a Syrian from Damascus is any better than an Egyptian, even if he *is* free. Just because I was bought in the market-place doesn't make me——

SARA (*with less than her usual tolerance*) Hagar, you talk too much. You have your place in this household, and Larsa has his. There is no question of comparison or competition. Tell

Larsa to come in. (*Raising her voice without turning her head and going on with her sorting*)

[HAGAR *goes.*]

And you can say to the cook that if the sauce is not too bad he might try pouring it into another pan and adding some wine.

[*Almost before she has finished talking,* LARSA *appears in the doorway. He is young, earnest, attractive, intelligent, unselfconscious, and physically well-made. He has grown up in the household and is now the steward. His relation to* SARA *and her husband is, through long intimacy, almost that of a cousin.*]

Come in, Larsa. Did you ever see such a mess? It is very odd having to say goodbye to one's clothes. One is used to giving them away, but not to leaving them behind. One *grieves* for them. (*She is laughing at herself again*) What did you want to say to me?

LARSA I want you to speak to Abraham for me.

SARA Yes, if it is something that I can do.

LARSA You are the only person who can always persuade him into changing his mind.

SARA (*smiling at him; amending*) Persuade him that *he* has changed his mind, you mean.

LARSA (*agreeing with a faint smile to the amendment*) Well?

SARA And what do you want me to alter his mind about?

LARSA About my going *with* you. Make him see, *please* make him see that it is right for me to go. That it is best for all of us.

SARA Best? Not best for you, surely, Larsa?

LARSA Yes, for me.

SARA What could be better than an appointment to the royal household?

LARSA Being part of the family I grew up with.

SARA Abraham obtained you that appointment so that you might be settled for life.

LARSA So that I might be off his conscience. He has a very active conscience.

SARA Oh, come! That is——

LARSA He can say: Larsa was educated in my household and grew up in it like a son and I love him. It is true that I lop him off like a branch that spoils the look of the tree, but have I not seen to it that he will have bread, honour, and fine raiment as long as he lives?

SARA And is that such a little thing? It is surely better than wandering through the world at the bidding of a Voice. (*In spite of her, the faintest tinge of irony creeps into her tone*)

LARSA I ask nothing better than to go wandering.

SARA Believe me, it hurts Abraham to leave you—it is like tearing off a limb—but he thinks it right. As you remarked, he has an uncomfortable conscience. Because you are not of his blood, there is no promise for you, and he will not be responsible for taking you from the good things that are naturally yours.

LARSA The *good things*. Sauce to my meat and servants at my call. A percentage for today and a pension for tomorrow. Are these the good things? *You* know better than that. Life must have purpose and savour. What savour and what purpose would life have for me deprived of all I love?

SARA But you are young, Larsa. You will make new friends. (*It is apparent from the slight effort in her voice that she does not relish the prospect*) And a new life for yourself. Presently you will marry. (*With an effort to be light-hearted and practical*) I have thought that the Third Secretary's daughter—the youngest one—would——

LARSA (*interrupting; repressive*) I can marry equally well a thousand miles from here and ten years from now. As for friends, do you imagine that any friend can be to me what you and Abraham are? You say that it is like tearing off a limb to part with me. For me, it is like having my heart cut out.

[*There is a little silence. Presently, in a new, practical, and somehow childish tone:*]

Besides, what is Abraham going to do without me?

SARA (*relaxing—smiling a little*) There is that. But you can hardly expect me to use that as an argument.

LARSA (*agreeing*) No.

SARA (*more to herself than to him—incautiously*) I suspect—— (*She stops*)

LARSA You suspect what?

SARA No.

LARSA (*amiably*) Shall I tell you what you were going to say?

[*As* SARA *does not answer.*]

You suspect that part of his reason for leaving me behind is to prove to himself how little he needs me.

SARA (*eyeing him*) It occurs to me for the first time that he may be right in leaving you.

LARSA Why?

SARA You know us both too well. (*Dropping her teasing and taking to sheer light-heartedness*) You are a great comfort to me, Larsa; Hagar never knows what I am talking about.

LARSA She is a poor thing, the Egyptian. It would be well if you left *her* behind.

SARA And do my own hair half across Asia? Certainly not.

LARSA Someday she will be a grief to you. You will see.

SARA I wish you didn't quarrel so much, you two.

LARSA I don't ' quarrel ' with slaves.

SARA She may be a slave, but she is a charming child, and you ought to have more patience with her. It will not add to the gaiety of life to have you glaring at each other all the way to Babylon.

LARSA Am I going to Babylon?

SARA And beyond, I hope.

LARSA You will speak to Abraham?

SARA Of course. But I can promise nothing; you understand that.

LARSA (*happy*) If you speak to him, you can persuade him.

SARA I did not persuade him to stay in Ur.

LARSA (*confidently*) You did not try.

SARA (*considering him*) So you know that too.

LARSA You could have persuaded him. If you had cared less for his happiness. It is because you understand how precious happiness is that I believe you will not stand by and see me deprived of mine.

SARA I shall do my best, Larsa. But it will not be easy. He was very pleased with that Household appointment. And moreover, he longs to have you with us; and Abraham always suspects that something he wants very much must be wrong. However——

[*As* LARSA *begins to thank her.*]

What arguments have you wasted on him?

LARSA (*with a ghost of a rueful smile*) I tried to persuade him how useful I would be to him.

SARA (*agreeing with his implied comment*) Yes, that was wrong.

LARSA He was so busy doing the right thing by *me* that he had no ears for that. By the time I noticed my mistake he had my future all settled.

SARA I see. Well, I shall——

[*There is the noise of voices off;* HAGAR *and* MILCAH *in conversation as they approach.*]

That sounds like Milcah.

[HAGAR *shows* MILCAH *in, or rather, does so technically, but* MILCAH's *impulsive entrance leaves her no time for any announcement. She pauses a moment to listen to* MILCAH's *reason for coming and then goes.*]

Good-day to you, Milcah.

MILCAH (*plunging straight into it*) Sara, you *must* talk to Lot. You are the only person in the whole Euphrates valley who can—how are you, Larsa?—who can persuade a little common sense into his silly head.

LARSA I think it is time I got back to the steward's room.

MILCAH Don't go on my account. It is no secret that I'm married to the biggest fool in Ur.

[LARSA *goes, but she does not even notice it.*]

MILCAH You *must* talk to him, Sara. Tell him that he is being——

SARA (*patient and kind*) Sit down, Milcah, sit down; and compose yourself. Whatever is wrong I am quite sure that it is not as bad as you are thinking at this moment. Sit down and let me give you something.

MILCAH (*sitting down*) No, I couldn't swallow anything. I am much too—— (*She catches sight of a familiar garment*) Oh, I remember that blue frock; you got it for Mimi's wedding—much too upset. You must persuade him, Sara.

SARA But what has Lot done?

MILCAH It is not what he *has* done, it is what he proposes to do.

SARA And what is that?

MILCAH He has decided that he must go with Abraham.

SARA Oh.

MILCAH For the last week he has been mooning about like a lost dog. I thought he was sickening for something, and I went to my woman and got three separate charms for him, and not one did any good, not even the one I gave her my topaz bracelet for. And now this morning he broke the truth to me. He wants to go with Abraham. As if it wasn't absurd enough that one family should be uprooted without any reason! You will speak to him, won't you?

SARA Persuade him against it, you mean? But——

MILCAH Now don't say 'Why?' *You* don't want Lot with you any more than I want him to go; so it is in both our interests to——

SARA Why should I not want him?

MILCAH (*with finality*) Nobody wants Lot.

SARA Oh, nonsense. He is quite popular with his own crowd.

MILCAH Oh, them! Of course he is. They love him. He shoots dice worse than anyone in Ur. Lot practically supports them, if you must know. They send their sons to school in Babylon on what they win from Lot. He can never bear to stop in case the next throw will be a good one. *That* is why he is crazy enough to think of going with Abraham, in case Abraham stumbles over a gold-mine, or is made King of Assyria, or something equally unlikely.

[*Enter* ABRAHAM.]

ABRAHAM (*gaily—he is very happy these days*) What is this about Abraham and a gold-mine?

SARA Milcah has come to say that Lot is going with us.

MILCAH (*amending*) *Proposes* to go with you.

ABRAHAM So! (*Genuinely glad*) Well! That *is* good news, *very* good news.

MILCAH *Good* news! *Good news!* My husband has a fit of insanity and you are glad about it? You don't imagine for a moment that he believes in that god of yours, do you? That he wants to go with you for the love of it? Not he. But the thought of what he may be missing if this turns out to be a good thing—that eats him like a toothache.

ABRAHAM (*mildly*) But if this, as you say, 'turns out to be a good thing' surely you too would be glad to share?

MILCAH I have put up with Lot's gambling for ten years. He has gambled with my housekeeping money, with my dress allowance, with the money my parents sent to buy a silver cup when Timna was born, and with anything else that came handy, but he is *not* going to gamble with my whole future!

[LOT *appears in the doorway.*]

LOT (*coldly*) They can hear you out in the street, Milcah. She has been going on like that ever since daybreak. You would think that I was proposing to drag her out to die in the desert.

MILCAH And how do you know you are not? Does anyone know where we are going? Or where we shall end up?

ABRAHAM Oh, come, Milcah. You women are always complaining that your life is nothing but a daily round. Now is the chance——

MILCAH In a round you at least come back to the same place. You know where you are. If you go out endlessly in a straight line you can end up anywhere; in a jungle being devoured by animals, perhaps. (*She begins to mop her eyes*)

SARA My good Milcah, we are not going hunting wild beasts.

MILCAH How do you know? If Abraham's god says: Hunt wild beasts, we'll be hunting wild beasts.

SARA Nonsense. Abraham's god is a kind and sensible one.

MILCAH In that case he won't want to have anything to do with Lot. And neither do I. I shall leave him, that is what I shall do. I shall take back my dowry—the law says that I may —and go and—(*struck by a sudden suspicion*) You haven't gambled with my dowry, by any chance?

LOT (*sullenly*) No. Your dowry is safe.

MILCAH (*resuming*) —and go and live as a widow in one of those little houses by the park.

SARA (*with a mendacious air of considering*) Well, I have always thought all-women parties very dull.

MILCAH Of course they are. What are you talking about?—parties?

SARA If you lived alone you could have no men in your house.

[*As this gives* MILCAH *pause; sitting down by her.*]

Come, Milcah, you are distressing yourself without real cause. What is so frightening about going out to see the world? Going out in good company, with food and drink and money for lodging, to see what new glories the earth holds.

MILCAH I don't want any glory that is further than a mile from the centre of Ur. (*But in spite of the stubborn words the tone is less certain*)

SARA Personally, I look forward to seeing the fashions of other cities.

MILCAH (*pausing in the mopping of her eyes*) Fashions? Shall we be going to cities? (*Her glance goes to* ABRAHAM)

ABRAHAM (*amused*) It would be difficult not to. The roads of the world are studded with cities.

MILCAH (*considering it*) Oh. That is different, of course. If we were to live in civilised places. I thought perhaps your god would want you to build a temple in some remote place and spend your life serving it. You don't think that something like that is likely to happen?

ABRAHAM I am commanded to seek out a new country and to found a family. I think that will take me all my time. And that it is most unlikely that I shall turn into a temple-builder.

SARA (*comforting*) So you see, Milcah, it is not so alarming. It is an adventure, not a tragedy.

MILCAH (*not maliciously—she is incapable of malice—but with her usual obtuseness and self-absorption*) It's all very well for you; you have no children. How are those daughters of mine to find husbands if we go wandering up and down the world? What standing will they have, or what friends? Am I to have them marrying a mule-driver?

LOT Oh, give me patience! Our daughters are still eating bread-and-milk—one has no teeth yet—and you are thinking of husbands for them. They may not even live to grow up——

MILCAH Lot!

LOT (*genuinely penitent*) Oh, I am sorry, Milcah. That was callous, but it was not meant so. You exasperate me when you invent difficulties——

MILCAH (*mollified*) And you exasperate me with real ones. (*After a pause*) Lot, if you must go with Abraham, couldn't it be for just so long? If one could set bounds to the thing, it might not be so dreadful, don't you see? Half a year, or a year, or even two years. But not just—without end or plan.

ABRAHAM Yes, why not? Why not come with us and see how you like it? You are free to come back to Ur at any time. (*He includes* LOT *in this*) Indeed, I shall *send* you back if at any time you want to go. Provide the transport for you. Is that good enough?

MILCAH (*wearily*) Oh, you are a good man, Abraham; no one doubts it. And you would treat us well. I just wish I saw some sense in all this. It is a very odd proceeding, and no amount of kindness, or argument, or talk of adventure makes it any less odd. We have a nice home here, and friends, and a position, and fine gay society in the best of taste—not vulgar like Babylon. Why can't Lot be content with what we have instead of hankering after riches a thousand miles away? (*Preparing to go*) However, perhaps nothing will come of it all, and Lot will grow discouraged and come back to live here.

He grows discouraged very soon. (*Seeing the expression on the faces of the others*) I expect it is unkind of me to hope for a bad end to your plans.

[*To* ABRAHAM *and for once aware of other people in relation to their own lives and not in relation to her.*]

It means a great deal to you, doesn't it? This Promise?

ABRAHAM Yes. A very great deal.

MILCAH You mustn't think that I am just being selfish and tiresome. For you it is exciting; you have the Promise but for me it is nothing but being torn up by the roots. (*Her eyes going to the garments round the trunk on the floor*) For me, and for Sara too, I expect. All those lovely things that she will never wear again.

SARA There will be others. Finer ones.

MILCAH (*unheeding; her eyes on the clothes*) That yellow silk; that was for the reception at the Syrian Ambassador's. And that silver thing—Oh, I must go home. If I begin to cry now I shall cry so much that I shan't be able to go through the streets with my face. I'll go home and cry in peace. (*She makes for the door*)

SARA (*going to the door with her*) Yes, Milcah, do that. A very satisfying occupation and very clearing to the head. Once you have got that over, you'll be surprised how much interest you will find in your new future.

MILCAH Goodbye, Sara; you are very kind. (*Over her shoulder to* ABRAHAM) Goodbye, Abraham; forgive me if I have been silly but I am so very miserable. And I gave away my topaz bracelet to my woman for a charm, and it did no good whatever——

[*The remembrance of this is the last straw and she begins to cry again.* SARA *is about to go out with her when* LOT *detains her and takes her place.*]

[MILCAH *goes.*]

LOT (*to* ABRAHAM *and* SARA) I'll go with her. You must not mind her; she is upset.

SARA (*with a shade of tartness*) It is natural that she should be. It is not every day that a woman is told that her home is to be broken up.

ABRAHAM Goodbye, Lot. I am glad that you decided to come with us.

LOT Goodbye.

[*Exit* LOT.]

ABRAHAM Poor Lot!

SARA Poor Milcah! (*She begins to go back to her packing*)

ABRAHAM (*watching her*) I suppose that for a woman it *is* more difficult to leave behind the familiar things.

[*He picks up a sandal and considers it; it is a fragile thing, not meant for the roads of the world.*]

I have asked a great deal of you, Sara.

SARA You have asked still more of Larsa. Asked too much, I think.

ABRAHAM Larsa? I have not asked anything of Larsa, surely?

SARA To leave things behind is difficult. But to be left behind must be a grief unbearable. (*She is still busy with her things, not looking at him*)

ABRAHAM (*surprised*) But, Sara, he is not a child, to cry at being left. I have obtained him one of the best appointments in Ur. He has a great future in front of him.

SARA (*agreeing, apparently preoccupied*) Oh, yes, I know. I have no doubt you are right.

[ABRAHAM, *left in the air by her agreement, cogitates for a moment in a disconcerted silence.*]

Did you see the man about the camels? Did he think ten would be enough?

ABRAHAM I have not seen him yet.

[*After another pause.*]

You think that Larsa's hurt is more than a passing thing? That he will be—scarred by it, so to speak.

SARA (*considering a problem and a frock together*) I don't know that scarred is the right word. Maimed, I should say.

ABRAHAM (*beginning to protest*) Oh, Sara, I refuse to——

SARA (*cheerfully*) But a great many people have lost legs for their own good, and found life at a hobble fair enough.

ABRAHAM (*who is simple but no dolt; catching* SARA *by a hand and pulling her to her feet to face him; amused*) What *is* all this? Is there a plot to work on my feelings?

[SARA *laughs a little at him, and her charm, so close to him and so potent, absorbs him.*]

You still want Larsa to come with us?

SARA What matters is that Larsa wants to come. And that snug little pigeon-hole in the royal establishment is so much poison. You had better let him come, my dear.

ABRAHAM (*with good-humoured exasperation*) Oh, very well. Though I shall have a fine time explaining to the Chief Secretary that I don't want the appointment after all. It took me five weeks and half a year's income to work that.

SARA You meant well, my dear. You always mean well.

[*It is doubtful to the listener whether this second sentence is the stronger form of the first that it would appear on the surface.*]

ABRAHAM (*contemplating her*) My beautiful Sara, what have I done to deserve the years we have had together?

SARA (*covering her bone-deep grief with lightness, as befits the moment*) Anyone but you would have divorced your beautiful Sara years ago, and had eight children by some fine fertile wench.

ABRAHAM I am content to wait.

SARA (*abruptly ; her lightness dying on her*) Wait?

ABRAHAM I believe in the promise.

SARA Did the promise make mention of Sara?

ABRAHAM (*stubborn and angry*) I tell you, I have no life apart from you. My God knows that. He would not promise fine things in which you had no share, for they would cease on the instant to be fine. We are one person, you and I, and the promise is for us both!

SARA (*gently, with recovered poise*) Very well, my dear; you have belief enough for two. I can borrow a little now and then without your missing it.

ABRAHAM (*confidently*) Some day you too will hear the Voice and then all will be well.

SARA Who knows? Who knows?

[*But there is no echo of his confidence. She puts her cheek against his in a caress, to make up for the barrenness of her response.*]

CURTAIN

ACT II

SCENE I

The interior of a tent near Bethel in Syria, some years later.

Bethel is in the high country to the west of the Dead Sea, but the tent is no nomad affair of black goatskin. It is hung with silk and floored with hide, and its shape and proportions might be those of any room in a town. Indeed, what we are looking at is merely one portion of the tent; there are at least two more rooms of the same kind adjoining.

It is the hour of siesta, and the room is darkened and quiet.

On separate couches are resting SARA *and* MILCAH. *Presently a curtain L. over the tent mouth is drawn aside, letting in the light, and* HAGAR *comes in with a small tray bearing cups and a jug. She sets it down on a low table near* MILCAH*—she being the guest—and goes out quietly R., leaving the curtain drawn back.*

MILCAH *is the first to stir. She moves over from her side to her back with a pettish movement.*

MILCAH Another day over in this waste of boredom! (*She yawns miserably*) Are you awake, Sara?

SARA (*who has not been asleep—mildly*) Yes, I'm awake.

MILCAH (*not to* SARA, *merely continuing her grumbling*) The only thing that tells me I'm alive is the fact that my foot is asleep. What a life! Nothing to do till bedtime but eat and sit around. (*She yawns again*) When I remember that once upon a time the fun of the day *began* at sundown, my very skin creeps with weariness. I sometimes——

SARA (*without anger, but as one at last saying something that has been in her mind for a long time*) Milcah, I have listened to your complaint all the way up the Euphrates, through the long months in Kharran, on the hilly way to Damascus——

MILCAH Damascus! There was a town! Why couldn't we have stayed in Damascus, and——

SARA All the long road south to Goshen and back again; day after day the same complaint; and I am very tired of it.

MILCAH (*swinging her feet to the floor and sitting on the edge of her couch*) Now don't *you* go back on me, Sara. You are the only comfort I have. No one else listens to me. I used to depend on old Terah for sympathy—*he* didn't like being dragged away from his home any more than I did. He would be alive now, I don't doubt, if he had been left in peace in the place he was born in. Alive for another twenty years, maybe; poor old man. We would grieve together by the hour in Kharran; at least, I would grieve and he would listen, but I knew what he was thinking. 'Abraham knows best,' he would say; 'good-night, my daughter.' But he died rather than go any further. Didn't he? And me, I die a little more every day——

SARA Nonsense! you were never better.

MILCAH One of these days I'll yawn my head off, and just expire. (*She pours some liquid out of the jug, and begins to drink it gloomily*) Why don't we sell all these thousands of stupid beasts and go and live in Damascus and be civilised again? Lot has enough now to live on for the rest of his life; yes, and to buy each of our daughters a prince for a husband, into the bargain; but what does he do when he sells some sheep? Does he buy a house in Damascus with the money? No, he buys more sheep with it. He even *gambles* in livestock nowadays. 'Bet you my two best rams.' It's monstrous. And you needn't try to persuade me that *you* like it, either.

SARA (*lazily*) It has its compensations. It is good to stand in the tent door of a morning and look at the new clean world that the night has left. So washed and shining. To smell the grass drying in the sun, and watch the flocks grazing over the far pastures——

MILCAH Yes; creeping like lice over the grass. Believe me, those two daughters of mine are beginning to *look* like sheep. I wouldn't be surprised any day if they started to bleat.

SARA (*good-humoured*) They couldn't bleat worse than their mother. Really, Milcah, you ought to be ashamed of yourself. We came into this country strangers, and we have prospered far beyond dreams. You are wife to one of the richest cattle-owners in Syria.

MILCAH And what good does that do me? That is just what I am saying. For all the amusement I get I might be a black slave in the back streets of Ur. No society but natives; uncouth creatures that quarrel all the time with the herdsmen and speak no language but their own.

SARA The quarrels, it seems to me, are not between our men and the Syrians, but between our herdsmen and yours.

MILCAH Do you wonder, when Lot never sells a beast without buying two in its place. There just isn't room for them all.

Every day there is a row about watering, or grazing, or what not. If only a miracle would happen and he would sell the lot and settle in Damascus! I would give ten years of my life to see the streets of a town, and hear——

SARA (*sharply*) Don't say that!

MILCAH Say what?

SARA (*recovering ; more mildly*) Don't use your life as a stake when you gamble with the gods. They may hear you and take the offer.

MILCAH In that case, I repeat it. Ten years of my life to live the rest of it in a town.

SARA Have you forgotten how stuffy the streets are? The wells of hot dead air between the houses? The gasping nights, and the sweat? Here in Bethel the air never stops up your mouth so that you can hardly breathe.

MILCAH No, that is true. But it is thin and dry, and oh, so *ageing*.

[SARA *moves one arm abruptly, as if someone had laid something hot against it. She sits up.*]

SARA Ageing?

MILCAH (*with no malicious intent ; matter-of-factly*) There is no moisture in it. Haven't you noticed? It dries one's skin as it dries a hide. We grow desiccated, you and I. Like that dead thorn tree on the hill.

[*In silence* SARA *comes over to the table and pours out her drink. She stands where she is, drinking slow mouthfuls while she is busy with her thoughts.*]

SARA At least Abraham is happy.

MILCAH (*again without malice*) Is he?

[*As* SARA *glances at her.*]

MILCAH It has seemed to me lately that there are traces of that old sickness that overtook him in Ur. That absent-mindedness. Haven't you noticed?

[*There is a short silence.*]

SARA (*breaking it with deliberate lightness*) Well, you must admit that there is one good thing in Syria; they make wine. (*She lifts her cup a little*)

MILCAH Yes, and Lot gets drunk on it.

SARA (*laughing a little ; she is determined to forget that remark about the ageing climate*) Oh, Milcah, you are hopeless. Aromatic wine instead of heavy Euphrates beer, aromatic air instead of the thick Euphrates heat, half a province for playground instead of a courtyard in Ur——

MILCAH (*who can see out of the tent door*) Here comes Lot.

[*Enter* LOT, *ruffled, heated, and very angry.*]

LOT (*as he comes to the tent door*) Abraham! Where is Abraham?

SARA (*coolly*) Good evening, Lot. Abraham is still in his tent, I expect. It is early yet. You look like a man who has bought a pound of walnuts and found them all empty.

LOT If I am angry it is with good reason.

SARA What is it now? Trouble over the wells again?

LOT No. Your men have killed one of my sheep.

MILCAH (*happily*) Well, that is *one* less.

SARA For food, you mean?

LOT No, just killed it, for murder's sake. Cut its throat.

SARA Oh, Lot, you know very well that last time you accused someone of that it proved to be the work of a wild dog.

LOT That was at night. Wild dogs don't kill in the middle of the afternoon; the thing is freshly done. I want Abraham to come and see it for himself. (*He turns away to go to* ABRAHAM'S *tent*) This time he'll have to believe me.

SARA (*moving quickly to follow him*) Lot, I won't have you disturbing Abraham over silly details and petty quarrelling. He is not well these days, I think, and I——

[*She has moved out of earshot, after* LOT.]

[MILCAH, *left alone, adjusts her dress and hair, as she rises and slowly follows them.*]

MILCAH (*as she goes, drawling*) Sheep and cattle! Cattle and sheep!

[*Enter R.,* HAGAR. *She crosses to the tent-mouth to watch the departing figures, and then comes back to the small table bearing the tray and picks up* MILCAH'S *cup. She finds that it still contains some wine, and begins to sip it, standing where she can contemplate the view beyond the tent door.*]

[*Enter back*—LARSA.]

LARSA (*standing in the entrance*) May I come in?

[*As* HAGAR *turns and he sees who it is.*]

Oh, it is you. Where is your mistress?

HAGAR Sara? She has gone with Lot to Abraham's tent, to tell him all about a sheep that was killed.

LARSA He is not in his tent. He is up on the hill by the little thorn tree—praying.

HAGAR Is it the sun he prays to?

LARSA (*repressive*) Certainly not. He prays to his own god.

HAGAR It is so like Abraham to have a god of his own. (*Indicating the other cup*) Have some?

LARSA Thank you, but I do not drink out of other people's cups.

HAGAR Not even out of hers? (*She picks up the other cup*)

LARSA Hers?

HAGAR That is Sara's. You have never any chance of touching her lips; would you not like the cup for proxy? Look, that is where her mouth came, where her lip rested——

LARSA (*snatching the cup from her and banging it down on the table*) Stop it! You have a mind like a dunghill—just as filthy and fertile and abominable.

HAGAR (*unruffled*) It knows a great deal about your mind, nevertheless. That is why you are so angry. For a Damascene you are a strangely dull young man, aren't you, Larsa? There are all sorts of delicious iniquities in Damascus, one hears.

LARSA There is more iniquity inside one skull I know than in the whole of Damascus. If her heart were not so empty . . .

[*He does not use her name because there is no other woman in his world : ' she ' is* SARA *and no other.*]

. . . her need so great, she would have seen you as you are long ago.

HAGAR Why don't you stop thinking about her, and take Maza to your bed one night? She is longing for you.

LARSA (*not listening*) She has squandered love on your worthless little body—teaching for your voice because it was sweet, music lessons because your hands were small and looked well on a harp, clothes with stitching as fine as her own—and what do you do with it?

HAGAR Well, what do I do?

LARSA There was a woman by the dry-stone wall of the fold last night, with one of the herds.

HAGAR A Syrian, no doubt.

LARSA No Syrian woman wears an anklet.

HAGAR And if I can't sleep, is there any crime in walking over the cool night grass and leaning on the wall of the fold?

The nights send me crazy, I tell you. They are so quiet you can hear the moments pass. In Ur there was always some sound; a man going home singing, or the mice in the rafters, or even the house itself just talking. But here the silence lies like a blanket over one, a blanket that grows thicker and thicker, until one must rise quickly and do something or scream.

LARSA You have a wonderful imagination.

HAGAR You don't believe a word I say, do you?

LARSA No.

HAGAR That just shows how stupid you are. Nearly half of what I say is true. (*With an air of egging him on*) Why don't you tell Sara about me, if you think I am bad, 'm?

LARSA So that you can make trouble between us? Oh, no! What a wonderful performance you would put on then—and how you would enjoy it. The tears, the protestations—(*his imagination seeing the picture and his voice growing bitter*)—and she comforting you in her arms; and looking askance at me ever afterwards for having doubted you. No! One day she will find you out for herself. Even your talent for dissimulation must have its weak places. It is my hope that before that time comes she will have found something more worthy to fill her heart——

HAGAR You, for instance?

LARSA (*pausing to look at her consideringly*) It is not often that you are stupid.

HAGAR Oh, I know; she yearns for a child. (*There is no sympathy in her voice*) If she took a lover she might have one. Someone young and handsome—like Larsa.

[*He begins to advance on her as if to do physical violence, and she retreats before him, amused.*]

Who is a very staid young man to all appearances, but who is all the same a Damascene and must have talents.

[*In her retreat before him she has come near the tent door and now sees* SARA *coming back. With a sudden change of tone and attitude.*]

Here is Sara.

[*She crosses quickly to the table, snatches up the tray with the cups and jug and disappears into the further tent R.*]

LARSA (*going to meet* SARA *as she comes to the tent-mouth and struggling to adjust his emotions*) Oh! I was coming to say that

Abraham is not in his tent, he is up on the hill by the little dead thorn.

SARA (*walking past him into the tent, her mind only half on him*) Yes. The desiccated thorn that is like me. (*Realising* LARSA) Yes, they know, thank you. They have sent to fetch him. All this fuss, when he is not—— Come in for a moment, Larsa; I want to talk to you.

LARSA Yes? Are you troubled about something?

SARA Yes, I am troubled. So troubled that my blood runs back to my heart when I think of it.

LARSA Is it the sheep-killing? If it is that——

SARA No, it is not that. It is Abraham.

LARSA (*who knows that it is more than the quarrel with* LOT *that ails his master, unready*) Oh.

SARA (*in a small voice*) He is not well. He is not happy.

LARSA (*coming to the rescue*) He is worried about those quarrels. Lot is being very difficult, you know. And Abraham has a strong family sense. It hurts his pride that—(*he catches* SARA'S *eye*)—that—— (*His voice dies away*)

SARA (*in a dull voice*) You know as well as I do what is wrong. He is losing faith in his Voice. He has prospered as it was foretold to him—gold and silver and flocks and herds in abundance —and there are no children to fulfil the promise. He looks at the riches, and doubts. 'I grew rich in Ur,' he thinks. 'That I have grown rich again in Syria is no evidence of divine care. The promise has not come true; and every day it grows less likely of fulfilment——' There is only one thing for me to do, Larsa.

LARSA What?

[*He sounds apprehensive.*]

SARA What the Law allows me to do. If I cannot give my husband a child, the Law says that I may give him someone in my place. The time has come to do it.

LARSA (*gently*) No. Wait yet a little, Sara. His god has done well by him——

SARA (*bitterly*) But not by me. No, it must be done now. It is not as if I had to bring a stranger into the house. There is Hagar. (*This is not a suggestion, but in relief*)

LARSA (*shouting his astonishment and repudiation*) No! (*As the full enormity of it comes home to him*) No!

SARA (*surprised by his vehemence ; looking at him ; quietly*) Are you in love with her?

LARSA With *that*?

SARA (*sharply*) Larsa! How dare you use that tone about Hagar?

LARSA (*quietly*) You see? That is what she does.

SARA What?

LARSA Makes strife where there was none. You have not spoken like that to me since I was an apprentice in the counting-house.

SARA Forgive me, Larsa. I was hurt by your—crudity, shall we say. You are implacable when you hate. You do hate Hagar, don't you?

LARSA Yes.

SARA Why? Has she harmed you in some way?

LARSA No, but she will. She will bring grief to us all one day.

SARA But that is absurd! What ground have you for—— (*The suspicion is still in her mind*) I should have thought that someone so young and delightful would have won a place in your good graces if not in your heart.

LARSA (*understanding the implied question*) Oh yes, she is a lovely thing, and I am a man. I know the way her eyebrows curve, and the way her lashes grow long at the corners. I know, too, the way her eyes watch from under those lashes, and what the eyes themselves look like. As bright, and impersonal, and cruel as those of a wild animal. Have you never noticed?

SARA What you see in her eyes is your own antagonism. You are quite unreasonable about Hagar. (*Accepting the position*) Very well, you dislike her, and you will no doubt go on disliking her. There is nothing we can do about that. But I hope that in her new position you will give her the same loyalty and service that you have——

LARSA She is unworthy. I tell you! I know her.

SARA And do not I?

LARSA No! When she is with you she plays a part. The devoted slave, the happy innocent. I tell you she is a——

[SARA *lays a hand on his, and he stops.*]

SARA (*quietly*) Don't go on, Larsa. Nothing you say will make any difference, and you might regret it later. Better have no barrier of things said between us. Let us accept that you and Hagar are enemies, and make the best of it. At least be glad for me that my supplanter will be someone I love; someone who is part of my household and part of my heart.

(*With determined brightness*) Who knows, it may have been to this end that I happened to walk past the rostrum that day, when they were selling an Egyptian child—who behaved like a wild-cat and was the loveliest thing in Ur that morning.

LARSA You were the loveliest woman in Ur.

SARA 'Were.'

LARSA I think now that you are the loveliest woman in Asia.

SARA (*casting him a smile*) Dear Larsa.

[*Enter, from the back*, ABRAHAM.]

ABRAHAM Is there no peace in the camp nowadays? I go up the hill and find serenity there—it is so clear this evening that you can see the very dropping-off edge of the world—and then I come back to . . . back to find the camp frothing with accusations and offence. Have we become barbarians that we cannot live quietly with one another?

LARSA (*murmuring*) There are always those who can't carry their corn.

SARA Lot has found a banner of revolt. It is a sheep.

[LOT *appears at the tent-mouth.*]

LOT A *dead* sheep. Another one. That makes twelve in the last three weeks.

ABRAHAM And you think that my men are responsible? Why should they do anything so strange?

LOT Because they think my flocks too numerous for the watering-places.

ABRAHAM And aren't they?

LOT No; they are jealous of my prosperity, that is all. And nothing is done to discipline them. You did nothing about the earlier cases——

ABRAHAM I am not satisfied that my men had anything to do with the matter.

LARSA How do we know that it is not done by your own herdsmen, to stir up trouble for ours?

ABRAHAM You have offered no evidence.

[*Enter, behind* LOT, MILCAH.]

MILCAH It is bad enough to breathe sheep night and day, year in and year out, but I draw the line at having carcases spread out for exhibition at my tent door.

SARA My poor Milcah.

LOT I don't know what evidence you want. It is my beasts that are being killed, isn't it?

ABRAHAM But it was my herdsmen that were knifed and left for dead on the low grazing last month.

LOT That was the work of thieves.

ABRAHAM Thieves who took nothing. And every day there is now trouble between our men. Not only about the grazing grounds and the watering, there is nothing they do not quarrel over; breeding, branding, shearing—even over the fashion of crook heads. It must end, Lot. Our whole lives are being poisoned by it.

LOT And how do you propose to end it?

ABRAHAM I suggest that we part company.

LOT (*who has not anticipated this*) Part?

ABRAHAM There is not room for us both in the same territory, Lot.

LOT You are going to turn me off your grazings?

MILCAH (*happily*) If Abraham refuses to let you use his wells any more, you can sell your herds and we can go and live in Damascus like civilised people.

LOT (*ignoring her; to* ABRAHAM) Let me tell you, they were your grazings once, but I have more cattle than you and more men too, and if you try to turn me off we shall fight, and if it comes to fighting my men will——

ABRAHAM (*mildly*) Yes, I know! Your men are mostly cut-throats. You misunderstand me completely, Lot. What I suggest is that the territory should be divided.

LOT Divided! Oh. And who is to do the dividing? Do we cast lots for it?

ABRAHAM No. No, I——

LOT No, I thought not! I get the thin grass and the muddy wells, I suppose.

ABRAHAM If you do it will be your own fault. I give you your choice. If you elect to have the eastern half, then I shall take the west. If you want the west, then I take the eastern portion.

LOT You are giving me first choice? Why?

ABRAHAM I don't want you coming to me in the future and complaining of the hard deal you had. Whatever your fortune it will be on your own head.

LOT (*still incredulous*) And if I choose the east and all the rich low grazing in the plain there, you will not encroach and claim sympathy when the high pastures are thin?

ABRAHAM No. If you choose the plain, it is yours, and I keep to the high country and to my bargain.

LOT And where will the boundary be between my country and yours?

ABRAHAM That we can decide in the morning before we part.

LOT Tomorrow?

ABRAHAM The sooner the better; before murder is done in the camp and our names disgraced. Will you decide in the morning which direction you go in?

LOT I choose now. I take the eastern half.

ABRAHAM Very well. I hope you will have the sense to keep your herds down to what the land will carry. Even the fine green plain supports only so many beasts per acre.

LOT Never fear; I know my business.

[*He turns to go.*]

ABRAHAM I suggest that you tell your men tonight that we are parting. That may save someone a knife wound.

[*Exit* LOT.]

MILCAH Oh, Abraham, I am sorry it happened like this, but I am so glad. Do you know what it means? Sara, do you know what it means? I can live in a town! I can live in a town like a human being.

SARA So you can, Milcah. Oh, my dear, I am pleased for your sake. I am quite sure the drains in a Syrian town must be primitive in the extreme, but——

MILCAH Oh, no! Those places in the plain are very fine; not Damascus exactly, but very fashionable. I can have a really fine establishment there. And Lot can come and go while he looks after his herds, and the girls will have some society at last, and it will all be lovely. You must come and stay, Sara, when we are settled. You won't hold it against us, Abraham, that Lot chose the rich half, will you? After all, you did simply hand it to him, didn't you?

ABRAHAM I did indeed, Milcah. Of course I bear you no malice, and of course Sara will come to visit you one day.

MILCAH I shall miss Sara very much to begin with. Now I must go and tell the girls the good news. I expect their faces will grow an inch shorter and less sheeplike on the instant. Oh, you don't know how happy I am.

[*Exit* MILCAH, *and at the same time exit* LARSA, *amused, at the back.*]

SARA (*watching her go*) Poor Milcah; she has been miserable. (*With benevolent tartness*) She has also been a misery. The atmosphere will be a great deal lighter in the future.

ABRAHAM More peaceful, I hope. (*He sounds weary and discouraged*)

SARA You sound tired.

ABRAHAM No; just disappointed. This is the parting of the ways. We have come so far together, shared so much, I had hoped that we would have been together to the end, that——

SARA If you think you are saying goodbye to Lot, comfort yourself. In a twelvemonth you will be rescuing him from the pickle he will have got himself into.

ABRAHAM (*half amused, half reproving*) Sara, you are unfair.

SARA In the difficult times, it was *your* wisdom, and *your* courage, and *your* strength that saved Lot. Now that times are easy he thinks that he can stand alone. (*Remembering*) Don't you think it was a little *too* generous to let him have the good grazing in the plain?

ABRAHAM Oh, no. The plain is more than a green and fertile country, you know. It is also a highway. Not ten years go by without some army or other tramping over it on their way to some place or other. Burning and pillaging, and confiscating, and generally making a nuisance of themselves. The high country is a more peaceful place for a man getting on in years.

SARA (*eyeing him*) Abraham. You *wanted* Lot to choose the plain.

ABRAHAM (*running his hand over his chin with a slightly embarrassed smile*) Well, I rather *hoped* he would.

SARA (*dry and amused*) For a good man, you have a surprisingly live business sense.

ABRAHAM Talking of business, you know that Lot was my nominal heir. Now that he will no longer be that, I have thought of appointing Larsa. There must be someone to look after you if anything should happen to me, and Larsa has been almost a son to me.

SARA (*feeling that the moment has come*) Abraham—— (*Her voice fails her*)

ABRAHAM Well? Is it that you don't like my decision about Larsa?

SARA No, of course not; I welcome it. But I too have made a decision.

ABRAHAM Yes?

SARA It is about Hagar.

ABRAHAM Yes? Do you want to make a match for her? She is a pretty thing. (*He sounds quite indifferent*)

SARA No. I want you to take her in my place.

ABRAHAM (*quite unprepared for anything like that*) Sara! Are you out of your mind?

SARA What is so surprising about it? The Law allows it, and custom expects it. I have wronged you in waiting so long. Now that I make tardy amends, you won't refuse what I ask?

ABRAHAM (*still dazed*) Take another woman to my bed?

SARA You could do that without putting me out of your heart, couldn't you?

ABRAHAM (*with vehemence*) Even God himself could not put you out of my heart.

SARA Well, then, there is nothing in the promise that says the children were to be the children of Sara.

ABRAHAM I will have no children that are not yours.

SARA And if you never have mine?

[*A pause.*]

No; take Hagar and make the promise good. I love Hagar like a daughter, and a child of hers will be almost my own. If I cannot have the happiness of a child, I shall rejoice in the possession of a grandchild. A grandson. It will be a boy.

ABRAHAM (*at a loss*) But—but—— (*Trying to shelve it*) You must let me think this over, Sara. The thing is too new in my mind.

SARA No! I know you. You will pray to your God, and grow thin and tired with searching your soul, and in the end decide that something so obviously to your advantage must be wrong. All your life you have looked askance at obvious good, suspecting and refusing, peering behind to find out what was wrong that a thing should be so commendable. You will do this thing for *me*. So that I shall no longer be a reproach to you.

ABRAHAM (*stunned but less heated*) No.

SARA (*looking at him*) You don't mean to be cruel, I know.

ABRAHAM Cruel!

SARA All the sorrow of the years is packed into this moment. The longing, the jealousy, the humiliation, the slow torture of knowing that I must renounce at the last; it is all in this moment, and you prolong it.

ABRAHAM Oh, Sara.

[*She takes this cry of grief for her, rightly, as capitulation. She claps her hands together to summon* HAGAR.]

SARA (*companionably, into the silence*) There is a path on the mountain with a narrow ledge; you look down and see the backs of birds wheeling away below you.

ABRAHAM (*watching her; also companionably*) I know it.

SARA I was terrified of that path. My whole life was blackened by the thought that one day I might have to cross it. And then, last winter, when the low road was flooded, I used the path. And it was not so difficult after all.

ABRAHAM (*quietly*) I love you very much, Sara.

[*Enter* HAGAR, *R.*]

SARA Come here, my dear.

[*As* HAGAR *comes to her she puts an arm round her.*]

Child, I have a great honour for you.

HAGAR An honour?

SARA You know that if a wife fails to give her husband children she may, by the Law, give him her handmaid in her stead.

HAGAR Yes, I know.

SARA Hagar, you have grown up in my house, in my heart, and I love you like a child of my own. It is for that reason that I give you with a goodwill to Abraham if you are willing.

HAGAR To my lord Abraham?

SARA Yes.

HAGAR To take your place?

ABRAHAM (*in a burst*) No! That of a certainty not!

SARA She did not mean it like that.

ABRAHAM If there are any ideas like that in your head, the matter ends here and now.

HAGAR Oh, my lord, I have offended you!

ABRAHAM You have a rash tongue, it seems.

HAGAR Not rash, my lord, but stupid. It is not supple to express my thoughts. My lord shall teach me and I shall be his servant, as I have been Sara's. In all things I am my lord's. (*She bends to kiss his hand*)

[*She drops neatly to her knees, and bows herself at his feet. Over this ready obeisance the eyes of* ABRAHAM *and* SARA *meet, almost as if they were taking farewell of each other.*]

[*As* ABRAHAM *puts out a hand to lift* HAGAR *to her feet the*

CURTAIN FALLS

SCENE 2

The Scene is the same, about a year later.

HAGAR *is alone, chopping herbs.*

SARA (*off*) I hope you are keeping your eye on that salve, Hagar.

[HAGAR *casts a bored glance towards the brazier.*]

(*coming in*) Oh, Hagar, you are letting it burn. I wish I had brought old Tina with us when we left Ur. It was she who knew all the best ingredients of a salve. (*She examines the mess*) It *looks* all right, but it would be too sad if it took the skin off a man instead of healing his wound. (*Looking across at* HAGAR) I think you ought to chop those herbs more finely, Hagar.

HAGAR (*pauses in exasperation, and resumes her bored chopping*) There may be no wounded man at all. Why should we make so much salve?

SARA The gods grant that it is only wounded we have to deal with when they come back.

HAGAR *If* they come back.

SARA Hagar!

HAGAR Well, why not? It is war, isn't it? (*She chops for a moment*) A very silly business, but it does put a little excitement into life. It is surprising how much better men look going to war. That dull stick Larsa looked like a god, riding away. Even Abraham looked young.

[SARA's *hand pauses for a moment and then moves on.*]

HAGAR I wish I could have gone with them. To ride out on a horse like a man—not bundled up on a camel—and see all the foreign kings in battle array, and the banners, and the bright armour, to look down from the hills and watch them crossing the plain like a bright snake, and to mark where they had the prisoners—the poor silly prisoners that had no bright armour any more and were being led like sheep—and to wait until all the bright army was hemmed in a gorge of the hills, and then to fall on them and to rescue the prisoners and be away, away, through the secret passes, before the long bright snake of the armies knew that its dull bit was missing. (*Coming back from her campaigning*) That is how Abraham will do it, isn't it?

SARA I don't know. I expect so. (*Still preoccupied with the salve—doubtfully*) As I remember it, Tina's salve had a greenish tinge.

HAGAR I wish I could see Lot's face when they rescue him. He will try very hard to look as if he were not really a captive at all. As if he and Milcah and their people had just joined up with the Mesopotamian army by chance. For the ride. That will save him from having to thank Abraham for rescuing him.

SARA (*amused at this accurate summing up of* LOT) Speak respectfully of your elders, child.

HAGAR He is not so very old; and he is only Lot.

SARA Only Abraham's nearest relation.

HAGAR He is of no importance now that the war has ruined him.

[SARA *casts a glance at the unconscious face. Every day she is learning new things about* HAGAR's *mental processes.*]

HAGAR Anyhow, Abraham loathes him.

SARA I can't imagine why you should think that.

HAGAR Abraham told me so.

SARA Oh, nonsense, Hagar. He would never——

HAGAR How do you know what Abraham tells me?

SARA (*reasonably*) I don't, of course. But I know Abraham.

HAGAR Then you think that I am telling a lie?

SARA No, my dear; exaggerating.

HAGAR Stop patronising me!

[SARA *looks at her in astonishment. Before she can find words, a man's excited voice can be heard in the mid-distance outside, shouting.*]

VOICE They are coming! They are coming!

[*Other* VOICES *join him, calling.*]

VOICES Yes, look, look, they are coming back. Look, everyone.

[SARA *drops the spoon into the bowl and makes for the tent door.* HAGAR *puts the plate and knife on the couch beside her with more an air of relief at being able to stop chopping than of eagerness to welcome anyone, and joins* SARA. *An elderly woman runs in from R., to peer over their shoulders for a moment or two and then runs away to spread the good news.*]

SARA Yes, they are coming.

[*It is evident that they are still a long way away.*]

HAGAR You can't see with the dust. It might be anyone.

SARA (*her hands cupped round her eyes to exclude the light beating up from the ground*) No, that is Larsa riding ahead. I hope it is good news that he is bringing, and that they are all safe.

HAGAR How do you know that it is Larsa?

SARA He rides with his elbows out and his reins flapping.

[*She shakes her head indulgently, smiling a little; her joy at having* ABRAHAM *back again centred for the moment on the advancing* LARSA.]

Dear Larsa.

[HAGAR *withdraws her gaze from the distance, and runs her eye speculatively over* SARA; *quite unable to visualise the relationship which exists between* SARA *and* LARSA—SARA *watches a moment longer.*]

(*remembering suddenly*) Oh, and we haven't finished the salve!

[*She snatches up the plate from the couch preparatory to adding the contents to the bowl, and then sees the result of* HAGAR'S *handiwork.*]

Oh, really, Hagar! They are *lumps.* I can't put them in like that!

[*It is a wail of despair, not a piece of scolding.*]

HAGAR I hate chopping things. If you wanted them chopped why didn't you ask your maid to do it?

SARA (*controlling herself*) I suggested your doing it because I thought it would give you——

HAGAR It would give me something to do with my hands! It annoys you to see me sitting about doing nothing, doesn't it?

SARA I was going to say: Because I thought it would give you a share in the making. And because, of course, I thought it would give you pleasure to help.

HAGAR Well, it may give you pleasure to play at work, since you never had to do any, but it doesn't amuse me.

SARA Work? You call preparing healing stuff for the wounds of our own men, work?

HAGAR Oh, what a fuss! A handful of spiders' webs and a piece of linen is all they need. That is all my mother used; and all her men expected.

SARA (*amiably, making the best of it*) Well, we are short of spiders' webs. Really, Hagar, you are very lazy. It is not good for you to lie about all day doing nothing.

HAGAR I have been running about all my life; I can afford to put my feet up now.

SARA I see your point of view. But position has duties as well as privileges, you know.

HAGAR I won't have you lecturing me!

SARA (*achieving a smile*) Was I lecturing? I'm sorry.

HAGAR The days are gone when you could scold me for my shortcomings. I please myself nowadays. (*With a transition of thought*) I please Abraham too. And if it were not for you I should have a child by now.

SARA (*astounded*) If it were not for me? What have I to do with that?

HAGAR You know very well. You have bewitched me.

SARA Hagar!

HAGAR You don't want me to have one, and so you put a spell on me.

SARA What nonsense is this? You must know that the dearest wish of my life is that you should give Abraham an heir. That it was to that end I sacrif—— (*She stops there, unwilling to parade that sacrifice*)

HAGAR (*snatching the word from her*) Yes. You sacrificed yourself! And you have hated me ever since for it.

SARA What possible reason have you to think any such thing?

HAGAR (*as one producing an unanswerable argument*) I should hate you if you were in my place.

SARA (*contemplating the monstrous simplicity of this*) I see. But do me the kindness to believe that it *is* possible to love unselfishly; to rejoice in a good-fortune that is not one's own.

HAGAR Words! Fine words! I know very well how you feel. Have I not seen you go white round the mouth when Abraham dropped a caressing hand on me in passing? Have you not had to rise of a sudden and go out when he doted over me as I played his favourite songs—songs *you* taught me; go out and walk, and walk, and walk until you had walked the rage and passion out of you? And you expect me to believe that you don't hate me! Of course you hate me. You have hated me since the hour you gave me to Abraham. So you work against me. You go every month to old Bekka the wise-woman and buy spells against me. I know! She told me. Five gold pieces a spell you pay her.

SARA Really, Hagar; is there no silliness too great for you to believe?

HAGAR I told Abraham about it. I asked him to send you away. But he only laughed. Well, he won't laugh this time, because I am the one who is going away. And I am going now, before he comes, and it will be you who will have to tell him why. Tell them all why! That you were very fine and noble as long as it didn't hurt you, but once it hurt you you were like other people. That you were as cruel as a thousand devils. So cruel that I couldn't stay any longer in your household. Explain that to Abraham and see if he laughs.

[*She disappears at speed, R.*]

[SARA *makes a very small movement to go after her, and then is still.*

[*Outside, the first greetings to the arriving* LARSA *are heard; welcome and inquiry and answer.*

[SARA *turns to face the tent opening and begins to move forward.*

[LARSA *appears in the opening, breathless, laughing, flushed and pleased with himself. He seems to have come from another world, a fine, spacious, generous, masculine world instead of the close, petty, emotional world in the tent.*]

SARA (*delighted to see him*) Larsa! Tell me! Did you get them? And are they safe? All of them?

LARSA (*pulling off his gloves and hitting the dust off himself with them*) Yes, we got them. And not a prick among the lot of us. It was as easy as cutting out cattle from a herd, and a deal more fun. We swooped on them at the end of the day, when they were tired and half asleep and thinking of nothing but their supper. And we were out from among them and away before they realised that we were there. You never saw anyone as surprised as Lot. I think he was already seeing himself carting bricks for a Mesopotamian builder.

SARA And no one hurt?

LARSA Not a soul—unless you count Lot's saddle-chafes. They made him ride a donkey.

SARA And Abraham?

LARSA Abraham has dropped ten years, and is thinking of

having a little private war of his own once a year just as a piece of diversion.

[THEY *turn as they talk to watch the approaching cavalcade.*]

SARA Not if I have to sit at home and wonder if I am going to see any one of you again! You will have to think of a less expensive amusement. (*She gives a big sigh of relief*) Oh, it is good to have you all back and safe. (*Reading off to herself the people she recognises as she searches the column*) Milcah. And Lot. Where are the girls?

LARSA Still at home. The invader took one look at them and left them where they were.

SARA (*looking at his brown, laughing face*) I have never known you so gay, Larsa. Hagar was right; war is a becoming thing to a man.

LARSA (*his face losing some of its brightness, as it always does at the thought of* HAGAR) Oh, Hagar. She would think that. (*With a glance backwards at the empty room*) How is *she* missing the fun?

SARA (*turning back into the room*) She is not here. She has just this moment run away. I have been oppressing her.

[*As* LARSA *receives this with nothing but the ghost of a snort.*]

I am not very sure whether she has gone for good or whether she will be back by supper.

LARSA She will be back in half an hour.

SARA Why half an hour?

LARSA That will give her enough time to work up the little scene she is preparing.

[*As* SARA *does not rebuke him.*]

Well?

SARA Well, what?

LARSA No rebuke?

SARA (*quietly*) No rebuke. (*Picking the spoon out of the mess in the bowl on the brazier*) Look what I have been wasting my day over. Salve for your non-existent wounds.

LARSA (*sniffing the stuff doubtfully*) For the first time it occurs to me to be grateful that I am whole.

SARA Oh, how can you, Larsa? That is that wonderful stuff that old Tina made, in Ur. At least that is what it is supposed to be. (*Still playing with the salve*) I was very unfair to you once, Larsa.

LARSA (*trying to shelve it*) Only once?

SARA I should have known that your integrity was as great as Abraham's. That no personal prejudice would taint your judgment. Will you forgive me?

LARSA There is nothing to forgive.

SARA Well, let us clear away this mess or Abraham will laugh at me.

[*She claps her hands and the* ELDERLY WOMAN *appears.*]

I would like to have known how Tina got it a greenish colour, but I suppose that will remain one of the unsolved mysteries of my life.

[*She gives the bowl and plate to the* WOMAN *and* LARSA *picks up the small brazier and carries it out.*]

LARSA (*going*) You can try again next year when Abraham has the first of his private wars.

[*Exit with* SERVANT.]

[*From outside the sound of voices, and* ABRAHAM'S *hail.*]

ABRAHAM (*outside*) Sara! Are you there?

[*Appearing as she goes to meet and embrace him.*]

ABRAHAM Well! We have done it! Safe, and not a scratch in the lot.

SARA Oh, my dear, I am so glad.

[*Enter* MILCAH, *behind.*]

(*embracing her*) Milcah, my dear, what a horrible experience for you.

MILCAH Oh, no, it wasn't horrible at all, Sara; it was most enjoyable.

[*Enter* LOT *behind her.*]

LOT Milcah is quite furious at being rescued, if you want to know the truth.

SARA Furious? Welcome, Lot.

LOT In another fortnight or so she would have been back in Ur, if no one had interfered.

SARA I hadn't thought of that! I thought you were very happy in the plain, Milcah, and quite resigned to Syria.

[*The* WOMAN SERVANT *comes in with a basin of water scented with herbs and a bundle of small hand towels over her forearm, and ceremoniously offers it to each arrival to dip hands into, giving each a separate towel.*

[LARSA *brings in wine to the side table and* SARA *dispenses it.*]

MILCAH Oh, Syria is well enough, but I must say that the finest experience it has ever provided me with was being carried off to Babylon. When Larsa appeared beside me and took my rein and dashed me away before I could utter a word, I was so angry I could have murdered him. I didn't even have a chance to say goodbye to anyone.

SARA Goodbye!

MILCAH Yes; there were some very charming people among them. One of the regimental commanders knew a cousin of mine in Kharran. *You* remember her—Nahor's daughter, who married the Pileser man. One of the few good things about war is that it is so international. One is always running up against people one knows.

LOT (*gloomily*) You wouldn't think, to listen to her, that we are ruined, would you?

MILCAH Oh, no, Lot, we are not ruined. We have got rid of the cattle, of course, but it was always a repellent way of making money. There is still my dowry—— (*To* ABRAHAM *and* SARA) We hid it behind the kitchen stove—and you will find something else to do.

LOT What, for instance?

MILCAH You could be an agent for something. There is always money in an agency.

ABRAHAM There is no need for Lot to change his business. I have more beasts than my grounds will carry this season. I shall be glad to hand some over to Lot.

MILCAH Oh no, Abraham! Not when we have just got rid of what we had.

LOT (*who does not relish the prospect of being a small-herd man after being a big owner*) It is kind of you, Abraham, but I don't think I have the heart to start again. Perhaps Milcah is right—she *is* sometimes right by accident—perhaps it would be easier to do something else altogether. Unless—you were advertising for a man to take charge of your south territory.

ABRAHAM Yes. Would you care for that?

LOT Yes, I think I should like that. I am sick of the plain.

MILCAH Come back to live in this wilderness! Never! It is bad enough to be brought back to Syria when I was half-way home to Ur, but to come back to living in a tent again, that would be too much.

LOT But, Milcah——

MILCAH If Lot does that he can do it alone, and I shall live on my dowry in the town. Though it will be a *very* odd situation and not too good for our daughters' social well-being.

SARA I hear the girls are safe at home.

MILCAH Yes. I did hope that one of the young Mesopotamian princes would become interested in them. There were at least fifteen of them at one time or another during the occupation, and all of them very rich, even if one doesn't count the booty they were taking out of Syria. Any of them would have been a good match for the girls. But they didn't even bother to capture them. Just left them where they were. *That* is what comes of bringing up girls among sheep. (*In a more pleading tone*) You don't really mean it, Lot, do you, about wanting to come back here?

LOT But it is a fine position, Milcah—manager to Abraham. Much better than scraping a living in town. And we could——

MILCAH Oh, no, Lot, please. Please, Lot, I don't mind how modestly we live in town—we could drop the weekly parties and things like that—but not back into this wilderness. Please, Lot.

ABRAHAM If you really feel that you would be happier in the plain, I have a suggestion to make. For a long time now I have wanted an agent for my wool. Someone to live in town and meet the buyers and arrange the disposal of the clip to the best advantage. What about it, Lot?

MILCAH An agency. There! I told you. (*She sounds as if she had produced it from a hat*) What could be better than that?

LOT It sounds very good.

MILCAH It is a nice, elegant, indefinable thing, an agency. Not positive, like cattle. When my friends said: 'And what does your husband do?' and I said: 'He's a cattle owner,' there was a sort of cloven-hoof atmosphere in the gathering.

ABRAHAM (*amused*) When you mention the agency you will have to keep the wool side of it dark.

MILCAH Oh, an agency is one of those vague, confidential things that no one ever inquires about; we should be quite safe. (*Becoming aware that her remarks might not be considered the height of tact in view of her host's occupation*) You don't think for a moment that I am running down your business, do you, Abraham?

ABRAHAM (*gravely*) Nothing was further from my thoughts.

[*Aware that if he catches* SARA's *eye he will laugh, he turns his attention to* LOT.]

Lot, we must get you a change of clothes. Perhaps some of Larsa's would fit you.

LARSA Yes, I am sure they would. (*With a glance at his own campaigning clothes, with armour on forearms and shins*) I shall be very sorry to get out of these things even after sleeping in them for a fortnight. It was the best fortnight of my life.

SARA You men!

ABRAHAM Well, this fortnight discovered to me one of the mistakes of *my* life.

SARA What was that?

ABRAHAM Putting Larsa into the counting-house in Ur. A great general was lost that day.

LARSA (*smiling*) Ah, well; wars are seasonal, but money is constant.

ABRAHAM Yes. As Hagar says: No one snubs a penny. (*Missing her for the first time*) Where *is* Hagar?

SARA She has fled the household. I am sorry to break it to you after all these years, Abraham, but I am a monster of cruelty.

ABRAHAM (*his brow clouding*) A tantrum? What was it about?

SARA I doubt if tantrum is the just word. She seems to be labouring under a burden of odd beliefs. It is very strange to live a lifetime with someone and to love them very dearly, and then one day, without warning, to find out how you look to them. How little they like you, how little they have ever liked you.

MILCAH It sounds as if she had just been very rude.

SARA 'Rude' is no more accurate than 'tantrum'. I was a whited sepulchre, it seemed, who pretended to be fine and noble and was nothing but a seething mass of iniquity inside. I hustled her, hated her, pursued her with spells and witchcraft, and generally tried to compass her ruin. (*To* MILCAH) Tell me, does she sound crazy to you?

MILCAH (*without need for consideration, indifferently*) No; just pregnant.

SARA (*her mouth opens slowly and shuts again*) Do you know, that never occurred to me!

[*They laugh at her a little.*]

ABRAHAM (*delighted*) I think even I could have diagnosed rightly after a tirade like that. Come, Lot, and we shall find you some clothes.

[*Exit with* LOT *and* LARSA, *back.*]

SARA (*her mind on the scene with* HAGAR) Why didn't I think of that?

MILCAH (*with unusual tartness for her*) If I know anything of Hagar you were probably deaf and dumb with shock.

SARA (*curiously*) Don't you like Hagar?

MILCAH No, my dear, I don't; and never have.

[*She doesn't embroider this in her usual fashion, and the simplicity of it makes it impressive.*]

SARA (*contemplating the fact that all these years other people have seen a different* HAGAR *from hers*) Oh.

[*It is a pensive sound.*]

MILCAH (*eyeing her with sympathy*) Her words are stuck in your mind and burning holes there, aren't they? (*It is not a question*)

SARA (*surprised and touched by this unexpected objectiveness on* MILCAH'S *part*) It's just that I feel so—— (*She lifts her hands in a helpless gesture*) so lost. So unsafe. How am I to judge, any more, if appearances can be so—— (*Not wanting to discuss it with* MILCAH; *pulling herself together cheerfully*) Come! It is time we found some clothes for *you*. Though you look so elegant, Milcah, that you might be walking down a street in Ur. I wonder what the fashions in Ur are nowadays; whether fringe has gone out, and where the waists are? Do you remember a red frock I had, ruched at the neck, with a long fringe?

MILCAH I do indeed.

SARA I was *very* fond of that frock.

MILCAH And there was a silver thing you had that used to cause me the most intense—— (*She breaks off, her eyes on the tent-mouth*)

[*Enter* HAGAR *L., apparently recovered and quite at her ease.*]

HAGAR (*with her best special graces*) How are you, Milcah? I should have been here to welcome you.

[*The tone implies in an odd fashion that* SARA *is merely doing proxy.*]

But I have been to the wise-woman.

MILCAH (*with her usual indifference to social niceties*) I thought you were running away.

HAGAR (*unabashed*) I was, but the wise-woman said not to.

SARA Very sensible of her.

MILCAH (*guessing what the wise-woman has said*) Sara tells n that you are going to have a child. That is very good news.

HAGAR *Sara* told you? How could *she* know? It is on just now that old Bekka said—— (*She breaks off*)

SARA A woman would have to be very stupid to fail in th diagnosis. People who make scenes about chopping a fe herbs can hardly be responsible for their actions. (*Gaily*) We now that my spells have failed, I hope that we can sett down to——

HAGAR (*airily*) About those spells; it was a misunde standing.

SARA Yours, or mine?

HAGAR Oh, mine, of course. I misunderstood old Bekk She has no teeth.

SARA Ah, that explains it, of course.

[HAGAR *looks at her doubtfully*

Well, what could be more joyful?

[*She begins to shepherd them to the entrance, R.*

Lot rescued from carting bricks in Mesopotamia, Milcah save from her cattle, and Abraham looking forward to an heir What rejoicing there will be tonight. We must send out som wine to the men, to wash down their roast carcase.

[*As they go out.*

And something soft for old Bekka who has no teeth.

CURTAIN

ACT III

SCENE I

he Scene is the same, but it is nearly eight years later, and the hangings of the tent are different.

RA *is on her knees in the middle of the tent bandaging the foot of a very small boy who, by his dirty streaked face, has been crying but is now quiet except for the sudden involuntary sob which succeeds a fit of tears. He is sitting on a stool; and on the floor beside it is the bowl in which* SARA *has been washing the injury.*

RA *is telling him a story while she bandages.*

SARA (*in the low, impressed voice in which one tells stories to small ildren*) 'And the old man said to the Prince: "How is it, rince, that you know my name?" And the Prince said: I know you because we have met before." And the old man as very surprised, and said: "Never before have I talked to a rince, I promise you." And the Prince said: "No, but once ng ago you took a thorn from the foot of a beggar boy, and at beggar boy was me." So the Prince went back to his own nd and to his father——' (*She pauses to look at the child*) Are ou Aran's son?

[*The* CHILD *shakes his head in denial, and after a moment's puzzled look at him, she suggests another name.*]

osrah's, then?

[*Again the* CHILD *shakes his head, and she goes back to the story.*]

Back to his father who was so glad to see him that he killed his est calf for the feast.' You do *know* whose son you are?

[*The* BOY *nods.*]

ell, that's a good thing! (*Setting down the bandaged foot, and tting up*) Now then! That is better, isn't it? (*Crossing to the nall table by the R. wall*) 'And he showed his father all the ophies and spoils of war that he had brought home with him.'

[*Holding out to the* CHILD *in each forefinger and thumb the two sweets she has taken from the dish on the table.*]

ne jelly one, and one made of almonds.

[*The* BOY *takes them, one in each hand, and moves slowly to th door, looking from one sweetmeat to the other. At the tent doo he turns, transfers the one sweetmeat with care to the other hand and gives a solemn little obeisance with a movement of his fre hand to forehead and breast.*

[ABRAHAM, *followed by* HAGAR'S *son* ISHMAEL, *a boy of seve or so, comes in R., in time to see the last of him.*]

ABRAHAM (*amused*) Who is the child?

SARA (*rolling up linen and clearing away*) I don't know. One of the herd's sons, I think. He was limping along with a thorn in his foot the size of your thumb.

ABRAHAM (*at the door, looking after him*) It looks like Bosrah's boy.

SARA *He* thinks *not.* Ishmael, you must not help yourself to my sweets without asking.

ISHMAEL You gave some to the herd's son.

SARA Yes, and if you ask I shall give you some.

ISHMAEL Why should I ask? They are mine.

SARA Yours?

ISHMAEL They are made of honey, and nuts, and gelatine, are they not?

SARA Certainly.

ISHMAEL It was my father's servants who gathered the honey, and it was my father's money that paid for the nuts, and it was from the feet of my father's calves that the gelatine was made. And everything that is my father's is mine.

ABRAHAM A fine logical tale! There is only one fault in it. Everything that is mine is not yours, including your manners.

ISHMAEL It will all be mine some day. I take a little on account, that is all.

ABRAHAM (*without emphasis*) Put them back.

ISHMAEL What?

ABRAHAM Put them back.

ISHMAEL (*trying a new tack*) No one will eat them now that I have had sweaty hands on them.

[*There is a silence, and he puts them back.*]

(*Having restored them, in a burst*) If *she* wasn't here you would have let me have them; I would have taken them and you would have said nothing. It is because she doesn't want me to have them. She doesn't want me to have anything because I am

Hagar's son and not hers. She is jealous of the very air I breathe. Jealous! Jealous! Jealous!

[*He flees out of the room—back.*]

ABRAHAM (*into the silence*) I know. You think I spoil him. But it is difficult not to. He is a child of such spirit.

[*As* SARA *ignores this fatuousness.*]

You are very patient with him, Sara—and with me.

SARA Oh, Abraham, it is not the present that matters. But what is to become of him? How will he be fit for a great place if you do not discipline him? You would not ruin a colt so.

ABRAHAM (*still at the tent door*) Do you smell something like tar burning?

SARA No. It is probably the stuff the men are using to brand the cattle. What are you looking at?

ABRAHAM (*his hands circling his eyes, binocular-wise*) That cloud on the plain. I have never seen a cloud lie there so long. It has been like that since yesterday morning. By noon yesterday at the latest it should have risen. (*Making a movement to go*) Well, I suppose I must seek out Ishmael and bring home to him, if possible, the error of his ways.

SARA No. He will only say that I asked you to punish him. It is not for any rudeness to me that you should punish him, but when he disobeys your own orders. When he rode the white stallion, for instance, and upset the whole camp.

ABRAHAM I know. But I was so proud of the lad's courage. Half the men will not go near that stallion. (*Turning for a last look at the cloud as he goes*) That cloud looks like smoke more than anything else. But you can't have a smoke ten miles square.

[*He goes out, still puzzled, back.*]

[SARA, *her shoulders drooped with depression, takes out a piece of embroidery and the coloured threads for it.*

[*Enter from R.,* HAGAR, *no longer the soft kittenish girl that we have known till now. The bones of her character are showing through the hardness, the opportunism, the preoccupation with material things.*]

HAGAR So you grudge my son an ounce of nuts and honey now?

SARA (*in a weary revulsion*) Oh, Hagar, don't be absurd.

[*She takes her embroidery to a low seat near the tent door.*]

HAGAR A ragamuffin at the tent door, oh, yes. Sweets galore for him, but for my son, no.

SARA Ishmael took the sweets without asking, that was all. Perhaps he did not tell you that.

HAGAR And why should he ask in his father's house?

SARA (*dryly*) It is a pleasant convention.

HAGAR You and your superiority. Do you think I cannot train my son in my own house without your interference?

SARA (*lifting her head for a moment to look at* HAGAR) I find it difficult to believe that you were ever trained in mine.

HAGAR And what a training! 'No, Hagar, one does it *so*.' 'Hagar, your laugh is too loud.' 'Bring this, Hagar.' 'Fetch that, Hagar.' 'A new frock for you, darling, to match your eyes.' 'My sweet Hagar.' 'My lovely kitten.'

[*As this produces no speech from* SARA.]

Well, I fetch and carry for no one now, and when I want new clothes I choose them for myself. And my son, thank the gods, does not have to wait on your charity for sweets.

[*Exit R.*]

[SARA'S *hands lie still for a moment, although her head is still bent over her work. Then she resumes it, drawing the thread through the cloth with a kind of slow hopelessness.*

[*After a moment there appears in the tent-mouth a* MAN *in desert clothes; that is, in the heavy robes and the head-covering of a nomad. He is apparently elderly, since the small pointed beard is streaked with grey, but he carries his tall figure straight and gracefully. His clothes are plain, but made of rich stuff, and he has an easy and relaxed dignity.*

[*He approaches against the sun, so that his shadow falls behind him, and since his sandals make no noise there is nothing to warn* SARA *of his presence. He stands for a long moment contemplating her before she becomes aware of him.*]

SARA (*noticing him*) Oh. You startled me.

THE SCRIBE (*for that is what he is*) I am sent to say that your nieces are safe.

SARA (*at a loss*) My nieces? You mean Lot's daughters?

SCRIBE Yes. They are safe in Zoar.

SARA What are they doing in Zoar? And why should they not be safe?

SCRIBE Have you not heard? It rains burning oil down

there. (*With a faint movement of his head he indicates the distance behind him*) The cities are in flames. You can see the cloud of smoke from here, covering all the plain and——

SARA Burning? The towns? Wait! (*Running to the doorway, back, calling*) Abraham! Abraham, come! Listen! There is dreadful news.

[*Enter* ABRAHAM.]

It *is* smoke, the cloud on the plain. Smoke of the towns burning.

ABRAHAM Burning? Whole towns?

SCRIBE Yes. Whole towns like torches. You can hear the roar of the burning six miles away.

ABRAHAM But how? Is it war?

SCRIBE No. The ground began to break open and send jets of burning oil into the sky. The oil came down like rain and could not be put out. Even where it fell on water it went on burning. The people fled out of the cities to get away from the fires, but even as they ran the ground would open in new places under their feet, and the flaming gases flare up, and the burning rain fall on them. The plain is strewn with corpses burnt ash-white, like pillars of salt. I came to tell you that your nieces are safe. They were sent to Zoar when the trouble began.

ABRAHAM And Lot?

SARA And Milcah, and their people?

SCRIBE No one knows. (*Into the dismayed silence*) There was a pause after the first explosion and, like most of the others, they decided to stay.

ABRAHAM (*pulling himself together*) I must collect some of my men. There is surely *some* rescue to be done—people to be gathered to shelter—reassured——

[*He goes out hastily, back.*]

SARA (*to the* SCRIBE) It was kind of you to bring us the news. You must be weary. Sit in the shade for a little and rest, and I shall bring you some food.

SCRIBE No, thank you; it is kind of you but I want nothing.

SARA (*offering refreshment lighter than food*) Some cold curds, to take the dust from your throat? Or some wine, perhaps.

SCRIBE Thank you, but I must be on my way.

SARA Have you, too, fled from there?

SCRIBE No, I travel the countryside, writing letters.

SARA (*a little surprised*) A scribe. (*With a glance at his clothes. In friendly fashion*) It would seem to be a prosperous trade.

SCRIBE (*with a little smile*) It suffices. The wordiness of the human race is unfailing.

SARA I think often that a public letter-writer must have more power than a Grand Vizier.

SCRIBE More knowledge, perhaps. But just as much discretion.

SARA (*eyeing him as she sinks on to her seat again*) Yes. It is strange. I never saw you before, and yet there is probably not one thing about me that you do not know.

SCRIBE (*agreeing*) Very little, my daughter. Though rumour lied in one respect.

[*As she looks inquiring.*]

It said that you were no longer beautiful.

SARA Perhaps it lies in other things. What *do* you know about me?

SCRIBE That you are the most unhappy woman in Syria.

SARA (*beginning to flare*) Is that what they say?

SCRIBE No. That is what I know. I saw you before you were aware of me. One so royal as you should not look defeated.

SARA (*her flare of antagonism gone*) But I am defeated. You know my story. The whole countryside knows it. Half Asia knows it, I don't doubt. It is an after-supper tale for full stomachs to belch over, a tit-bit for the women's tents on hot afternoons, a jest to lighten the boredom of a cattle trek. What a fate for Sara who lived in Ur, and was proud and beautiful and unpitied and mistress of her household—and of herself.

SCRIBE The world is a black misery to you, isn't it? Nevertheless, next time that I see you it will be with a son in your arms.

SARA (*in a low fury*) How dare you mock me. (*In a sort of weary contempt*) Oh, I know; you want to sell me a charm. You waste your talents, my friend. There is no spell, no invocation, no stratagem, no quirk that I am unacquainted with. I have slept with my feet to the north and my feet to the south. I have made pilgrimages and consulted oracles. I have done penance and made promises, I have swallowed messes, breathed vapours, abstained, indulged, made of myself a crucible for all the arts and magic of a silly world.

SCRIBE There is one thing you have not done, my daughter.

SARA Oh, yes, I have crossed people's hands with silver, too.

SCRIBE (*unperturbed*) You have not done your part.

SARA (*practically speechless at what seems to her the enormity of this statement*) Not done——!

SCRIBE Abraham, your husband, had faith; and for him the promise came true. But you! What faith had you? Because the promise was unlikely you laughed at it in your heart. You went from longing to despair, but not once did you think of having faith.

SARA (*considering him anew*) You did not read *that* in any letter.

SCRIBE No; that I know of myself.

SARA (*still mocking a little, but more as a guard against her own emotions than in contempt for him*) You are clever, scribe. If the human race ever stop writing letters, you can make a living at divination. And now, I suppose, you sell me your charm.

SCRIBE I don't sell it. I tell you what it is.

SARA And what is it?

SCRIBE A small piece of the little dry thorn on the hill.

SARA I knew that you were mad.

SCRIBE A fresh piece every day. Fetched by no one but yourself.

SARA (*beginning to see method in his madness; quite seriously*) You want me to go up there?

SCRIBE Yes. It is surprising what new hope grows on the top of a hill.

SARA New hope is not faith.

SCRIBE No. Not quite. It is the shadow that faith throws in front of it.

SARA (*having considered this*) You think that I shall find Abraham's God, up there?

SCRIBE No, my daughter. Your own.

[*There is a moment's silence while they look at each other.* SARA *gets to her feet and stands face to face with him.*]

SARA (*searching his eyes; all her sophistication and mockery gone*) Do you believe what you said about—about——

SCRIBE About the child in your arms? If I had not believed I would not have said it.

SARA How do you—have you a gift? Can you see——

SCRIBE No. It is simple. The promise was made to Abraham, and he believed, and it was so. The promise was made to you, but you did not believe, and it was not so. It is not the promise that has failed, but you. The missing piece in the pattern is faith. Find faith, and the promise comes true. I see a beggar coming to claim your charity; I shall leave you to your good works. (*He pauses a moment*) When I come again it will be to celebrate your son's first birthday.

[*He goes.*]

[SARA *stands where she is, inside the tent, busy with her thoughts.*]

SARA Faith. (*Still with her mind on other things, she claps her hands to summon a servant*)

[*Enter an elderly* WOMAN SERVANT.]

(*Without looking at her, automatically*) Bring me some food to give to a beggar.

[*The* WOMAN *goes.*]

[SARA *moves to the tent-mouth slowly. She stands for a moment or two idly watching the* BEGGAR *approach. Then her indifferent attitude changes to attention.*]

SARA (*tentative, incredulous*) Lot. (*Certain*) Oh, Lot, my dear!

[*She disappears to meet him, and brings him in with her, a broken, ragged, distracted creature.*]

Oh, Lot, my dear, dear Lot! Sit down, sit down.

[*She half-guides, half-supports him on to the seat she has been using. He sits there, his elbows propped on his knees and his head in his hands.*]

Poor Lot. I shall get you——

[*Enter the* WOMAN SERVANT *with bread in one hand and a carafe of wine in the other. She stares at the tableau.* SARA *snatches the wine from her, tilts back* LOT's *head and puts the mouth of the carafe to his lips. He drinks eagerly.*]

(*As he pauses*) Your girls are safe. You know?

[*He nods.*]

(*Hardly daring to put it into words*) And Milcah?

[*He shakes his head, not as one not knowing, but as one when the worst has happened.*]

Poor Lot! Poor Lot! (*To the* WOMAN) Make a meal ready as quickly as you can. Something light.

[*The* WOMAN *goes.*]

[LOT *puts his head back in his hands and begins to sob.* SARA *takes this rightly as a sign that the strain is breaking and that the worst is over. Partly her sympathy, partly the more physical relaxation of sitting down, has ended the nightmare world he has been walking through.*]

LOT (*through the sobs*) I *told* her not to go.

SARA To go where?

LOT (*by degrees*) Not to go back. She went back for her charm. A silly thing of blue beads. (*This overcomes him afresh*)

SARA But if she went back, Lot, perhaps in spite of everything she is still safe. She may——

[*The head between* LOT'*s hands is shaken vigorously.*]

LOT (*by degrees*) The whole earth opened in a wall of flame. I was standing there watching her. She had got to the corner where the camels unload. I was furious with her. Thinking how silly she was. Blue beads. And then—— (*he rocks himself in grief*)

SARA (*whispering*) Poor Lot!

LOT (*presently; calmer, but still with his face hidden*) They are saying in the plain that this is a judgment. I know it is a judgment on me.

[*He means: Whether it is a general judgment or not, I, personally, have deserved it.*]

SARA But why, Lot? What have you ever done to bring anything so horrible on your head?

LOT I mocked Abraham's God.

SARA (*thinking he must be slightly deranged, comforting*) Oh, no, Lot.

LOT (*half following her thought*) Not with words, but in my life I did. I shared the Promise without believing. I took all the benefits and gave nothing in return. I was not even grateful for what I got. I took it all for granted. Abraham thought that he had a Promise, and I—cashed in on it.

SARA But is that so grave an offence? Grave enough to——

LOT If an unbeliever comes to the altar he dies. That is

so in all religions. Without faith one has no right to the blessing.

SARA (*thinking how oddly this echoes what the* SCRIBE *has said*) Faith. Yes. Perhaps it is as you say. Without faith, nothing. (*Her mind going on to her own problem*) And with it—— (*Her thoughts go soaring*)

[*Guilty at her own preoccupation, she comes back impulsively to* LOT's *plight.*]

Come, Lot. Come and lie down in the cool darkness for a little. I shall give you something to make you sleep.

LOT Sleep? How can I ever sleep again and not see the flames—and the burning rain—and the white corpses on the road——?

SARA We shall send word to Zoar that you are safe, and your daughters will come to be a comfort to you. For there will be comfort, believe me. There is no gulf of despair so deep that one cannot be rescued from it. I know.

CURTAIN

SCENE 2

The Scene is the same, about two years later.

Some of the tent hangings are different—to emphasise the interval—but the furnishings are the same.

The entrance to the inner tent R. is open, and there is much coming and going of SERVANTS *bearing plates of fruit, cakes, jars of honey, wine, sweetmeats, bread, and all the other ingredients of a feast. An air of excitement and satisfaction pervades the scene. At the side of the tent opening is a small cot; half in the open air but still in the tent.*

ISHMAEL *is lounging near by, making sounds on a reed pipe in a bored and tuneless fashion.*

When we have sufficiently absorbed the scene and the fact that a feast is toward, and noted with satisfaction the presence of the cot, the more immediate action begins.

A passing SERVANT, *noticing* ISHMAEL's *eyes on a decorated cake that she is carrying past, breaks off in a surreptitious fashion a projecting piece and offers it to him.*

ISHMAEL (*in offended scorn*) I don't take stolen pieces, thank you. If I am no longer my father's heir, I am nevertheless his son.

[*The* SERVANT, *well aware that* ISHMAEL'S *morals are not normally so rarefied, shrugs a resentful shoulder at the refusal of her proffered kindness and goes on.*

[LARSA *comes in slowly from the tent entrance, his eyes and mind on the clay tablet with dampened surface he is holding in his left hand—it is about the size of his palm—and on which he is making notes with a pencil. He stands a moment busy with his tablet, while* ISHMAEL'S *mournful performance on the pipe goes on.*]

LARSA (*coming to, mildly*) Do you have to make that horrible noise?

ISHMAEL I am playing a tune for my brother.

LARSA Your brother is asleep; and if he is not going to howl the place down when the guests are here, he had better be allowed to have his sleep out. Postpone the melody.

[*As* ISHMAEL *sullenly desists,* SARA *comes in R., from the inner tent. She is very happy, and there is a bloom on her that one associates only with youth.*]

SARA (*slipping her arm through* LARSA'S, *laughing*) Tell me, Larsa: If a chief eats enough for a chief-and-a-half at a wedding, how much will ten chiefs eat at a child's first-birthday party?

LARSA (*laughing too*) Why worry? There must be enough food in there to feed all Syria. Food to make their eyes fall out.

[*They stroll together to the tent-mouth.*]

It can't be often that the world is ransacked to make a meal. Wine from the islands, honey from Thrace and Iran, strange berries from the Black Sea.

SARA Still stranger fruits from Africa.

LARSA Spices from Hindustan.

SARA Potent syrups from Smyrna.

LARSA Some still more potent liquid from the far north that looks like water and tastes like wood-shavings.

SARA To say nothing of some very odd-looking nuts from the Caspian. I hope they don't poison anyone.

LARSA This feast will be the talk of Syria for a hundred years—and part of its history for ever.

SARA Well, as gossip it will be a pleasanter tale than I once provided them with. (*She moves over to adjust the shadow on the cot and pauses to look down at her son*) He is an ugly little wretch, isn't he?

LARSA (*with an amused jerk of his head, considering the child*) Yes.

SARA Oh, Larsa, you are hopeless! The correct reply to that is: 'But *so* full of *character*!'

LARSA Yes, he has that in plenty. He will make a fine man some day.

SARA And I shall not be here to see. It will be for you, Larsa, to see that my son is a credit to his father. You must promise me one thing.

LARSA (*protesting at the intrusion of death at this joyous moment*) Oh, no, Sara! Not on this feast day.

SARA Oh, I am not being sad about it. I have been blessed too greatly to have time for regrets. But one is mortal, and one speaks while one still has a tongue. Promise me that when the time comes for him to take a wife, you will go back to Ur and choose one for him; from among some of the families we used to know.

LARSA (*surprised and sympathetic*) You still think of Ur, then?

SARA In Ur there was tradition, and a philosophy of life, and standards to live up to. I don't want him to mate with this restless and polyglot people. (*After a slight pause*) I have learned in these years how much more the blood counts than the training.

[*There is a moment's silence while each contemplates what sorrow lack of breeding has brought to the household for the last ten years.*]

LARSA Yes, Sara: I promise.

[*Enter* ABRAHAM *in his best clothes, back.*]

ABRAHAM (*exhibiting his magnificence obediently*) Well? Am I fine enough for you?

SARA (*admiring critically*) Yes. Turn round.

[*She turns him round and back again.*]

Oh no, Abraham! Not that belt!

ABRAHAM What is wrong with it? Except for my every-day leather one, it is the only one in my box.

SARA (*briskly*) Oh, nonsense.

[*Sweeping him out in front of her, back.*]

There is that beautiful one I embroidered for you with the silks from Serica—

[THEY *go.*]

[LARSA *goes back to his tablet and presently strolls into the further tent R., still busy with the tablet.*

[*As he goes,* ISHMAEL *reappears, twanging a catapult, and taking imaginary aim at various objects in the same desultory fashion as he indulged in melody.* LARSA, *coming back, finds him so engaged.*]

LARSA Can't you find some way to make yourself useful, Ishmael, instead of just hanging about this tent? (*Seeing the catapult*) I thought that you were forbidden to play with that catapult inside the camp bounds? You know what happened six months ago.

ISHMAEL That was an accident.

LARSA (*his attention arrested by this strange reaction*) Of course it was an accident. I didn't suppose you half-killed your brother on purpose.

[*He stares at the boy, a new thought darkening the back of his mind. Putting out his hand, decidedly.*]

You had better give me that catapult.

ISHMAEL (*flurried by the thought of losing his treasure*) But I won't use it. I promise I won't. I don't need to.

LARSA You *don't need to*? What does that mean?

ISHMAEL (*retrieving*) I mean: there are no targets to aim at here. I have no need to use it.

LARSA (*puzzled, but quite sure that the weapon should not be left where it is*) You had better give that thing to me.

[*Intimidated by the tone,* ISHMAEL *hands it over without a word.*]

And don't let me catch you hanging round here any more this afternoon. Find something useful to do and do it—if you can. (*He sits down to con his tablet*)

[ISHMAEL *disappears sulkily to the outer world.*]

[*From the opening behind him, R.,* HAGAR *strolls into view. She is like her son, idle and detached and outside the rejoicing. She stands for a little regarding* LARSA'*s back with antagonism.*]

HAGAR (*strolling forward*) You didn't need a pencil and tablet to reckon the cost of *my* son's first birthday party.

LARSA (*glancing up at her*) No. Abraham bought you the

necklace you are wearing. (*Going back to his tablet*) It cost a king's ransom. (*His mind suddenly realising what the tail of his eye has seen; looking up again*) You are *not* wearing it.

HAGAR (*her hand going automatically to the empty place*) No, it was stolen.

LARSA (*incredulous*) It was stolen? And you did nothing about it? A necklace worth a fortune!

HAGAR I—I lost it, perhaps. It is missing, and I didn't want Abraham to know.

LARSA (*dryly*) Then if I were you I should be intelligent enough to wear another in its place. Otherwise even Abraham will notice.

HAGAR Always very free with advice, aren't you, Larsa?

LARSA (*offering her the catapult*) This belongs to your son, by the way. I thought he was forbidden to play with it in camp?

HAGAR (*snatching it from him*) Was he playing with it today? The little fool. Spoiling everything. (*She sounds furious*)

LARSA (*surprised at her reaction*) Spoiling everything? Spoiling what?

HAGAR (*retrieving*) Spoiling the peace of this happy day, of course. (*Through a smile that goes no deeper than her teeth*) It would be too sad, wouldn't it, if anything happened to mar the rejoicings; to take the bloom off the triumph. Yes. Very sad that would be.

[*She stalks out into the sunlight leaving an odd impression of threat behind her. As if something she had been unable to repress had shone through her words in spite of her.*

[LARSA *stares after her for a moment and goes back to his reckoning.*

[TWO SERVANTS, *separately, cross from opposite sides, busy with the food traffic. They lark with each other in passing and disappear.* LARSA *rises and follows the one through the opening R.*]

[*The room is now empty.*

[ISHMAEL *appears in the tent-mouth from the opposite direction that* HAGAR *has taken. He strolls in humming in a would-be casual manner that is more guilty than any silence would be. On the threshold he reassures himself that the room is empty. He then makes his way to the entrance, back, casual but quiet, his humming stopped for the moment and his eyes on the open entrance R., ready for any invasion from that direction. He listens at the upper entrance, and is evidently reassured by the sound of* SARA *and* ABRAHAM *in conversation.*

[*From there he comes down to the entrance R., and from there surveys the inner tent. It is apparently empty. He takes from the folds of clothing at his waist a small metal box. He makes sure again that he is alone and darts across the room to the cot in the tent-mouth. He is preparing the box in some fashion, and is bending over the cot preparatory to leaving the contents there, when* LARSA *comes back R.*]

LARSA (*seeing him*) I thought I told you not to hang about this tent any more this——

[*The* BOY'S *sudden straightening and alarm have given him away.* LARSA *crosses quickly to him.*]

What are you doing? What have you got there?

[*The* BOY *makes a motion to run, but is a fraction of a second too late.* LARSA *has hold of him.*]

ISHMAEL Leave me alone! Let me go!

LARSA (*trying to reach the little metal box in the boy's hands as well as keep him from escaping*) What have you got in that box?

ISHMAEL It's just a brass box, that is all. It's mine, and you can't have it. (*He is struggling and kicking*) Leave me alone! How dare you lay hands on me?

[*His voice, between terror and rage, is rising rapidly.*]

LARSA What is in the box? That is what I want to know. Give it to me. Give it to me, I say!

[*He manages to snatch it from the boy, and to open it has to let* ISHMAEL *go. But now that the box is in* LARSA'S *hands* ISHMAEL *can no longer help himself by running away. He must stay and brazen it out.*]

ISHMAEL (*with a pretended air of superior scorn*) I don't know why you had to make all that fuss. It's only a spider in the box.

[*Shrieking suddenly, as he sees* LARSA *about to open the box.*]

Don't open it!

[LARSA *pauses.*]

(*Conversationally again, trying to retrieve the mistake of that involuntary shriek*) It's only a spider I tell you.

LARSA And why shouldn't I open it?

ISHMAEL If you do it will get away. I don't want to lose it. (*But it sounds very lame*)

[LARSA *begins to open the box, slowly and with care.*]

ISHMAEL (*yelling*) No! No, don't! No! No!

LARSA (*shuts the box quickly, having seen—a little breathless*) A spider, yes. But what a spider!

[SARA *and* ABRAHAM, *alarmed by* ISHMAEL'S *shrieks, come in hastily from back.*]

ABRAHAM What is this? Is murder being done?

LARSA Oddly enough, yes.

SARA Yes? What do you mean, Larsa?

LARSA (*holding out the little box*) Do you see this?

SARA Yes. It's the little brass box that Hagar bought in Damascus. She keeps her pins in it.

LARSA What is in it at this moment is a Black Enchanter.

ABRAHAM (*puzzled*) A spider? A *poisonous* spider? Who put it there?

SARA (*always quicker of perception than* ABRAHAM *and with, therefore, less question and less puzzlement in her voice*) And why?

LARSA (*to* ABRAHAM) I found your son putting the box in his brother's cot.

ABRAHAM (*refusing it*) Oh, no.

ISHMAEL It is only a spider. I just wanted to frighten him. To make him cry.

ABRAHAM You put it there—you were going to put it there, knowing it had a Black Enchanter in it?

LARSA If you didn't know, then why did you shriek like that when I was going to open the box?

SARA Black Enchanters are very rare. It may be true that he never heard the name. On the other hand, the chances of his having come across it by accident are very small. Where did the spider come from, Ishmael?

[*Enter* HAGAR, *from outside. She is brazen, as usual, but somehow apprehensive; a quicker rate of breathing than usual, a wariness.*]

HAGAR Was that Ishmael who was shrieking?

LARSA Ah! Welcome, Hagar. Perhaps *you* can tell us how death got into your pin box?

HAGAR (*deciding that the best defence is the boy's ignorance*) How should I know what is in the box? Ishmael has been playing with it for days.

ISHMAEL (*thinking he is being deserted*) No!

HAGAR (*turning on him in quick warning*) Leave this to me!

[*But the boy is past reasoning. All he can see is that the onus is being placed squarely on his shoulders. His overwhelming instinct is to place it elsewhere.*]

ISHMAEL No! *She* gave it to me! She got it from one of the herds. He promised it to her when he found one. She gave him her necklace for it.

HAGAR You little fool!

ABRAHAM Hagar! You—you *ordered* a poisonous spider? With this in your mind?

HAGAR If you believe the word of an hysterical child.

ABRAHAM Then you still have your necklace?

HAGAR Of course I have.

LARSA A few moments ago you told me you had lost it.

HAGAR I did no such thing.

LARSA (*relentless*) You said you had not mentioned its loss because you did not want Abraham to know, and I advised you to fill up the missing space with something else.

[*He indicates the space, but her guilty hand is already there in an automatic gesture.*]

ABRAHAM I have never known Larsa to lie, Hagar.

HAGAR Well, he is lying now.

ABRAHAM Why should he?

HAGAR He has always hated me. He has hated me from the first day I came into this household. He was jealous!

SARA Jealous?

HAGAR He was jealous because I was Sara's pet. I took away the interest that might have been his. Until I came he had it all to himself, but once I was there she had no eyes for him any more. He was just a piece of furniture. And he went on being a piece of furniture and hating me more every day. He has spied on me all my life, and there is no lie he would not tell if he thought it would harm me.

SARA Believe me, Hagar, if Larsa ever took to lying the lies would be intelligent ones. Not ones that could be disproved by the production of a necklace.

ABRAHAM (*in a sort of groan*) Hagar, you *couldn't* have done this thing. You couldn't have planned injury to the child, death perhaps, to the child who meant so much—even if you were envious of his prior right, disappointed, even so you *could not* have *planned*—you must have some explanation, some defence.

HAGAR I tell you, the boy found the spider and had no idea it was poisonous. He put it in the box and planned a piece of mischief, that is all. How was he to know that it was a Black Enchanter?

LARSA (*quietly, taking his ample and complete revenge*) How did *you* know?

[*There is a moment's silence.*]

SARA (*with quiet decision*) Hagar, nearly twenty years ago I bought you in the market-place. Today I give you your freedom and you will go out of this family for ever. And take your son with you.

ABRAHAM Oh, no, Sara; not the boy.

SARA The boy too. The boy most especially.

ABRAHAM But it is partly my fault—the boy.

SARA It is very largely your fault.

ABRAHAM If I had not spoiled him, failed to punish him——

SARA It is too late to think of that now. It was not the boy you indulged, but your own love for him.

ABRAHAM Yes, I know. It was selfishness. But don't punish the boy for my fault. He is young yet, and there are years in which to train him to better things.

SARA No. He is Hagar's son. I will have none of Hagar's blood in my house.

HAGAR And if I refuse to go?

SARA The men in the camp will be told the story of this afternoon, and you and your son will be turned out to them an hour later.

[*As* HAGAR *appreciates this.*]

Not only will you leave this family, but you will go out of the country. You will go south until you are over the borders of Syria, and you will never come back. As long as you stay outside Syria a pension will be paid to you—and to your son after you. Abraham will make it a generous one, I have no doubt; and from that I would not dissuade him. Twice a year the money will come to wherever you are—outside Syria.

HAGAR (*cheerful and relieved at such a fortunate ending from her point of view*) Very well, I go. It is not every woman who is given money and her freedom in the same five minutes. I shall be a great deal better off in the future than I ever was in your household. Even when I was mistress of it the air suffocated me. I shall have what I always wanted; freedom. Freedom to do as I like. To take what road I like, what lover I like, and my leave when I like. Abraham went out from Ur to inherit Syria, but his son goes out from Syria to inherit the world.

[*She takes her son and goes, L.*]

ISHMAEL (*just audible as he is dragged off*) But you betrayed me! You betrayed me!

SARA Give her money, Abraham, and send her away. Let them have camels, so that by sundown they may be below our horizon.

[ABRAHAM *follows* HAGAR *out, L.*]

(*Sits down abruptly—to* LARSA, *but even more to herself*) He will forget.

LARSA Who?

SARA He will forget the boy when our own son grows up.

[*She is reassuring herself against inner doubt.*]

LARSA (*comfortably*) He will forget long before then.

SARA You think so?

LARSA Ishmael's manners were beginning to strain even Abraham's tolerance. Hadn't you noticed? His pleadings for the boy came from a tender conscience, not a doting parent.

SARA Oh, Larsa, you are a great comfort to me. You have always been the greatest comfort. And how can I ever thank you for what you did just now?

LARSA Staying Ishmael's hand? Oh, that was mere chance. I came in to—to—— (*He can't remember*) I can't remember what I came in for. It doesn't matter. I came in at the exact moment to—to—— (*He is still puzzling with half his mind about what it was he had come in for*)

SARA To save the child.

LARSA (*amending*) To achieve Hagar's ruin.

[*There is an unregenerate satisfaction in his voice.*]

SARA You sound as if you had waited for years to do that.

[*She does not believe that he has, and is taken aback by his answer.*]

LARSA I have.

SARA Larsa!

LARSA All the long years when you loved her, all the slow bitter years when you suffered at her hands, I knew that one day she would make a mistake; that she would go too far; and that I would be there when the time came.

SARA Was it true what she said: that you were jealous; that that was why you hated her?

LARSA In the beginning I think it may have been. But not for long. Hagar provided so many reasons for hating her that the choice became embarrassing. She—— (*He stops abruptly*) (*Looking scandalised*) Great Astoreth!

SARA What is it?

LARSA I have just remembered what I came in to do! I came in to tell you that a guest had arrived.

SARA Oh, no, Larsa; not already, surely?

LARSA What is worse is that it is someone I don't know. I am quite sure he was not invited.

SARA A chief, is he?

LARSA No, he says he is a letter-writer. And that you know him.

SARA (*getting to her feet, her face lighting*) Yes, I know him. Bring him in, Larsa.

LARSA In here?

SARA Yes; he has come to see my son.

[*While* LARSA *goes to fetch the* SCRIBE, *she goes over to the cot to dote on her boy.*

[*The* SCRIBE *comes in by himself, R., and after a pause on the threshold crosses the room to her as if he were at home, and joins her at the cot.*]

SARA My friend!

SCRIBE My daughter.

[*She smiles at him wordlessly, and together they contemplate the child of faith.*

[ABRAHAM *comes in behind them from outside L., full of a still more revealing scene off with* HAGAR.]

SARA Abraham, our first guest has come. You remember that he came once to bring us the good news that Lot's girls were safe.

ABRAHAM (*welcoming the guest with the air of a kind host whose mind is elsewhere*) But of course, of course. We are glad to see you again. I feel that our thanks that day were not as generous as your kindness deserved. It was a very distressed moment.

SCRIBE (*in a tone that makes a question very nearly into a statement*) And—this?

SARA How did you know?

SCRIBE It needs no pool of ink, or pattern in the sand, to divine that.

(*Note: Keep 'or', the more grammatical 'nor' makes too many N's.*)

ABRAHAM I am harvesting my folly, friend. It is a bitter crop.

SCRIBE (*agreeing*) Yes. (*There is a sort of qualification to the word*) There *are* those who have harvested a bitter crop, with no folly sown.

ABRAHAM (*quickly*) I know: I know. (*Going to her*) Sara, can you ever forgive me for those blind years?

SARA (*gently*) My dear. This is no time for humility. We have a great triumph, you and I. A great happiness. Let us take it greatly—and forget the bitter crop. (*After a pause of communion she looks back at the* SCRIBE *and puts out her hand to him—smiling at him*) Come and be the first to share our feast.

CURTAIN

NOTES

To look at, this play should be a miracle of light and colour. The lovely colours in the soft reflected light, and the brilliant light outside; a white, heavy, hot light pouring down on the green well of the courtyard in the first act, and the clear diamond light of the Syrian uplands in the second and third.

The costumes vary from the scanty clothes of urban Mesopotamia—bare arms and necks, and oddly modern-appearing frocks—to the heavy cream-wool folds of the Nomads in Syria.

Place-names are not always chronologically true. They have been chosen for their sound or for convenience; to avoid a too 'Biblical' atmosphere, for instance, it is useful to use the Babylonian rather than the Israelitish form of a word, although its use may not have been contemporary. All the places mentioned did exist at the time, of course; the only liberty taken is with the form of the names.

With regard to the story:

It is likely that Sara picked up Hagar during their stay in Egypt, long after they left Ur and before their final settling down in Canaan. But, dramatically, Hagar could not appear when the play was half over. So, since there is no information one way or the other as to when she joined the household, she is allowed to be there from the beginning. Similarly Larsa (Eleizar in the Bible form) no doubt joined them in Damascus, but, since we don't know, he, too, is allowed to be part of the household in Ur.

Where Ishmael's attack on his brother is concerned: the Bible word 'mocked' is also translated as 'did injury to'; and since a mere mocking could not have had the results recorded in the story, the second is the more likely version.

'An angel of the Lord' is too often taken literally, as a supernatural visitation (with wings or without according to taste) instead of the metaphorical phrase for a bringer of good which it undoubtedly is. (Just as 'the Lord was with him' is used for a mere material prospering.) The Scribe in this play is no angel, but very much an 'angel of the Lord'.

The tent in the second and third acts is open almost entirely on L., the roofing stretched out on poles to make an open place of shade beyond the tent proper.

Note on Milcah

Milcah is not a scold. *Nor* a shrew. She has neither passion nor venom. There is no heat in anything she says. Indeed, if one were not listening to her words, one might conclude that she was talking about the weather.

She is the type of woman who is despairing long before she is angry. Tiresome, but likeable in a way that a scold or a shrew could never be.

VALERIUS

CHARACTERS

C. VALERIUS VALENS, *Centurion of the Second Augusta*
RUFUS SITA, *Camp Prefect*
FLAVIUS BETTO, *Centurion of the Second Augusta*
DEMETRIUS, *Officer Commanding Artillery*
TI. CLAUDIUS PAULINUS, *Centurion of the Second Augusta*
M. COCCEIUS FIRMUS, *General Officer Commanding the Wall*
AEMILIUS, SALVIUS, VARUS, CANDIDUS, PETRONIUS, MARIUS, JULIUS — *Soldiers*
VIRIUS LUPUS, *Governor of Britain*
COGI, *a Caledonian trader*

Non-speaking Parts

GAZA, *a tongueless servant*
LOSSIO, *a soldier*
PATRICIUS, *a soldier*
SANCTIUS, *a soldier*
OTHER SOLDIERS, *unnamed*
TAMINIUS, *a doctor*
TWO YOUNG TRIBUNES

SCENES

Except for the second scene, on the ramparts of the fort, the whole action takes place in a room in the infantry post of Vindobala, on the Great Wall, in the late autumn of the year A.D. 196.

AUTHOR'S NOTE

It has pleased the author, for a whim, to use in this play the names of men who actually served in Britain in the years when Britain was part of the Empire.

To the shade of Marcus Cocceius Firmus, sometime Centurion at Auchendavy on the Antonine Wall, the author offers apology for having taken his name in vain.

ACT I

SCENE I

A room in the infantry post of Vindobala, on the Great Wall, in the late autumn of the year A.D. 196. *The fort is about twenty miles west from the mouth of the Tyne, and is set on a hill.*

It is a square, bare room, with plastered and painted walls. In the middle of the back wall a widish doorway gives on to a veranda and thence to a courtyard; the inner courtyard of the principia, or headquarters building, of the post. The other side of the courtyard, which can be seen in the distance, is an arcaded wall with sloping roof. One cannot see the door to the outer courtyard because the room is not the middle one on our side of the courtyard. The middle one (through the R. wall) is the 'chapel' of the fort, where the standards are kept—and from which they are visible, through the lengths of the two courtyards, to every man passing along the main street beyond.

Up L. is an entrance to the room on the L.; which can also be entered from the veranda.

Normally the room we are looking at is an office, but since Clodius Albinus, Governor of Britain, drained the Wall of troops to fight for him in Gaul, the more-than-halved garrison of Vindobala is commanded not by a Tribune but by the Senior Centurion (a Company Officer), and he finds it pleasanter and more convenient to use these two rooms as his quarters than to occupy the empty and echoing rooms of the Commanding Officer's house.

It is at the moment about an hour before sunset, and the courtyard outside is filled with the reflected light of a western sky that is growing, unbelievably, more magnificent minute by minute. In the room it is quiet. A distant bugle sounds, and now and then a soldier crosses the courtyard outside.

Seated on a stool at a table, L., his back to the L. wall, is C. VALERIUS VALENS, *the Centurion in command. He is a young man, only twenty-six, but he looks as though it is a long time since he was a boy. He has a well-bred face, an air of natural command, passable looks, a controlled and unexpectant expression. When he smiles, however (which is not often), one is surprised by the revelation of an inward charm. He is engaged in making a map from a smaller rough copy which is a by-product of one of his hunting expeditions. There is no urgency in the process; it is obviously a hobby, not his work.*

Beyond him, up L., is an easy-chair of leather slung on wood. Hanging on the L. wall, above it, is his equipment: a leather jerkin, a belt with short sword, a metal helmet, and a woollen cloak.

In the opposite corner, R., is a couch of leather and wood, and down from it a low table.

A heavy curtain hangs at one side of the doorway.

Standing in the middle of the floor, slightly to R., and down from the couch, is RUFUS SITA, *Camp Prefect; in command of Details and responsible for supply, medical services, and similar bits and pieces. He is in early middle-age, but like many service men is practically ageless: square, upright as a rush, lean-faced, hard-bitten; his calm, intelligent eye as clear as sea-water; never exalted, never despairing, never at a loss; observant, tolerant, experienced. Son of a Thracian father and a Neapolitan mother, he has seen the Empire from end to end, and has served it contentedly and with great success.*

He has just come in, and is taking off his cloak before sitting down on the end of the couch. From habit he folds it length-wise four times and doubles it over, before dropping it to join his helmet on the couch. VALERIUS *takes no notice of him. They have served together for nearly three years, and are old friends by now. As Senior Centurion of the detachment of regular troops from the Second Legion which forms the garrison of the fort,* VALERIUS *is nominally the superior in rank, but neither remembers it except on general parade.*

It may be said here and now that neither of them looks in the least like Roman soldiers in a Shakespearean production. Nor like firemen who have forgotten to put their clothes on. They are both wearing trousers of a drab woollen material, laced into the ankle by the thongs of their shoes, and tunics of a lighter cream shade, short and belted in to the waist, with sleeves ending above the elbow. RUFUS, *who has come in from duty, is wearing a thick padded-leather jerkin, like the one hanging on the wall, and a heavy belt with short sword. That, with cloak and helmet, constitutes the uniform for every-day life on the Wall. Breastplates and plumes are left for ceremonial parades and for action. Except that their tunics are drab instead of cream, the men's uniform is the same as that of the officers.*

RUFUS (*breaking the comfortable silence as he begins to take off his belt*) It is going to freeze tonight. The line of the hills against the sky is as hard as the edge of a tile. (*His eye lighting on the buckle as he automatically rolls up the belt; absently*) I wonder if Solomon would give me anything on that buckle. That is the first frost this autumn. (*Sitting down on the end of the couch*) When I was a ranker, serving on the Danube, we had the worst frost for a hundred years. We carved blocks of ice nine feet thick out of the river before we could get to the water. And what do you think we found in one block? A girl. As fresh and bright-coloured as the day she fell into the water. It turned out that she froze before she drowned. When we thawed her out she proved to be quite chatty. Married a man in the Seventh. Why do you bother making maps that no one is ever going to use?

VALERIUS (*amiably, still not looking up*) Why do you bother telling stories that no one ever believes?

RUFUS It passes the time.

VALERIUS Quite so. It passes the time.

[*From the inner room has come* GAZA, VALERIUS's *servant, with a bowl of hot soup for* RUFUS.

[GAZA *is a strange creature: stunted, simian, awkward. His eyes have the listening expression that deaf persons' have. He is not deaf, but he is dumb. His tongue was cut out by the barbarians beyond the wall, and it was among them that he was found by a Roman-British punitive expedition, and saved from abandonment by* VALERIUS.

[*He is not a soldier, of course, and his garments are a collection of 'odds'. No one has ever discovered his nationality. He wears all the garments he can lay hands on because he is never warm enough, and this has led to a belief that he belongs to some southern clime. His speech is a series of grunts in different keys, but even his grunts are few and far between.*]

RUFUS (*taking the bowl*) Thank you, Gaza. (GAZA *offers with a gesture to bring soup for* VALERIUS, *and* VALERIUS *refuses with a head-shake*) Oh, Gaza; if you go into town this evening, get the Greek to give you a bottle of Spanish olive oil, and one of fish sauce. A large bottle of oil, and a small one of sauce. (*As* GAZA *grunts acquiescence, and makes a tentative movement with his hand*) Tell him to chalk it up. The army always pays. Eventually.

[*Exit* GAZA.]

VALERIUS Town! We call that bastard collection of wooden booths a town, and we don't even smile when we say it.

RUFUS (*busy with his hot soup*) Cheer up. There were worse losses at Cremona. Though I can think of better places than the Wall in winter. At this moment—contemplate it—fat profiteers are lolling in the sun on warm terraces, looking at the blue sea and dropping oysters down their throats to give them an appetite for their fourteen courses. While we keep the Wall for them at a shilling a day. (*He sounds quite unresentful*) And fat grapes with the bloom on them, to keep them from being too hungry between courses. It makes my teeth water!

VALERIUS (*who has more personal experience of profiteers*) It makes me sick at the stomach.

RUFUS (*comfortably*) Oh, well. I expect they all have dyspepsia. I never turned from my victuals, thank the gods, and my victuals have always done right by me. (*After another mouthful*) But if I'd had any sense I would have got me a job in my uncle's wine shop in Puteoli, and lived on the fat of the land, instead of sitting on the border of civilisation with nothing to look at over the Wall but barrenness and barbarians.

VALERIUS (*looking up at him with a slight smile*) You know very well that you would not exchange those twenty years of soldiering for a consul's pay.

RUFUS (*pausing in his soup to consider* VALERIUS, *who has gone back to his map; affectionately*) I shall miss you, Valerius.

VALERIUS (*not looking up; uninterested*) Am I going somewhere?

RUFUS One of these days a letter will come from Rome saying: All is forgiven; a commission in the Praetorian Guard awaits you; return at once.

VALERIUS One of these days the moon will fall out of the sky and prove to be green cheese.

RUFUS A letter with a lovely pink travelling warrant attached. And you will auction your ponies, and pay your debts—always supposing pay has come up—and you'll drop a keepsake here and there, and be half-way down the road to York before a man can say Julius Caesar.

VALERIUS Is it from your Thracian father or from your Neapolitan mother that you get your imagination?

RUFUS Well; you must see that I have a good tombstone as compensation.

VALERIUS (*surprised into interest*) Tombstone?

RUFUS If I am going to rot on the Wall, I insist on rotting in style. I make only two conditions. The stone must be the handsomest ever seen; and it must be outside the Wall.

VALERIUS Outside?

RUFUS (*jerking a thumb over his shoulder towards the door behind him, and so to the North*) Facing Caledonia. I never turned my back on the barbarian alive, and I shall not do it dead.

VALERIUS (*moved suddenly by the faint breath of seriousness that has blown into the light exchange*) You and your tombstones! (*Changing the subject*) I think we grow stale, Rufus. Let us have the cavalry over from Condercum (*the slight movement of his head to the wall behind him indicates that Condercum is somewhere east of them*) one night for supper.

RUFUS (*deserting his dream of a tombstone and coming hastily down to brass tacks*) Feed a lot of Auxiliaries when we have not enough food for respectable Legionary stomachs?

VALERIUS We still have some of the Falernian wine left, haven't we?

RUFUS Yes, but it is not going down the throats of any Spanish horse-copers.

VALERIUS You served with Auxiliaries once.

RUFUS I did, God help me. I was seconded to them in Dalmatia. On the first day of every month they ate a baby for breakfast. And at ten o'clock every morning they practised telling lies for half an hour.

VALERIUS Did they need to?

RUFUS Oh, no. Merely exercising their art.

VALERIUS So that is where you learned. (*Giving it up*) Well, I am sorry you will not spare the wine. I think they are amusing. And it is bad for our souls to be the only regulars on the Wall.

RUFUS (*mock submissive*) Of course, if you command it, sir—— As your subordinate——

VALERIUS (*smiling at him*) We will keep the wine; and entertain old Cocceius with it next time he comes up from the depot. If we give him enough he may sign a pass for leave, who knows?

RUFUS (*sadly*) With ten men and a cobbler to hold seventy-three miles of Wall! Even Cocceius doesn't get as drunk as that.

[*They both pause to listen to a distant man's voice singing in a hearty baritone the 'rage' song of the moment.*]

VALERIUS I wish that he would get a new song.

RUFUS (*without malice*) Bird brain, bird song.

VALERIUS (*as the song approaches*) Which of his two subjects do you think it is going to be? His home town? Or his beloved battery?

RUFUS Oh, Tarsus.

VALERIUS I say the battery.

RUFUS Bet you my last gold den. it is Tarsus.

VALERIUS Done!

[*Enter from the courtyard* DEMETRIUS, *the young officer in command of the various forms of catapult on the ramparts of the fort. He is dark, full-blooded, handsome, callow and insensitive. Because of his limited outlook, his energies are canalised, so that he cares passionately for the thing that interests him. Now it may be a girl, and now a piece of bargaining; but permanently it is his battery, his pride and obsession.*]

DEMETRIUS (*to his superior officer, politely*) Good evening, Valerius.

VALERIUS Demetrius.

DEMETRIUS Rufus, if those spare parts for my battery do not come soon, we shall be at a standstill. That main catapult is practically an ornament right now.

[*Without remark and with his usual economy of gesture,* RUFUS *picks a coin from the purse on the inner side of his belt, where it is lying beside him, and tosses the coin over to* VALERIUS, *who catches it expertly.*]

RUFUS My good Demetrius, why look with glazed eye at me?

DEMETRIUS You are responsible for supply.

RUFUS Responsible for its distribution, not for its arrival. I am a simple soldier, not a medicine-man.

DEMETRIUS But you could do *something* to get them out of store at the base.

RUFUS No one knows that they are in store.

DEMETRIUS Of course they are in store! They are probably mouldering there.

RUFUS For all we know the Governor has taken your bits and pieces with him to Gaul, to help make him a Caesar. You would not grudge a few spare parts to Albinus for such a worthy object, now would you?

DEMETRIUS You do not care in the least that the best battery on the Wall is slowly falling to pieces!

RUFUS There is only one thing that worries me about your

eapons, my friend. I am afraid that I shall come along one orning and find them tied up with ribbons.

VALERIUS (*hastily*) Can our own smiths not make the parts r you?

DEMETRIUS No. I tried that. The results were primitive. hey have no idea of making a spring.

RUFUS Have you suggested to the women of the town that ey sacrifice their hair in the good cause, like the Carthaginian omen?

VALERIUS Would you like some soup, Demetrius?

DEMETRIUS No, thank you, sir. If I cannot make anyone ten to me I shall ask for leave and go and get the parts!

RUFUS I have heard many excuses for a week at Headiarters, but collecting replacements was not——

DEMETRIUS Who said anything about Headquarters? I do ot want to go to York! I only want to go to the depot at orbridge.

VALERIUS Do you think what you need will be there!

DEMETRIUS I am sure of it.

VALERIUS Then write your request for leave. It can go to orbridge with the evening courier. (*Getting up from the table d offering* DEMETRIUS *his place*) Write it now.

DEMETRIUS (*accepting the invitation*) Thank you, Valerius. *Ie shoots a triumphant glance at* RUFUS)

VALERIUS (*to* RUFUS) Play you for a gold coin at the Baths ter mess.

RUFUS (*elaborately unconcerned*) No, I think I shall go down and in the back shop at Lucilla's. Perhaps she will make some nger biscuits.

VALERIUS Take care, or Lucilla may marry you.

RUFUS I propose to her every baking day, but she will not ve me.

VALERIUS You old liar! There is not a woman from here to the osphorus that ever held your interest for more than five minutes.

RUFUS (*considering it*) Ten minutes. I am not a god.

VALERIUS But some day you will be time-expired, and a ssible legal husband for every harpy in Britain. So do not ow too attached to Lucilla's ginger biscuits.

[*Enter from the courtyard,* FLAVIUS BETTO, *Centurion. He is young, earnest, quiet, efficient. As a personality a little dull, but as a junior officer comfortingly dependable.*]

s, Flavius?

FLAVIUS The working-party have come back, sir.

VALERIUS (*cynical where work-parties are concerned*) Have the lost anything?

FLAVIUS Only some weight, sir.

VALERIUS Weight? Don't tell me that they have bee exerting themselves!

FLAVIUS They have been chased, it seems.

VALERIUS (*sharply*) Caledonians?

FLAVIUS Caledonian cattle, sir.

VALERIUS (*relaxing*) Oh. Another disgrace to Rome.

FLAVIUS Another grievance for the troops. (*In answer t* VALERIUS'S *eyebrows*) They are soldiers, they say, not gladiator They engaged to fight men, not horned animals.

VALERIUS They must write to their favourite politicia about it.

FLAVIUS (*with a grin*) Varus will see to that, sir. It will soo be time for rounds, sir.

VALERIUS Yes, Flavius; I shall be ready.

FLAVIUS That Caledonian trader from beyond the Wall i here, sir. Will you see him?

VALERIUS Cogi? What has he got?

FLAVIUS Oh, the usual things. Dogs; furs; cheek.

VALERIUS Send him in. We might as well see them.

[*Exit* FLAVIUS.

[DEMETRIUS *rises, his letter finished, and* VALERIUS *takes his pla at his map again.*]

VALERIUS Cogi is losing his tact. Until now, I have neve known him to arrive before the pay-wagon.

RUFUS Perhaps he was afraid that the dogs' teeth would dro out before anything like a pay-wagon appeared again.

DEMETRIUS The men always seem to have enough to gamb with. I don't know how they do it.

VALERIUS They borrow it from Solomon at sixty per cen interest.

RUFUS (*agreeing*) Ah. The first to cheer that pay convoy int the fort will be old Solomon.

[*Enter* COGI, *escorted by* FLAVIUS.

[*He is a small, dark, elderly man; sly, friendly, persuasive, sof tongued. He is wearing garments of soft leather, worn and n too clean, and a wisp of cloak, like an undergraduate's gow flung about his shoulders. He is leading on a leash a wolf-hound like the present Irish breed, and over one shoulder are several mixed skins.*]

VALERIUS Well, Cogi, you old rascal. Your judgment is failing.

COGI (*not following*) You say?

VALERIUS You ask us to buy and you know as well as we do that no one on the Wall has had pay for four months.

COGI (*placidly*) Pay come.

VALERIUS Oh. Do you have spies on the roads to the south too?

COGI Not by road. By sea.

VALERIUS (*attentive, puzzled*) Sea! Why by sea?

COGI (*with a shrug*) Safer, maybe. Who knows?

RUFUS Safer by sea!

COGI Gentlemen buy fine dog, fine skins. Pay when money come.

DEMETRIUS (*answering the puzzled cogitative expressions of his companions*) The old beggar is doited. Sea, indeed.

RUFUS Perhaps it is coming from Gaul.

FLAVIUS If Albinus has had a victory in Gaul, we may get more men, as well as pay, and then we can have leave at last.

COGI Gentlemen buy, never mind pay. Fine beautiful skins. Feel! Thick. Soft. Shiny. No smell. (*He puts it dramatically to his nose, shrugs, and amends his description.*) Very little smell. (*As* VALERIUS *is uninterested he passes them on to the others.* GAZA *appears at the inner door and stands glowering on the hated Caledonian*)

VALERIUS What do you want for the hound?

COGI Five gold pieces.

VALERIUS You don't want the province of Britain as well, I suppose.

COGI Fine hunter. Full of faith. Walk at your heel. Lovely, lovely dog.

VALERIUS Can he retrieve?

COGI You shoot arrow, miss beast, he bring back arrow.

DEMETRIUS A circus performer.

COGI And smell! He smell a spider in a pony-load of hay.

DEMETRIUS A magician.

COGI He smell the very thought in your head.

DEMETRIUS A fortune-teller.

VALERIUS Be quiet, Demetrius.

COGI (*to* DEMETRIUS) Pretty soldier has pretty girl?

RUFUS (*looking up from where he and* FLAVIUS *are examining the skins*) No, he has a battery.

COGI (*producing some pearls from his pouch*) Pearls for pretty ears. (*He exhibits them on his palm under* DEMETRIUS'S *nose*)

FLAVIUS (*who has a girl*) Let me see those.

DEMETRIUS (*not interested until then*) No, he showed them to me first. (*They examine them, while* COGI *turns back to* VALERIUS)

VALERIUS One gold piece for him. (*He is playing with his map again*)

COGI (*dismissing this with a gesture that says that Valerius is of course jesting*) Famous hunter like Valerius need fine dog.

VALERIUS I have a dozen dogs.

COGI Away, away (*a sweep of the arm to the north*), beyond Tava, beyond the high hills, men round fires tell of Valerius, hunter.

VALERIUS You should take lessons from Rufus. He tells much better lies. (*Catching sight of* GAZA *in the doorway; in a new voice*) Go away, Gaza. (*The tone is kindly enough but stern*) The man (*he means* COGI) is harmless, I promise you. Go away. (*As* GAZA *retreats into the doorway, still glowering at* COGI) Since your friends cut his tongue out he dislikes Caledonians.

[COGI *greets this also with his usual shrug, moves round the up side of the table and twists his head so that he can see what Valerius is doing.* VALERIUS, *amused, tolerates him.*]

COGI (*having looked*) Picture?

VALERIUS In a way. (*Stabbing his forefinger downward above the paper in an explanatory gesture*) Picture looking down. Your country. (*Indicating*) Bodotria. Trimontium. Alanus.

DEMETRIUS (*pausing to watch*) It doesn't mean any more to him than it would to a monkey.

COGI (*having considered*) Summer picture?

VALERIUS Summer? Or winter.

COGI (*indicating*) Summer picture, no river.

VALERIUS Oh. Dry in summer, is it? Thank you, Cogi. (*He makes a note on the map*) For that I shall buy your doubtful-looking hound. And I shall give you three pieces for him. Which is one more than you expected to get. Take him to——

[*He pauses to listen to the distant hubbub of laughter and talk that comes from the outer courtyard.*]

What is that, Flavius? Are there other traders with the men?

FLAVIUS No, sir. I think it must be a demented creature who came in at the same time as Cogi.

COGI (*with an eloquent gesture of his forefinger round the top of his skull*) Mad. Very mad.

VALERIUS What is he selling? Religion, prophecy, or physic?

FLAVIUS I think he is quite genuinely mad, sir.

VALERIUS (*coldly*) In that case, he should not be sport for the men. Go and see that he is put outside the fort safely.

FLAVIUS Yes, sir.

RUFUS Oh, let us have a look at the madman too.

VALERIUS Why, Rufus? It is not a pretty spectacle, and——

RUFUS It is a good thing to run the eye over all visitors. Especially one who is not too crazy to get himself inside the fort.

VALERIUS Very well. (*He nods to* FLAVIUS)

FLAVIUS (*giving the pearls to* COGI) Keep the pearls, Cogi. I shall bargain with you later.

[*Exit* FLAVIUS.]

VALERIUS Take the dog to my groom at the stables, Cogi. Tell him to see whether it will do the things that you say it will. If it does, come for your money later.

DEMETRIUS (*bargaining for one of the skins*) Two silver pieces.

COGI (*gathering up the skins and throwing them on his shoulder*) Pretty soldier make jest. (*He turns to* VALERIUS *again*)

RUFUS What do you want the skin for? You can get just as good south of the Wall.

DEMETRIUS No. You can't. Look. (*He takes back the skin from* COGI'*s shoulder, shows* RUFUS *the thickness ; they discuss it while* COGI *talks to* VALERIUS)

COGI (*to* VALERIUS) When pay come, you go hunting?

VALERIUS Perhaps.

COGI Go on leave, maybe?

VALERIUS Not likely. Why?

COGI Better you go on leave, when pay come. Better you go.

[*He turns to retrieve his skin.*]

DEMETRIUS Two and a half.

COGI (*taking it from him*) Ah no, pretty soldier. Ah, no. (*He puts the skin on his shoulder with the others, and with a bow to* VALERIUS *takes himself out, followed by the eager* DEMETRIUS)

DEMETRIUS Well, what *will* you sell the thing for? After all, it is only a mangy bit of rat-skin——

[*They go out of hearing to the L. as* FLAVIUS *brings to the door from the R. the ' madman '.*]

FLAVIUS This is the man, sir.

[*The man comes in submissively under his guidance. He is young, apparently; haggard and unshaven, wild-haired, and without clothes except for a ragged tunic, a cloak, and shoes. His dull eyes move absently over the objects in his immediate line of vision, never rising to the faces of his questioners. In fact he seems quite unconscious that other people exist. His lips move constantly in what seems to be a repeated phrase, but the phrase is inaudible. His expression is neither mad nor wander-witted, merely withdrawn, intent on some secret end.*]

VALERIUS Who are you, and where do you come from? (*Silence except for that inaudible repeated phrase*) Are you a Briton? (*No response*) What did you want in the fort? (VALERIUS *shrugs at* RUFUS)

RUFUS (*considering him*) He looks genuine enough.

VALERIUS How did he come to be in the fort, Flavius?

FLAVIUS The guard on the West Gate thought that he was with Cogi, sir. Cogi says that he has been drifting about the Wall for some days. The men were amused because he is wearing a woman's cloak.

VALERIUS So I observe. (*His eye runs over the man speculatively, and his attention is arrested by the man's feet*)

RUFUS What is it?

[VALERIUS *points.*]

VALERIUS Legionary's shoes.

RUFUS So they are. Probably stolen.

VALERIUS Yes. (*Considering the man again*) Looks as though he had been rough-handled sometime.

RUFUS No marks.

VALERIUS No, but he has that look. Oh, well. Ask the men's kitchen to give him some food and send him on his way. (*He is about to turn away when his attention is once more caught by the repeated phrase. This time, listening, it seems to make sense. He repeats it, still doubtful but with the air of someone on the edge of discovery*) Vindobala! (*To the man*) This is Vindobala.

[*The man's eyes lift, his head turns a little towards* VALERIUS, *he repeats the word still indistinctly but with an air of achievement, his chin drops on his chest and his knees begin quite slowly and deliberately to buckle.*

[VALERIUS *catches him expertly, directs the falling body over the couch and swings the man's legs up as the body comes to rest.*]

RUFUS (*as* VALERIUS *straightens from examining the man*) Is he dead?

VALERIUS Dead asleep.

FLAVIUS I shall call the guard, sir.

VALERIUS (*stopping him*) No, let be. (*Something in the battered heap of exhaustion on his couch appeals to him against his reason ; a hint of gallantry, of breeding—or perhaps of mere charm*) He looks clean enough. Let him sleep it out there. It must be some time since no one moved him on. (*A distant bugle sounds and he takes his equipment all but his cloak from the wall, and puts it on*) I am coming, Flavius.

[*Exit* FLAVIUS, *with doubtful glance at the couch.*]

RUFUS (*as* VALERIUS *buckles on his equipment*) For a hard-bitten soldier you have an independable heart.

VALERIUS I have no idea what you are talking about.

RUFUS Let us hope you have no valuables lying about.

VALERIUS The nearest valuables are in the first-floor room at Solomon's. The man is out on his feet. (*Pausing to look at the man again*) And he looks—— (*He breaks off. To say 'appealing' would be ridiculous. He would not even to himself acknowledge the possibility of such a thing*) Odd about those shoes.

RUFUS Cast-off, probably. They are very worn.

VALERIUS Worn—but new. Oh, well. He may have his wits when he wakens.

RUFUS (*picking up his own belongings from the end of the couch, and preparing to go too*) Talking of valuables, lend me a gold den. till next week.

VALERIUS (*throwing him the coin, laughing*) I was afraid of that!

[*He goes out, followed by* RUFUS.]

BLACK OUT

SCENE 2

The sentry walk on the north wall of the fort, about half an hour later. The Scene consists merely of a stone pavement, nine feet wide, a breast-high wall, and the sunset sky. Looking at it one has the feeling of immense space beyond the Wall; of a wide emptiness.

The near edge of the pavement is not abrupt; it slopes down in a ramp to the ground level of the fort, so that the walls can be manned from within at any point at a moment's notice.

Enter L., AEMILIUS, *private soldier of the Second, doing his turn of guard. He carries a spear on his shoulder, and his pace is a long, slow, leisurely one. He is young but not callow, intelligent, sensitive, and will probably end by commanding a company and doing it very well. He reaches the middle of the stage, pauses to examine the sunset and to look out over Caledonia, and turns to resume his beat to the L. again, when he notices that his fellow-sentry is within speaking distance. He waits.*

Enter from R., VARUS. VARUS *is a man of thirty; lean and disgruntled-looking. He is the eternal malcontent. However great the pile on his own plate, he would always imagine that another man had fared better. Like most malcontents, he has an exaggerated idea of his own importance and talents. To be ignored or taken for granted is, from* VARUS'S *point of view, to be ill-done-by. His mother began it by taking it for granted that no one quite as wonderful as her son had ever been born. The son naturally subscribed to the beautiful theory. When later he found that everyone else did not share that belief his resentment knew no bounds. Other men got promotion, other men got invitations, other men were elected and praised; no one seemed to realise how wonderful* VARUS *was.* VARUS *simmered in a perpetual stew of grievance. He adopted the grievances of other men and made capital out of them. He agitated for this and for that; but if the desired benefit was to be obtained at the cost of* VARUS'S *disappearance into the background he would be ready to forfeit it. For the desired benefit he cares not a whit, but a grievance he loves with passion; and even more he likes being a Big Man. Since his character and influence with the men make promotion impossible there is never any hope of his being a Big Man legitimately, and so the vicious circle is complete.*

AEMILIUS Hey, Varus. You could have saved yourself all that speechifying last night.

VARUS What do you mean?

AEMILIUS (*pleased about the pay and pleased to ' dot* VARUS *one in the eye'*) Pay is coming up!

VARUS How do you know?

AEMILIUS That Caledonian trader brought the good news.

VARUS How should he know?

AEMILIUS I should think he knows enough not to bring his goods to a moneyless market. (*As that shot goes home*) You have lost your audience, Varus.

[VARUS, *too full of chagrin to find ready words, turns abruptly on his heel and resumes his beat.* AEMILIUS *watches him go with pleasure. He begins to sing as he turns leftward, a son of his native Gaul.*]

[*Enter from below, R.,* VALERIUS. *He overtakes* AEMILIUS.]

VALERIUS Sentry, halt! (AEMILIUS *faces front immediately and stands to attention*) What is the password?

AEMILIUS Ballista, sir.

VALERIUS (*recognising him*) It is you, Aemilius. What was the song?

AEMILIUS (*relaxing*) It is a thing my people sing in the Loire valley.

VALERIUS I thought so. My mother used to sing it. Everything quiet?

AEMILIUS Everything but the sunset, sir.

[*They consider it.*]

VALERIUS Deafening. How is the home-sickness?

AEMILIUS It eats me less since you talked about it to me, sir.

VALERIUS Eats. Yes, it does devour, doesn't it. All the other griefs one can forget for a little. But nostalgia is all-pervading. Nostalgia blackens the very daylight. Have you heard from your people?

AEMILIUS I had a letter last month, sir. They are very well.

VALERIUS Give my remembrances to your mother when you write. Say I still remember the blackberry wine she made when I was a boy.

AEMILIUS Yes, sir.

VALERIUS Well, I shall leave you to your sunset. It is very companionable, not to say intrusive.

AEMILIUS It is a magnificent symbol, sir.

VALERIUS (*his attention caught, pausing*) Do you worship Mithras?

AEMILIUS Yes, sir.

VALERIUS I have not seen you at the ceremonies.

AEMILIUS You see, sir, I have only reached the second degree, and you are initiate.

VALERIUS I see. (*After a pause*) I am glad, Aemilius. It is good for a soldier to have a creed. An anchor; a framework; a—home.

AEMILIUS (*smiling agreement to the last word*) Yes, sir. A home.

VALERIUS I see your relief coming.

[AEMILIUS *resumes his official stance, turns on his heel, and disappears L., to go off duty.*

[*As he goes,* VARUS *arrives from R., and* VALERIUS's *expression changes.* VARUS *turns front and halts.*]

VALERIUS For a man whose chief interest is the bettering of conditions, Varus, you take little interest in bettering the condition of your equipment.

VARUS (*at attention*) It complies with regulations, sir.

VALERIUS Oh, yes, it does that. I have wanted for some time to talk to you, Varus. (*His tone, if not friendly, is reasonable*) Outside orderly-room, as it were. It seems to me that the talent you devote to stirring up trouble in your company might be employed to better ends. Your own promotion, for instance.

VARUS I am not interested in promotion, sir.

VALERIUS (*considering him*) Do you fool yourself, I wonder; or do you merely hope to fool me?

VARUS What talent I have is devoted to my fellows.

VALERIUS Devoted to making yourself as conspicuous as possible, you mean. My point is that with a tenth of the effort you could achieve a more worthy conspicuousness. You cannot nurse a grievance and a career at the same time.

VARUS My grievances are those of my fellow men, sir.

VALERIUS Your grievance, my good Varus, is that no one shares your own estimate of yourself. You are neither a Caesar nor a Cicero. But you have as many brains as the next man. Why not accept that standing and work for normal promotion? As a junior officer you could do more for your fellows than ever you could as a grieved and grumbling private. And until you deserve that promotion I cannot give it to you. To promote the company agitator might be good business, but it would hardly be fair to men who had served faithfully for their first step in rank.

VARUS I cannot be bribed, sir.

VALERIUS (*coldly*) You cannot be rescued either, it seems. I have offered you a chance; now I offer you a warning. What you do is within the law, and so I cannot punish you. But if you make yourself too much of a nuisance, I can have you transferred. Strange as it may seem, there are worse places than the Wall.

VARUS I have no doubt, sir, that as an officer it is in your power to dispose of me as you will.

VALERIUS (*considering him; quietly and finally*) I think, after all, you are right, Varus. You would be unbearably lonely without your grievance.

[*From R., to take* VARUS'S *place comes* PETRONIUS. *He comes to a halt, turns front, grounds his spear, and stands at ease.* VARUS *comes to attention, shoulders his spear, takes a step forward, a right turn, and marches slowly away.*

[PETRONIUS *is middle-aged, quiet, kindly, a little worn. He has had a clean record since he entered the service as a boy. Only his natural diffidence and his native content have kept him from rank.*]

VALERIUS (*greeting him*) Petronius.

PETRONIUS Good evening, sir.

VALERIUS No need to ask you for the password. How is the rheumatism?

PETRONIUS Oh, very fair, sir, very fair. Nothing to complain about.

VALERIUS Have you never thought of taking your pension, Petronius? Settling down on a nice piece of land near Colchester or Caerleon?

PETRONIUS I wouldn't know what to do away from the service, sir.

VALERIUS But they are all time-expired men there. You could talk service shop from morning till night.

PETRONIUS I expect it will have to come to that, sir, but it won't be the same. No bugles; no spit and polish; no routine.

VALERIUS You old die-hard.

PETRONIUS (*anxious and tentative, as* VALERIUS *is about to turn away*) You won't recommend my discharge, will you, sir?

VALERIUS With men worth their weight in gold! And anyhow, I may be said to share your point of view, Petronius. After all, I was not kidnapped into the army. (*They exchange a glance of understanding*) Carry on.

PETRONIUS Thank you, sir.

[*He goes out, R., on his beat.*]

[VALERIUS *turns L. and sees* AEMILIUS'S *relief approaching. He bursts into protest before we can see who comes.*]

VALERIUS Gods and gods, Candidus. (*Enter* CANDIDUS) Where did you get that jacket?

[CANDIDUS *is not a figure of fun, but he is a gawky, simple, self-effacing youth, whose uniform does not seem to belong to him.*]

CANDIDUS The storeman issued it to me, sir.
VALERIUS And you took it?
CANDIDUS I had no money, sir.
VALERIUS Money?
CANDIDUS He said that for two days' pay he could give me a better fit, sir.
VALERIUS And you did not say that for two pins you would—— (*His glance taking in the vacant, good-natured face; giving it up*) Oh, well; perhaps not. How long have you been with us, Candidus?
CANDIDUS One year and thirty-two days, sir.
VALERIUS And in all that time you have not learned—— (*Toning it down*) You must learn to stand up for yourself, Candidus.
CANDIDUS Yes, sir.
VALERIUS You are a soldier. Worth ten of any non-combatant barrack-loafers. Get that into your head.
CANDIDUS Yes, sir.
VALERIUS Tomorrow morning you will present my compliments to the storeman and say that I will not have any private of mine looking like a May Day effigy.
CANDIDUS Yes, sir.
VALERIUS That is all. (*As* CANDIDUS *goes out*) And get your hair cut. (*His expression as he watches the retreating soldier is tolerant and amused*)

[FLAVIUS *joins him, on the Wall, beginning the discussion of whatever has parted him from* VALERIUS.]

He said it would be all right, sir. Either tomorrow morning at ten, or the day after in the afternoon——

[*They go out together R.*]

[*After a moment* PETRONIUS *appears on his beat, and as he is going again,* CANDIDUS *appears from L.*]

CANDIDUS Petronius.

PETRONIUS Yes?

CANDIDUS Does this jacket look very odd to you?

PETRONIUS Well; it isn't exactly Praetorian Guard. Have you been told off about it? (CANDIDUS *nods*) Cheer up. As Rufus Sita says: there were worse losses at Cremona.

CANDIDUS (*placidly*) Oh, I don't mind. I would rather be told off by him than patted on the back by a lot of men I know.

PETRONIUS (*agreeing*) Yes.

CANDIDUS (*pausing as he is about to go*) Petronius, what properly comes after: For two pins I would——?

PETRONIUS Oh, many things. For two pins I would—knock your back teeth down your throat. Does that fit?

CANDIDUS Yes. That sounds fine. (*He resumes his beat murmuring ecstatically*) For two pins I would——

FADE OUT

SCENE 3

The Scene is the same as Scene I. *It is more than an hour later. The brilliance has died out of the courtyard; it is still daylight, but the light is cold and blue. On the table an oil lamp has been placed which makes a yellow glow in the room. The sleeper lies in the same position in which we left him.*

Outside the chapel (the room through the R. wall) a bugler sounds an evening call. It is longer than any of the 'business' calls which we have heard already; and of course much nearer. The sleeper's sub-conscious mind answers to it; even exhaustion such as his is not proof against habit. He stirs, and begins to waken. He sits up abruptly, swinging his feet to the floor, and pauses, at a loss, as the automatic reaction ceases.

He is still sitting bewildered on the edge of the couch, when VALERIUS *comes in, followed by* FLAVIUS. VALERIUS *comes in briskly, at a pace which takes him well into the room, and* FLAVIUS *follows, so that both have their backs more or less to the man on the couch.* VALERIUS *begins to take off his equipment, as* FLAVIUS *talks.*

FLAVIUS About that Syrian, sir. I suppose we couldn't run him out of town?

VALERIUS Why?

FLAVIUS The men will gamble there.

VALERIUS They gamble in the temples, in the latrines, and in the face of the enemy. Why not at the Syrian's?

FLAVIUS I told you, sir: the game is crooked.

VALERIUS Do the men know that the game is crooked?

FLAVIUS Oh, yes. But they let themselves be fleeced because of the girls.

VALERIUS I am afraid there is nothing that I can do about it, Flavius. It is the inalienable right of all free men to go to the dogs in their own way in their own time.

FLAVIUS (*ruefully*) Their rights make them very wrong-tempered.

VALERIUS Their temper would be much worse if I took their toy away from them lest it hurt them.

FLAVIUS (*submitting*) Yes, sir.

VALERIUS (*adding a word of comfort and advice*) It is very well to keep an eye on the young shoots, but don't wet-nurse the hard cases. (*His eye lighting on the stranger*) So! You are awake, are you. That is all, Flavius.

FLAVIUS (*with a curious glance at the stranger; willing to linger*) Will you be at mess, sir?

VALERIUS (*going to the inner door*) I think so.

FLAVIUS Very good, sir.

[*Exit* FLAVIUS.]

VALERIUS (*calling*) Gaza! A bowl of hot soup! (*He comes back and stands contemplating the stranger—who is hereafter to be known as* CLAUDIUS)

CLAUDIUS (*as much to himself as to* VALERIUS, *of whom he is only partly aware; slowly*) I remember now. I am Claudius Paulinus. I was sent from Caerleon. From the Second at Caerleon. I was sent to Vindobala.

VALERIUS Well, you have arrived.

CLAUDIUS (*his glance lifting to* VALERIUS) Are you Valerius Valens?

VALERIUS That is my name.

CLAUDIUS (*his consciousness sliding away from* VALERIUS *again to the memory of his recent experience*) I had a draft of twenty-five men.

VALERIUS (*sharply*) A draft! Where are they?

CLAUDIUS I lost them. Every man of them. (*It is a bare statement; devoid of emotion*)

VALERIUS You lost twenty-five men on the main trunk road! With a fort at every day's march!

CLAUDIUS No. We took the secondary road from York. Those were my orders. To give us practice in bivouac, it was.

VALERIUS (*bitterly; half to himself*) And so that your men should not see how the forts were garrisoned!

CLAUDIUS (*his attention coming back to* VALERIUS; *vaguely*) Garrisoned?

VALERIUS Most of them are held by three kitchen-details and an orderly-room clerk. If your men did not see the forts why did they mutiny?

CLAUDIUS (*roused to emotion for the first time; first puzzled and then protesting and indignant*) Mutiny! There was no mutiny! My men were the best—— (*His voice breaks and dies away for a moment. But he goes on; summing up in one phrase his admiration for and trust in his men*) They were fine. They are dead. Every one of them. We were ambushed.

VALERIUS (*incredulous, half suspicious*) Between here and York!

CLAUDIUS We had bivouacked for the night. (*Again he is living it in his mind rather than telling it to anyone, but his flicker of emotion has died out. It is plain statement again; detached*) It is thick forest there; before you come to the big river. They came without a sound.

VALERIUS Who did?

CLAUDIUS I don't know. They were in the middle of us before we knew they were there.

VALERIUS But your sentries?

CLAUDIUS I saw one of them, when they were carrying me away. He had his throat cut from ear to ear. I expect they all had. We were asleep, all but the sentries. There was no time even to draw a sword. They died on their feet, but not fighting. There was no time.

VALERIUS And you are alive.

CLAUDIUS (*accepting all that his superior's cold voice implies; simply*) Yes. I think they saw my badges in the firelight.

VALERIUS They kept you for ransom?

CLAUDIUS No. I think they planned to amuse themselves with me afterwards.

VALERIUS (*unsympathetic*) What makes you think that?

CLAUDIUS When they knocked the sword from my hand——

VALERIUS You said there was no time to draw a sword.

CLAUDIUS Oh, I was not asleep. I had not slept much any night, since leaving Caerleon.

VALERIUS Why?

CLAUDIUS It was my first command. I was excited—and pleased.

VALERIUS (*invaded abruptly by the friendliness that had seized him at first sight of* CLAUDIUS; *coldly*) Go on.

CLAUDIUS They stripped me and tied me up. And after they had carried me some way, they flung me down under some trees. On the edge of their camp, it was. (*He pauses, to contemplate it*)

VALERIUS (*pointing out*) But you are here.

CLAUDIUS Before dawn, while it was still dark, a woman came and cut the thongs. She said in my ear: The ford across the river is five miles to the north. When I could move I found that she had left me her cloak. After that, I don't remember. I think I was a little wrong in the head. All that I knew was that I had to go to Vindobala, and that I must not sleep till I got there. (*His mind running away again*) I have been in a great many places, I think.

[*Enter* GAZA *with the soup.* VALERIUS *indicates that it is for* CLAUDIUS, *and* GAZA *takes the small table from the end of the couch and places it in front of* CLAUDIUS.]

I would have killed myself that morning in the forest, but I thought it my duty to report what had happened. Now that the gods have allowed me to do that, I can finish it.

VALERIUS Eat first. It is bad to go to the gods fasting.

CLAUDIUS No. I cannot eat.

[GAZA *picks up the bowl and waves it slowly back and forth under* CLAUDIUS's *nose, setting it back on the table slowly as if drawing* CLAUDIUS's *will after it.*]

VALERIUS It is even worse to go to the Commandant fasting. And you have still that before you. Eat. It is an order.

[*But the famished boy has smelt the food and needs no more coaxing.* GAZA *watches for a moment or two, pleased, and retires.*]

VALERIUS (*after a little*) How did you know that it was a woman who freed you?

CLAUDIUS Her hair fell over my face.

VALERIUS When you have rested I must send you to Cocceius. He lives at the depot: Corbridge. Three miles south of Hunnum, the next fort west of here. What is your rank, by the way?

CLAUDIUS I am—I was Junior in the Eighth Cohort.

[*In the doorway, without warning other than his altercation with the sentry who tries to stop him, appears* SALVIUS, *private of the line, very large, very elated, and very drunk. He has a rough, good-natured, and rather stupid face, and red hair. Under one arm he is carrying a fighting-cock.*]

SALVIUS (*brushing the sentry aside like a fly, and advancing on* VALERIUS) Didn't I say I had the best fighting-cock on the Wall! Didn't I! The best cock in all Europe I have, and I've won a packet. Enough to bribe two consuls and a procurator. (*He has difficulty with 'procurator'*) And that's for you! (*He pours a little stream of gold coins into* VALERIUS's *lap*) You've a damned superior visage, Valerius Valens, but I like you! I like you! (*As he turns about, rocking back on his heels with the effort, his eye lights on* CLAUDIUS. *Looking down his nose from his rocked-back stance, in a good imitation of an officer's parade-ground manner*) How dare you come on parade without being shaved! Disgrace to the service! Ten days confinement to barracks, and get your hair cut. (*He weaves his way out, past the speechless sentry*)

VALERIUS (*making a little heap of the coins on the table*) Salvius will have a balance in his savings-bank account this month. That will be a nice surprise for him.

CLAUDIUS (*almost speechless with surprise*) But—is he not going to be punished!

VALERIUS (*cold again*) Punished?

CLAUDIUS He was insolent—and drunk. At Caerleon, he would have been flogged.

VALERIUS Perhaps. But on the frontier a man is judged by his quality, not by his manners. If I sent Salvius into Caledonia with ten men, he would bring ten men back.

[CLAUDIUS *flushes painfully, and goes back slowly to his soup-swallowing.* VALERIUS, *watching, is angry with himself.*]

I ask your pardon. It is a peasant's trick to bait a tired man. On the Wall one loses more than one's youth.

CLAUDIUS (*not looking up, murmuring*) I should not have said it.

VALERIUS What did you say your name was?

CLAUDIUS Claudius Paulinus.

VALERIUS Native born?

CLAUDIUS (*with the faintest hint of defence*) I was born in Britain, yes; but my family have been civilised for four hundred years.

VALERIUS (*disclaiming any superiority*) I congratulate you My family in Rome will not be civilised for a thousand.

CLAUDIUS (*naively interested*) Rome! (*He regards* VALERIU *with interest*) I think you are the first Roman-born Roman I have ever met.

VALERIUS (*amused and dry*) We are made of clay like other men.

CLAUDIUS My mother's brother went to Rome once. He was witness in a law-suit.

VALERIUS And what impressed him most in that home of privilege and perjury?

CLAUDIUS Its fairness.

VALERIUS (*at a loss*) Its beauty, you mean?

CLAUDIUS No. Its equity. He said that the greatest lawyers in the Empire sat for days considering the rights and wrongs of the case. A silly little case of no moment; a tiresome quarrel from a distant province, that held neither advantage nor glory for a judge. He could talk of nothing else when he came home. He is still talking of it. (*What with the food and his enthusiasm, he is coming alive*)

VALERIUS Is that all he saw?

CLAUDIUS All?

VALERIUS (*drawling*) Has he seen the mistress of the world and failed to observe the monuments to her wealth? The tenements crowded with paupers who have never worked because they are given bread for nothing. The villas with three gardeners for every flower and the loot of a dozen cities in the living-room. Millionaire slaves wallowing in their wealth, sick three times a day with their own gluttony. Condemned murderers fighting out their lives in the arena for the entertainment of the suburbs. Drivers of racing chariots laying down the law, and picking up the perquisites. Rich women who buy boys, and rich men who sell their daughters. Politicians who buy votes with their friends' money, and sell their friends for an enemy's vote. Priests who give the temple revenue to the dancing-girls, and dancing-girls who bribe their way to fame. The market of the world; where you can buy false witness for fivepence, murder for a song, and a province for two gold den. and an invitation to dinner. The finest gathering—— (*His unemotional recitation is interrupted by* CLAUDIUS'S *passionate refusal of the picture*)

CLAUDIUS It is not like that! (*Abashed by his involuntary protest, but sticking to his guns*) I have lost my men, and disgraced my name, and I shall die before sunrise tomorrow, but that is not the Rome I have served!

VALERIUS (*not unkindly*) No? What is your Rome?

CLAUDIUS I think (*he has not been prepared for exposition and his thoughts are still fragmentary*) it is the Rome of my father's house in the Mendips. (*Parenthetically*) My father is in the Civil Service. Department of Mines. It is a good way of life, the one we were bred to. To have work to do, and leisure after, and security for both. To make a song, or mend a shoe, or walk from Gloucester all the way to Greece, without any man's leave and with no man hindering. To till a field and know that one will reap what one has sown. To know that there is a future for one's children and a hearth for one's old age. To be no man's belonging and no man's sacrifice. That is Rome. Order and equity. And freedom—freedom from *fear*. It is to keep fear outside the Wall that we fight. (*In the silence that succeeds his speech he returns, abashed to his soup*)

VALERIUS (*quietly*) Perhaps you have the right of it, scarecrow. (*Lightly*) You must show me that home of yours in the Mendips one day.

CLAUDIUS (*eagerly; forgetting*) I should like to. It is lovely there among the—— (*he remembers and breaks off*)

VALERIUS (*going on as if he had not spoken*) I have not much knowledge of homes.

CLAUDIUS (*forgetting again in his eager curiosity about this Roman*) But your family—they have a home?

VALERIUS They have an address. My mother has a salon. (*As* CLAUDIUS, *not knowing how to deal with so detached and critical a view of one's parents, goes back to his soup*) My father is usually at sea with the fleet, but my sister looks in for her letters now and then. Have you a sister?

CLAUDIUS Yes. She is quite small; just eleven. I promised to send her a Caledonian brooch with my first pay. I suppose it would not be possible to let my people think that I had been killed in action? They were so——

[*Enter* RUFUS.]

RUFUS (*warning but with latent amusement*) Hold on to everything: here comes Cocceius.

VALERIUS The Commandant! What does he want?

RUFUS Somebody's blood, I have no doubt.

[*Enter* FLAVIUS, *showing in* COCCEIUS.]

FLAVIUS The Commandant, sir.

[*Enter* COCCEIUS, *attended by an elegant young tribune of the type referred to by retired generals as whipper-snappers.* COCCEIUS *is large, heavy, and impressive. He has a hot complexion and a cold eye.*

[*When* COCCEIUS *was a small boy he was terrified of everything. One day in sheer panic he shouted and made a face at the dog that was terrifying him, and the dog turned and walked away. Ever since then* COCCEIUS *has, so to speak, shouted and made faces. What began as conscious policy is now habit, but he still carries in the far recesses of his mind an awareness of the façade, and a malicious watchfulness of the effect he creates with it.*

[*His position as officer commanding one of the drearier parts of the Empire he owes to his unpopularity. That he is commander at all he owes to his power of impressing his personality on his superiors and his talent for terrifying the troops under him.*

[*Both* VALERIUS *and* CLAUDIUS *are on their feet to receive him.*]

COCCEIUS Ha, Valerius. That pony you sold me was unsound!

VALERIUS (*polite but no wise impressed*) I am sorry to hear that, sir. Will you sit down, sir?

COCCEIUS (*not moving from his stance inside the door*) Do I look as if my limbs were giving way!

VALERIUS No, sir. Certainly not.

COCCEIUS I want an explanation about the pony.

VALERIUS You had a veterinary surgeon's warrant with it, sir.

COCCEIUS What is that worth!

VALERIUS Is it the surgeon's talent you doubt, sir, or his word?

COCCEIUS Both! I doubt them both! *And* his eyesight!

VALERIUS (*smoothly*) Then I suggest that it is Rufus Sita's business, sir. (*He carefully avoids the eye of the outraged* RUFUS)

COCCEIUS And what has my pony got to do with the Camp Prefect?

VALERIUS The Prefect is in command of details, sir, and is responsible for the medical staff. It is intolerable that he should suffer an incompetent in so important a post.

COCCEIUS Ha. Think you are riding me off, don't you! Riding me off!

VALERIUS Oh, no, sir.

COCCEIUS You sold me that pony, and he is foundered in a fortnight.

VALERIUS (*silkily*) I did warn you that he was no weight carrier, sir.

COCCEIUS Are you suggesting by any chance that I am a monster?

VALERIUS Oh, no, sir. I am merely pointing out that the pony is country-bred, and cannot be expected to have the stamina of a thoroughbred from Gaul.

COCCEIUS (*feeling that he is again being ridden-off*) Stamina! The creature is fit for nothing but dogs' meat.

VALERIUS Then I suggest that I buy him back from you, sir.

COCCEIUS (*staggered*) Buy him back! You will?

VALERIUS As dogs' meat. That will do something to save your pocket, sir.

COCCEIUS I said you were riding me off! Riding me right off the course. First you sell me a pony you have no more use for, and then you buy it back for your hounds at a penny the pound! You have more impudence than the rest of the Wall put together, Valerius Valens. Come back to supper with me. (*This last with no change of tone or pace*)

VALERIUS Thank you, sir: but I have an engagement.

COCCEIUS Oh, well: next time you are in Corbridge. There are blades of grass showing through the tiles in the outer court-yard. Do something about it. And the guard on the East Gate gave me compliments instead of a challenge.

VALERIUS They recognised you, sir.

COCCEIUS Of course they did. They had no right to. That is all. (*He is turning away, and his eye falls on* CLAUDIUS. *Remarking en passant*) Company on the Wall grows stranger and stranger.

VALERIUS I was just going to send this man to you, sir.

COCCEIUS (*pausing in his departure*) To me!

VALERIUS Odd as it may seem, he is a Centurion of the Second.

COCCEIUS Jupiter! Is this what they are turning out now?

VALERIUS Not exactly. This is what remains of twenty-five men and an officer who set out from York.

COCCEIUS But——!

VALERIUS They were ambushed.

COCCEIUS You mean that a pack of thieves got the better of twenty-five regulars from the Augusta!

VALERIUS There is no evidence that they were thieves, sir.

COCCEIUS Of course they were thieves! The country is at peace, isn't it! What else is it but brigandage? (*As* VALERIUS *does not answer*) Well?

VALERIUS The loot from a handful of private soldiers is hardly a titbit to interest experts. They were expert, sir.

COCCEIUS Took it for a convoy, I wager. Pay for the Wall.

VALERIUS That is coming by sea, sir.

COCCEIUS By sea! What nonsense!

VALERIUS I have no doubt that your brigands knew that, sir. Everyone knows it but us. That is not important. What is important is that everyone knows how many man Albinus took with him to Gaul, and just how many men are left.

COCCEIUS It is not for us to criticise the actions of the Governor.

VALERIUS (*meekly*) No, sir.

COCCEIUS One can only deplore them. So you think the tribes in the south grow restless?

VALERIUS I suggest that someone went to great trouble to prevent a small reinforcement of the Wall.

COCCEIUS Spite, probably, just spite. Still, we can double the guards. (*His eye going back to* CLAUDIUS) Twenty-five men, indeed! And the officer without a scratch on him. What is your name?

CLAUDIUS Claudius Paulinus, sir.

VALERIUS He made his way north to report, sir. I do not think that it was any wish of his to survive his men.

COCCEIUS Just a piece of unexpected good fortune, huh?

VALERIUS He plans to fall on his sword, sir.

COCCEIUS (*regarding the unmilitary object with disfavour*) What sword?

VALERIUS One of the regulation pattern will be provided, sir.

COCCEIUS (*having swivelled a secretly appreciative glance at* VALERIUS *for that*) He will not fall on any sword until he has been court-martialled for incompetence.

VALERIUS Yes, sir; perhaps that would be most satisfactory from the troops' point of view. (*The accent is on 'would'; the tone agreeable*)

COCCEIUS Troops?

VALERIUS The men will look for a sacrifice. Moreover, the garrison is short of entertainment; and it always pleases them to see an officer going through the hoop.

COCCEIUS I object to your slang, Valerius.

VALERIUS I beg your pardon, sir.

COCCEIUS And I object still more to circuses for the men. Let the fellow have his sword.

VALERIUS Very good, sir. May I suggest that the sword be withheld from him until such times as he has repaid the Exchequer.

COCCEIUS Repaid it for what?

VALERIUS Loss of equipment, sir. If he is allowed to kill himself now, there will be no way of recovering the money.

COCCEIUS But——

VALERIUS It is both common sense and Regulations, sir. Not always the same thing. Section fifty-one, paragraph seven: Any officer or man losing any article of equipment shall have his pay stopped in whole or in part, according to the discretion of his commanding officer, until such times as the total value of——

COCCEIUS Very well, very well! Don't quote Army Regulations at *me*! I knew them before you were born. Though I never made such odd use of them, damn me if I did. Stop his pay till he has paid for every last shoelace, if you like. But see that a written report of the whole affair is waiting me at Corbridge tomorrow morning.

VALERIUS Very good, sir. It is understood, then, that Claudius Paulinus is in honour-bound to make no attempt on his life until he is free of debt to the State.

COCCEIUS That is the arrangement; and I wish you joy of him. Come along, Titus, we are going to be very late for supper. (*To* VALERIUS, *who escorts him out to his pony*) What is this nonsense about pay coming by sea?

[*He goes out with* VALERIUS, *followed by the* A.D.C. *and* FLAVIUS, *leaving* CLAUDIUS *with* RUFUS.]

RUFUS (*watching them go*) That puppy of a tribune! White buckskin boots on the Wall! (*Turning to* CLAUDIUS) It is fortunate for you, my friend, that Cocceius was in so good a humour. (*As* CLAUDIUS *casts him a glance*) Oh, yes; I have known men burst into flames merely through standing too near Cocceius in one of his rages. (*Referring to* GAZA, *who has come in and is grunting at* CLAUDIUS) He wants to know whether you will have some more.

CLAUDIUS (*having shaken his head; watching* GAZA *go with the empty bowl*) Is he afflicted?

RUFUS He has no tongue. We found him captive among the Caledonians during one of our expeditions. The others were for leaving him, but Valerius brought him along. No one has ever discovered his nationality. Valerius named him Gaza because he is a treasure fit for a king.

CLAUDIUS Is it often Valerius's pleasure to pick men from the mud?

RUFUS Cheer up, my son. There were worse losses at Cremona. Where were you ambushed?

CLAUDIUS Two days' march out of York; on the east road. Black forest as far as one can see. They caught us in bivouac. (*With sudden emotion*) Does Valerius Valens think it will be easy to go on living?

RUFUS No; I expect he thinks that one junior officer willing to work is better than twenty-*six* dead men. (*His voice is less kindly*)

CLAUDIUS (*half bewildered, half resentful*) He was laughing about it! 'Paying for equipment.'

RUFUS (*a shade coldly*) Valerius Valens, my young friend, laughs very seldom, and never at failure. If he joked with Cocceius it was not from light-heartedness. He saw some worth in Gaza: a dumb bundle of rags and dirt half crazy with terror. If he finds you worth saving, be thankful; he is probably right.

[*Enter* VALERIUS.]

VALERIUS (*to* RUFUS) I knew he would ruin that pony! (*His glance goes to* CLAUDIUS, *and then back to* RUFUS *over* CLAUDIUS's *head. They look at each other for a moment, eloquently*) Well (*he sounds cheerful and off-hand*) there will be a new face in Mess, thank the gods. We shall all have a chance of telling our stories over again. Where shall we put him? With Flavius?

RUFUS The quarters next mine are vacant; he could have those. They are the only ones where you cannot hear Demetrius singing.

VALERIUS (*referring not to* DEMETRIUS *but to the altruism of* RUFUS's *suggestion*) That would be a good idea. Thanks, Rufus.

RUFUS I shall go now and see about it. They have not been occupied since Vettius went to Gaul. (*He goes*)

CLAUDIUS (*emotion overcoming him*) I thought you understood! I thought you agreed that I should end it as any soldier would—as any Roman! I had earned the right to do that, hadn't I? And you played a trick on me: a silly cruel trick. Tying my honour to my lost equipment, when you know as well as I do that it died with my men! What were you trying to do? Save me from myself! (*Wild sarcasm and budding sobs in this last*)

VALERIUS No, I was saving you for duty. I am very short of junior officers.

CLAUDIUS Duty! What reverence will be paid by troops to an officer who has lost both his weapons and his men!

VALERIUS That is for you to say.

CLAUDIUS (*the sobs beginning to come up into his throat*) I cannot do it! I cannot do it!

VALERIUS You will feel better when you have had a longer sleep. I am going across to the Baths now. Come with me and I shall see about clothes for you, and a servant. You can have the man Vettius had. He is a half-wit, but very good at making mulled wine, I understand. (*He is giving* CLAUDIUS *time to control himself, but he is now ready to go and* CLAUDIUS *is still unpresentable. Reminding without emphasis*) There are sentries outside.

CLAUDIUS (*taking the hint, and running his fingers through his hair in a vague effort to tidy it*) Yes, sir. (*His chin comes up*)

VALERIUS (*taking his own cloak from the wall and tossing it to him*) Ready?

CLAUDIUS (*catching the cloak*) Yes, sir.

[*He follows* VALERIUS *out, putting on the cloak as he goes.*]

FADE OUT

SCENE 4

The Scene is the same, about ten days later. Pay has arrived, and the paying-out parade is nearing its end. Outside, on the edge of the veranda, is a table, past which troops are filing, and taking their pay as their names are read. RUFUS *is superintending this part of the proceedings. In fact, all one can see of it are the backs of* RUFUS *and his assistant, and the half-hidden figures of passing soldiers. And all one can hear is the murmur of the read-out names.*

Inside the room, at the table L., with his back to the L. wall is VALERIUS. *On the table is a very large, deep tray divided into numerous small partitions, and on the up side of it two leather money-bags, now nearly empty. On the down side of the table, on a stool, is a small strong-box with open lid. On the up side of the table, facing down, with a sheaf of documents in his hand, is* FLAVIUS. *R. from him, but L. of the doorway, facing down and standing at ease is* MARIUS; *a private soldier, young, superlatively smart, with that blend of alertness and control that is the mark of his calling.*

At the smaller table opposite, is seated JULIUS; *also a private soldier, but, like his friend* MARIUS, *due for his first step-up any day now. He is a less vivid edition of* MARIUS. *He is facing* VALERIUS, *and on the table in front of him are a sheaf of papers like the ones* FLAVIUS *is holding.*

FLAVIUS *is reading out the names of the garrison with the amount due to each man. At each name* VALERIUS *takes the due amount from the two bags, and drops the sum into one of the partitions, while* JULIUS *at the opposite table ticks the name on a duplicate list, and when necessary, where a man is dead or transferred, supplies the information, so that the amount goes not into the tray but into the strong-box to* VALERIUS'S *left.*

As each tray is filled it replaces the emptied ones on the table outside. This, however, is the last trayful.

FLAVIUS (*reading*) Terentius Probus: seventy-five forty. Frontinus Aquilo: eighty forty-five. Julius Severinus: eighty twenty-five. Liberius Fronto: eighty-five fifty. Flavius Martinus——

JULIUS (*interrupting*) Killed on patrol, September the 10th.

FLAVIUS (*continuing*) Seventy-nine sixty. (VALERIUS *puts the amount into the strong-box*) Oppius Felix: seventy-two ninety. Tabellius Victor: eighty-nine twenty. Salvius Otho: sixty-four twenty——

JULIUS Sixty-three twenty, sir. Stoppage for one lost entrenching tool.

VALERIUS (*adjusting the sum*) It surprises me that he has any pay coming at all.

[*Enter from the veranda* CLAUDIUS; *fresh, shining, and apparently confident. It requires a closer look to reveal that his face is still hollowed and his eye uncertain.*]

VALERIUS Claudius, you might relieve Julius.

CLAUDIUS Yes, sir.

[JULIUS *points out the place to* CLAUDIUS *and joins* MARIUS, *standing R. of the doorway.*]

FLAVIUS (*beginning a new sheet*) Dosennius Proc—— Oh, no; we have done that. I am sorry, sir. Just one moment.

JULIUS (*giving him the number of the required sheet*) Number eleven, sir.

VALERIUS Take that grin off your face, Marius. It is indecent.

MARIUS (*who has merely been looking pleased; smiling broadly*) I have not seen so much money, sir, since we raided the coiner's den in Corbridge.

CLAUDIUS (*half shyly*) What are you going to do with yours, Marius?

VALERIUS He is going to buy new polishing stuff. Marius is a barrack-brat. He has been in the army for—three generations, is it, Marius?

MARIUS Four generations, sir.

VALERIUS He polishes equipment in his sleep. Look at him. It hurts the eyes. (*He makes a slight gesture of protection*) He got himself those decorations just for an extra piece of bright-work. (*He refers to* MARIUS's *bracelets and necklet.* MARIUS's *hands go to them automatically*)

FLAVIUS (*having found the place*) This is the end, sir. Petronius Fidus: eighty-five eighty. Julius Magnus——

CLAUDIUS Promoted centurion and seconded to the 1st Batavians, sir.

FLAVIUS —Ninety twenty-five. Mannius Secundus: eighty twenty-five. Pontius Sabinus——

CLAUDIUS Died of fever, August the 6th.

FLAVIUS Seventy-five forty. Tannicus Verus: eight-four. Antonius Dardanus: seventy-eight fifty. Rubrius Pollio: seventy-four ninety. (*Dropping his papers and looking eagerly at the sacks*) Has it worked out, sir?

VALERIUS (*looking ruefully at the money still in the sacks*) No.

FLAVIUS Not!

VALERIUS There is enough for nearly thirty more.

FLAVIUS (*distressed*) I'll swear we made no mistake, sir.

CLAUDIUS (*who has risen from his seat at the table; into the dismayed silence; with obvious difficulty*) That is the pay for my twenty-five men, sir.

VALERIUS (*into an awkward pause*) Oh, marvellous Headquarters! Accurate even in their sleep. (*Putting the two bags into the strong-box*) Put it in the vault, Flavius. It can go back with the next convoy. Take the tray, you two. (MARIUS *and* JULIUS *lift the tray by the finger-slots in each end, and carry it out, placing it on the table outside as an empty one is removed.* FLAVIUS *shuts the strong-box, summons the sentry to carry it, and goes out with it to the chapel next door*) It will take the various Departments at least two years to decide who really owns that money. Showers of memoranda blowing back and fore across Britain like a snow-storm. (*Regarding his soiled fingers*) Filthy stuff, money!

CLAUDIUS May I speak to you, sir?

VALERIUS What is it, Claudius? (*He is attentive and kind*)

CLAUDIUS I want you to release me from my promise, sir.

VALERIUS Why?

CLAUDIUS I have done my best these ten days, sir.

VALERIUS You have done very well.

CLAUDIUS But it is more than I can bear. (*He is quite unemotional about it*)

VALERIUS I never imagined that dying would not be the easier thing.

CLAUDIUS If it was punishment you planned, sir, I have surely taken enough?

VALERIUS (*coldly*) What have I done to make you think it is punishment?

CLAUDIUS I cannot believe, sir, that you need a junior officer badly enough to crucify a human being for it.

VALERIUS (*touched; quite kindly*) What is so bad?

CLAUDIUS Today; and the memory of yesterday; and the thought of tomorrow.

VALERIUS The men have accepted you. Flavius told me.

CLAUDIUS They never really look at me. Their eyes look over my shoulder when I speak to them. When I pass they stop what they are doing, and idle with their backs turned until I have gone, as if afraid that I might speak to them. And every now and then, a dozen times a day, I catch sight of one of my draft.

VALERIUS (*startled*) Your draft!

CLAUDIUS But it never is, of course.

VALERIUS (*murmuring*) Soldiers do run to type.

CLAUDIUS And continually things happen—like the pay. There is never a moment, day or night, when one can forget. I cannot face any more of it, sir.

VALERIUS Not even for that Rome you serve? Not even to keep fear outside the Wall?

CLAUDIUS Rome has a million better men than I to serve her.

VALERIUS Perhaps. But not here. How will it satisfy your

pride to die like a Roman and leave someone else to do two men's work?

CLAUDIUS You think it is my pride that suffers!

VALERIUS I think it cries very audibly. Being young, you are egotist; being a soldier, you have a vulnerable pride; being a Roman, you have standards of conduct. A Roman is disgraced: a Roman falls on his sword. A fine gesture, say his friends. Well, I find the gesture contemptible. And in a soldier with duty still to do, unforgivable. I suppose you think that blasphemy?

CLAUDIUS No; but, with respect, sir, I think that if you had ever been disgraced you would see it differently.

VALERIUS I! (*exasperated by the boy's egotism and by the stab of reminder*) You fool of a boy, do you imagine that you are the only soldier to be disgraced and to go on living!

CLAUDIUS (*staggered; hardly articulating it*) You, sir!

VALERIUS I and a thousand others. The frontiers from here to the Tigris are full of men who are living down their mistakes. However, since you will have your gesture, I make a bargain with you. When you have paid back the price of your sword, come and tell me; and I shall give you leave to use it. That is all.

[*Enter* RUFUS, *from the courtyard.*]

CLAUDIUS (*a little bewildered*) Yes, sir. Thank you, sir. (*He begins to go*)

VALERIUS Finished, Rufus?

RUFUS (*beginning to tidy the sheaf of documents he is carrying, roll them up, and tie them with tape*) I have not seen so many shining faces since the local horse won the Spring Cup at twenty to one.

VALERIUS What! no grievances?

RUFUS Salvius thinks that he has been overcharged for an entrenching-tool.

VALERIUS Did you point out that he had been let off the fine for beating up the baker's assistant?

RUFUS No; I expressed surprise that he had any pay at all.

VALERIUS (*to* CLAUDIUS, *who is lingering by the door*) What is it, Claudius?

CLAUDIUS I shall pay for my equipment, sir. All of it.

VALERIUS (*accepting the capitulation matter-of-factly*) Very good, Claudius.

[*Exit* CLAUDIUS.]

RUFUS Talking of pay, did Cogi turn up for his money?

VALERIUS Yes; this morning.

RUFUS I think the little wretch can smell the stuff.

VALERIUS I would still like to know how he knew that that pay was coming by sea. And why he is so anxious that I should go on leave now that it has come.

[*Enter* FLAVIUS, *with keys which he lays on the table.*]

FLAVIUS The keys of the vault, sir. (*As an item of interest*) The sentry on the south-west tower reports a big fire burning, Corbridge way. (*A jerk of his head to the R.*)

RUFUS The garrison from Hunnum are drunk very early.

[*As* FLAVIUS *has come in the noise of an argument on the far side of the courtyard is just audible. This now rises to fighting pitch; that is to say, the noise of two people arguing changes into the laughter and encouragement of many men watching two fight.*]

VALERIUS (*sharply, to* FLAVIUS) Is that a brawl?

FLAVIUS I think it must be Salvius, sir. He was shaping for a fight as I came through the courtyard.

VALERIUS (*roused*) I will not have Salvius in the defaulter's parade tomorrow! I am sick of his face in orderly room. Send him here at once. And his partner in crime.

FLAVIUS (*going*) Yes, sir. Varus.

VALERIUS *and* RUFUS (*startled*) Who?

FLAVIUS Varus.

[*Exit* FLAVIUS.]

RUFUS (*regretful*) Could you not have waited a little!

VALERIUS Why?

RUFUS It has always been my regret that as an officer I cannot lay hands on Varus; and I could not imagine a better deputy than Salvius. There is the money I owe you. Thanks, Valerius.

VALERIUS (*taking the money*) One of these days I shall set up as a rival to Solomon.

RUFUS Someone ought to. Drive the old bastard out of business.

VALERIUS I think the only solvent persons in the Empire must be Jews.

RUFUS Anyone could be solvent at sixty per cent.

VALERIUS Not everyone would touch the business even for sixty per cent.

[*Enter* SALVIUS *and* VARUS, *ushered in by* FLAVIUS, *who goes again.*]

FLAVIUS These are the men, sir.

VALERIUS Salvius, are you responsible for the uproar in the urtyard?

SALVIUS It was Varus who was hollering, if that's what you ean, sir.

VARUS He attacked me without any provocation whatever, . (*He has come in mopping an eye, and now that he is standing to tention it is apparent that tomorrow the eye will be decorative, if not sed*) All that I had done was to offer him a little advice——

SALVIUS Be quiet, you.

VALERIUS Salvius, you must not use——

SALVIUS If I'm charged tenpence for an entrenching-tool at cost fourpence wholesale, that's a matter between me and e Emperor——

VARUS Which emperor!

SALVIUS Any one I choose to elect. And I don't need any rning barrack-lawyer to tell me my rights or my wrongs. A iserable wage-slave, he called me, and I don't take that from ny man, least of all from a miserable puling poor-mouth of an d woman who has been in the army ten years and doesn't even now his foot-drill.

VALERIUS Salvius, hold your tongue. You are not here to escribe Varus. You are here to be warned that if you appear efore me tomorrow you can expect no mercy. I am very tired f seeing you in orderly room.

SALVIUS (*not cheekily but with a hearty simplicity which is very hard to mbat*) I am always very glad to see you, sir.

VALERIUS I can promise you a change of mind next time we eet officially. Get along now, and do not get drunker than ou can help tonight. (*As they are going*) And in future keep our hands off old women and barrack-lawyers.

SALVIUS (*at the door*) His tongue goes like a bell-clapper, sir. ing-dong in your head like the morning after, till——

VALERIUS That is all, Salvius.

[SALVIUS *goes, but* VARUS *lingers at the door.*]

hat is all, Varus. You are an innocent victim as usual.

[VARUS *goes abruptly.*]

RUFUS (*delighted*) That eye is going to look quite beautiful morrow morning.

VALERIUS Odd, about Varus. He is rotted through a[n]d through with vanity and grievance until he is more stupid th[a]n Salvius himself.

RUFUS His mother thought he was a god, no doubt. Ju[st] when he had grown used to the idea he found that no o[ne] agreed with her. It is always mothers who make the wasters.

VALERIUS Hark to the philosopher.

[*Enter* FLAVIUS, *going to the papers on the table*

FLAVIUS That is a huge fire at Corbridge, sir. The sky to th[e] southwest is blotted out with smoke.

VALERIUS I had better have a look.

RUFUS (*lazily*) Corbridge is Hunnum's business. They a[re] always very proud to be living hand-in-glove with the depo[t]; let them deal with the depot fires.

[VALERIUS *has gone*

FLAVIUS (*busy gathering up his papers*) There are times whe[n] life is too much for me.

RUFUS What is it now, my poor Flavius?

FLAVIUS It is my company's turn to find the guard tonigh[t]. *Pay* night! The first pay for four months. My junior is of[f] duty, so I shall have to warn the men for guard.

RUFUS They will probably kill you. Have you heard of th[e] ghost who walks the ramparts of Deva crying and jingling [a] money-bag?

FLAVIUS No. What has that to do with it?

RUFUS It is the ghost of a chap who warned men for guar[d] on a pay night.

FLAVIUS (*going out*) You are a great comfort, sir.

[RUFUS *makes a leisurely tidying up of his own papers among th[e] varied piles that have been under the tray on the table. As h[e] does so his eye falls on something in the waste-paper basket on th[e] floor to his left.*]

RUFUS (*arrested*) Now, who throws away a travelling warran[t]? (*He is so surprised that it is a moment before he stoops to pick it out [of] the rubbish. It is made of thin waxed wood of a pinkish shade, an[d] has been broken by being crushed in a hand.* RUFUS *reads it, and as [a] result of what he reads begins a search under the more official documen[ts] on the table. He draws out what appears to be an opened lette[r]. Reading*) 'Everything is forgiven. A commission in th[e] raetorian Guard awaits you if you return on receiving this. o not delay, I pray you. A travelling warrant is——'

lowly) Well; I got the formula right, it seems. (*He puts the tter back, and pushes the warrant into the pocket on the inner side of his lt as he hears* VALERIUS *coming back*)

VALERIUS (*coming in*) Did Demetrius ever get those stores om Corbridge for his battery?

RUFUS They were to come tomorrow, I think.

VALERIUS It looks very much as though he will never get em at all. The depot seems to be going up in smoke.

RUFUS That will save me writing indents for some time to me. You might order some things for me as you pass through ork, though.

VALERIUS It will be years before I see York. What made u think——

RUFUS Oh; you are going all the way by sea.

VALERIUS Going where?

RUFUS To your future in the Guards.

VALERIUS How do you know anything of that?

RUFUS I am capable of reading Roman script with the st.

VALERIUS (*furious*) You are capable of reading other men's tters, it seems.

RUFUS Oh, yes. I have not been denied the pleasures of life being well brought up.

VALERIUS Well, you know about the letter. You may know so that I am staying on the Wall.

RUFUS Valerius, will you forget for a moment that you are y superior officer.

VALERIUS When have you ever remembered it?

RUFUS You are not going to throw away your future, are u, just because a silly young fool has got himself into trouble?

VALERIUS (*quickly, surprised*) Why should you imagine——

RUFUS (*interrupting, tolerant*) I know. I have watched you ese last ten days, watched you coming awake. Even Vindo-la in the winter began to blossom for you.

VALERIUS Do you think I am enamoured of the boy!

RUFUS No. I have known you too long for that.

VALERIUS Then why should you——

RUFUS No, it is that you see yourself again in him. You ent through the same hoop; made the same kind of mistake, ffered the same disgrace. So you—adopt him, and suffer erything all over again for his sake. I bet you lie awake at

nights worrying over him, while he snores. Well, he is a goo
boy in many ways, but not worth sacri——

VALERIUS You know as well as I do that he is the be
material that has appeared on the Wall for years. It was
bitter chance that he should have been overtaken by a fa
reserved for fools and blackguards. He has everything th
makes a good commander: courage, ability, and faith.

RUFUS Faith? Mithras?

VALERIUS No. Rome. (*As* RUFUS *lifts a shoulder in a gestu
half-doubting, half-cynical*) I am not sure that he is not rig
about that. Perhaps on the frontier we have our noses to
close to the mud for a long view. We see nothing but th
barbarian on the doorstep and the politicians in Rome. W
forget what lies between. Why do you fight, Rufus? Wh
have you fought these twenty years?

RUFUS (*equably*) I am paid to.

VALERIUS And?

RUFUS It is a man's life.

VALERIUS And?

RUFUS I don't like men who make a treaty in the spring, an
stick you in the back when the harvest is in.

VALERIUS 'To keep fear outside the Wall.'

RUFUS As you like. I don't deny that the boy is promisin
Valerius, but to think of giving up your chance of reinstatemen
your transfer to home service——

VALERIUS What is so desirable about service in Rome
Parades, parties, politics? Have I ever showed a passion f
any one of them?

RUFUS It is more than that; it is vindication. Every ma
wants that.

VALERIUS I prefer the Wall. And if I prefer it, believe m
it is not because one of my junior officers cries himself to sleep
nights.

RUFUS Oh, Valerius, why lie to an old friend——

VALERIUS (*suddenly angry*) You blind fool, have you——

[*From the outer courtyard comes the sound of* DEMETRIUS'S *son*
VALERIUS *breaks off with a gesture of impatience, and both m
wait* DEMETRIUS'S *arrival with resignation.*

[*Enter* DEMETRIUS. VALERIUS *greets him without enthusiasm*

DEMETRIUS Valerius, something odd has happened. Som
thing very odd. I have been down to the town to pay Solomo
what I owed him.

RUFUS Odd? It's unbelievable.

DEMETRIUS (*ignoring him*) But Solomon has gone.

VALERIUS Disappeared?

DEMETRIUS No. Gone away, without waiting to be paid.

VALERIUS There must be foul play somewhere. Half the ;arrison owed him money.

DEMETRIUS No; that is what is so odd. He left yesterday by ea from the East End of the Wall.

[VALERIUS *and* RUFUS *exchange a long look which says: 'Are things as bad as that?'*]

RUFUS (*after a pause*) Perhaps he has killed someone and is unning away.

VALERIUS Solomon squeezed his clients, but he would not quash a spider.

DEMETRIUS He has left all the pledges neatly labelled with the owner's name.

VALERIUS If even a Jew is cutting his losses—— (*Again he exchanges that speculative glance with* RUFUS)

[*Enter* FLAVIUS *in haste.*]

FLAVIUS The Commandant is here, sir. (*Troubled*) I think omething is wrong. They say that——

[*Enter* COCCEIUS, *attended by the same young tribune.*]

VALERIUS I thought you were in Corbridge, sir.

COCCEIUS I have been hunting for two days. I suppose half our men are in the town spending their pay?

VALERIUS More than half, sir.

COCCEIUS Recall them at once, and close the gates. Conider your command in a state of siege.

VALERIUS I know you would not risk mutiny, sir, for any but grave reason.

COCCEIUS Never more grave. The Caledonians have broken he Wall at Hunnum.

VALERIUS The Wall! But the Wall has never been broken rom the north, sir!

COCCEIUS No. The fort was taken by treachery from the outh, and the gates opened to the Caledonians. They have been pouring through since mid-day, and the Brigantes from he south are making common cause with them. Hunnum ried to signal the news, but the signal stations thought the men were drunk.

VALERIUS Then the fire at Corbridge—— (*He is afraid t put it into words*)

COCCEIUS They sacked Corbridge this afternoon. There i nothing there but charred bodies. When they are tired of loo they will try to roll up the Wall, and you are next in line. M orders are that you hold the post at all costs. There is to be n sortie whatever the provocation.

VALERIUS But the civilians in the town, sir?

COCCEIUS They must make the best of their own way t the east. I am bringing the cavalry from Condercum. O my way there now. That will be some kind of screen fo them.

VALERIUS Yes, sir.

COCCEIUS (*answering the doubt in* VALERIUS'S *voice*) You have— how many men?

VALERIUS Two hundred and twenty, sir.

COCCEIUS Quite so. And the normal complement of th fort is five hundred. I have sent to York for help. Until th Legion gets here there is nothing we can do but hold the Wall Meanwhile I shall find out how far the mischief goes. Is al clear?

VALERIUS Quite clear, sir. (*As* COCCEIUS *makes a move to go* But—your wife and daughter, sir?

COCCEIUS Yes?

VALERIUS They are in Corbridge!

COCCEIUS They were. Are there any other questions yo would like to put?

VALERIUS No, sir. I understand.

COCCEIUS (*as* VALERIUS *is about to accompany him*) Never min the honours; get your men out of the town. And I wish yo joy of the job.

[*Exit with his* A.D.C.

RUFUS (*into the momentary silence*) Old Cocceius has his points

VALERIUS Flavius, order them to sound the recall and to g on sounding it.

FLAVIUS Yes, sir.

[*Exit* FLAVIUS.

VALERIUS If I want these men back, I shall have to go fo them. (*He begins hastily to collect his garments from the wall*)

RUFUS I shall go with you, sir. I'll go and collect a picket.

VALERIUS Thanks, Rufus. I shall join you at the Sout Gate.

RUFUS (*taking the crumpled travelling warrant from his belt*) Much use your travelling warrant is now! (*He drops it on the table*)

VALERIUS (*smiling*) As much good as it ever was. (*He puts it into the waste-paper basket*)

RUFUS I don't understand. What was there to keep you here!

VALERIUS You, and Salvius, and the fresh air! (*There is a slight pause after the word 'you'*) Come on.

[*They go out together as the first bugle-call sounds. It is repeated urgently, at varying distances. The curtain comes down on the clamouring bugles and the distant voices of men calling to each other in the further parts of the fort.*]

CURTAIN

ACT II

SCENE I

The Scene is the same; ten days later.

Up by the inner door GAZA *is busy cleaning a breastplate. R., lounging on the inner side of the door to the courtyard, is* SALVIUS, *watching him with interest.*

SALVIUS (*after a little*) It would be more to the point if you blacked that over, instead of burnishing it. Do you think a man wants his harness winking like a signal light when every heather bush for fifty miles is bristling with Caledonians? (GAZA *takes no notice*) Now that the barbarians have come looking for trouble, you'll be able to get a bit of your own back, eh, Gaza? A tongue for a tongue. (*Considering it*) Maybe two tongues for a tongue. (*He hears* VALERIUS *coming, and leaps to attention as* VALERIUS *comes in, passing him towards the table.* VALERIUS'S *right forearm is bandaged*)

VALERIUS Salvius. Are you waiting to see me?

SALVIUS Yes, sir.

VALERIUS What is it? A petition?

SALVIUS No, sir. A complaint.

VALERIUS (*coldly*) Complaints should go through the orderly room in the proper manner.

SALVIUS Yes, sir; I know the routine. But the complaint is about you, sir.

VALERIUS About me!

SALVIUS Yes, sir. I volunteered for that scouting job, sir. (*His tone is rich with accusation*)

VALERIUS Your whole company volunteered.

SALVIUS Yes, sir, and you gave it to Marius, instead of to me.

VALERIUS Why to you?

SALVIUS Because I am the best shot and the most desperate character in the company.

VALERIUS You do yourself too much honour. Petronius is the company shot; and your character is not so awe-inspiring as you seem to imagine. In any case, I send out a scout not to terrify the enemy but to gather knowledge. To be self-effacing and discreet. Does that sound like you, do you think? Besides, your hair is too conspicuous.

SALVIUS That is my mother.

VALERIUS Your mother?

SALVIUS She was a very respectable woman, sir, but she could never resist Spaniards with red hair. I suppose it wouldn't make any difference if I dyed it, sir?

VALERIUS Not if you dyed yourself heather colour all over, Salvius. But one thing I promise you: when the Legion comes, and we settle with these gentry, you shall be first out of the fort.

SALVIUS That is very thoughtful of you, sir. Thank you. (*As he is going*, AEMILIUS, *on sentry duty outside appears in the doorway*) You watch me that day, sir!

[*Exit* SALVIUS.]

AEMILIUS Sir, Julius asks if you would see him for a moment.

VALERIUS No, Aemilius, no! If a man has business with me, there are the proper—— (JULIUS *has appeared beyond the open door.* VALERIUS, *resigned, relents; he likes* JULIUS) Oh, very well, Julius. Come in! What is it? A complaint?

JULIUS (*surprised and a little shocked*) Oh, no, sir. A petition. I wanted to ask, sir, if another scout is sent out that I should be the one to go.

VALERIUS But you have little experience, Julius. And you don't speak the local dialects, do you?

JULIUS Not very well, sir.

VALERIUS Then why do you want to go?

JULIUS Marius was my friend, sir.

VALERIUS I see. But you realise that I must choose men for their worth rather than their willingness.

JULIUS If a man's heart is in a mission, sir, he is good at it.

VALERIUS There is something in that. I cannot promise anything, Julius, but I will remember your request.

JULIUS Thank you, sir. Thank you very much.

VALERIUS (*as he is going*) How does the carving progress? The seagull. It is finished?

JULIUS Very nearly, sir. (*Lingering*) I suppose—— Perhaps you would care to have it, sir?

VALERIUS I thought it was for your girl in Olicana?

JULIUS The way things are, sir, it looks as if there will be time for me to carve several more birds before my leave comes up. You like such things, sir; and if you think it good enough——

VALERIUS Thank you, Julius. I shall be very pleased to have it. There is no doubt of its quality. If you were not a soldier, you might be the fashion in Rome.

JULIUS I would rather be a soldier, sir.

VALERIUS (*exchanging a smile with him*) There is no accounting for tastes, is there! (*As* JULIUS *is going*) You don't hope that your bird may be a decoy, do you?

JULIUS No, sir; oh, no. But you won't forget that I asked you, will you, sir? Marius and I were friends a long time.

VALERIUS I won't forget.

JULIUS Thank you, sir.

[*He goes out as* CLAUDIUS *comes in.*]

VALERIUS (*as* CLAUDIUS *is making for the table with the request on his lips*) No; you can't!

CLAUDIUS (*taken aback*) Can't what, sir?

VALERIUS Go scouting in Marius's place.

CLAUDIUS How did you——? Have others been——?

VALERIUS The whole garrison except for the master baker and the tailor's boy.

CLAUDIUS But I am different, sir.

VALERIUS They all are.

CLAUDIUS But, sir, this is what I was saved alive for. I have wondered so often why the gods—— And now I know. I can bring you any intelligence you want, sir. I did dialects at Caerleon, for my second step. And I have hunted since I was a boy. And——

VALERIUS Claudius, I have fifty good scouts, and practically no junior officers. Have a little common sense. (*Getting up from the table and giving his place to* CLAUDIUS) If you want to make yourself useful, duplicate these lists for me. It is a clerk's job; but every clerk is carrying a spear today.

[*As* CLAUDIUS *complies*, RUFUS *comes in.*]

RUFUS No word of Marius?

VALERIUS No. What of the stores?

RUFUS Oh, we have enough for the whole garrison for two weeks.

VALERIUS Ordinary rations?

RUFUS Yes.

VALERIUS That means enough for six weeks.

RUFUS (*judicially*) They would still be alive. I doubt if they could still shoot. Where do you think you are? Troy?

VALERIUS No one knows where we are. That is my point. All we know is that we are cut off. Relief may come tomorrow, or next week, or ten minutes from now. I want to know how we stand.

RUFUS The rest of the Wall may be too busy to help us, but it will take the Legion from York only a matter of days to reach us.

VALERIUS Half the legion in York are in Gaul. And the other half will have to fight their way here.

RUFUS The Sixth are very vain of their fighting powers.

VALERIUS Well, we shall present them with a detachment of the Second that will have been worth their while, I hope. Is that all?

RUFUS Demetrius is murderous because the spare parts for his battery did not arrive before the Caledonians. (*More slowly, with a change of tone*) There are not even heads of hair in the town to provide them now.

VALERIUS (*thoughtful*) No. (*As if driven to speech against his will*) I have seen the Legions loose in victory, and it was not a pretty sight. But there is an—inventiveness about barbarian massacre—— (*He breaks off*)

RUFUS Yes.

VALERIUS (*in a burst, not raising his voice but furious*) I wish you could hear the talkers in Rome! The reformers, the bright intellectuals, the vote-catching politicians——

RUFUS I have heard them. They come on tours of inspection.

VALERIUS (*imitating*) 'You must have been harsh with them; too rigid; too unimaginative. They are primitive, mere tribes; must be dealt with kindly. They must be led, not driven. They are children, who mean well, children who have only to be taught—— ' I wish they could see those children in the town! Their stomachs might speak more sense than their tongues.

[*Enter* FLAVIUS, *at speed, excited. His left arm in a sling. Outside, the murmur of voices.*]

FLAVIUS Sir! Sir, Marius is back. He is here.

[*This is tremendous news; its importance is reflected in their reaction.*

[*Enter* MARIUS, *a little weather-worn, but cheerful and collected, and still wearing, oddly, that burnished look which is characteristic of him.*]

VALERIUS Marius! I am glad to see you! We had given you up.

MARIUS Oh no, sir. I am all right. It was a longer beat than I had planned for, that was all, sir.

VALERIUS Well? What have you gathered for us?

MARIUS I have been east as far as the sea, sir.

VALERIUS Yes? Where are the nearest troops?

MARIUS There are no troops, sir. The Wall has gone.

RUFUS What do you mean: The Wall has gone?

MARIUS There are no troops between here and the sea, sir. The Caledonians are behaving like mad things. They are overturning the Wall stone by stone. They are even levering up the stone floors. I have never seen them work before.

VALERIUS But our men? There are five forts east of us!

MARIUS Yes, sir. The cavalry post at Condercum was empty——

VALERIUS Yes, we expected that.

MARIUS Pons Aelii was full of dead men. (*Parenthetically, in great admiration*) They fought, those Britons! There was a Caledonian body for every British. Segedunum was going up like a chimney, and the other two were burnt out.

VALERIUS (*into an aghast silence*) But—how!

MARIUS I think they rolled the Wall up from the sea, sir. A wounded Gaul I found outside Pons Aelii said they boasted how they had cut the Wall in two and rolled it up from either end.

VALERIUS *Either* end! The west too?

MARIUS So they said, sir. I hadn't dared to hope that I would find Vindobala still standing, sir. It was like a miracle. (*After a slight pause*) There is no one alive in the town at all, sir.

VALERIUS No. We knew that. The cavalry from Condercum came too late. We made a sortie—against orders—but—— (*He stops with a lift of his shoulder*) We have buried twenty men these last few days. (*Seeing the look on* MARIUS's *face*) There was no one from your section.

MARIUS Thank you, sir.

VALERIUS What happened to your wounded Gaul?

MARIUS (*simply*) He asked me to finish him, sir; and I did.

VALERIUS Very well, Marius. You must need some rest. I congratulate you on your report. We are glad to have it, and very glad to have you back.

MARIUS Thank you, sir.

VALERIUS (*as* MARIUS *is going*) How did you get into the fort alive, by the way?

MARIUS I came in from the north, sir. The heather is deep that side and fairly close to the Wall. And for the last half-mile

I crawled along in a wild boar's skin. That's the smell, sir. You may have noticed it.

VALERIUS I see. All right, Marius; get yourself some food and sleep and then we can go into details.

[*Exit* MARIUS *with* FLAVIUS, *to be received outside by a crowd of eager questioners. Their voices die into the distance.*]

VALERIUS Well, the Sixth are going to have a chance to show those famous fighting qualities. You had better double the guard on the stores, Rufus.

RUFUS I have done that.

VALERIUS (*half amused*) So. You were not as casual as you seemed.

RUFUS I have never been casual since my first season in camp. In Dacia, it was; late spring, but the nights were bitter. I came back to camp late one night, and lay next to the only man who had a fur rug.

VALERIUS And fleas the size of elephants trampled over your body all night. Go on.

RUFUS No. In the morning I found I had been sleeping with a bear.

[*Enter* DEMETRIUS, *excited.*]

DEMETRIUS Valerius, Marius has brought some wonderful news.

VALERIUS Wonderful?

DEMETRIUS When the Caledonians sacked the cavalry post at Condercum, they tipped the big catapult over the Wall. Marius says that it is lying there broken, but the parts are whole. We have only to collect them when it is dark.

VALERIUS May I bring to your specialist's mind the fact that we are no longer part of a Wall. We are an island, surrounded by seas of furious barbarians, with whose amusements of pillage and murder we have interfered so long, and who are now making up for lost time.

DEMETRIUS Oh, I know the country is up. That is all the more reason we should have those parts. It is only six miles, and there is no moon. I need only a couple of ponies and a dozen men.

VALERIUS You wouldn't care for a litter and a camp kitchen as well?

DEMETRIUS I thought if we took the ponies we could save the whole catapult. It is the best on the Wall.

RUFUS We thought yours was.

DEMETRIUS (*ignoring him*) I have always wanted that catapult.

VALERIUS When the Legion arrives you can indent for the pieces.

DEMETRIUS You mean you won't give me permission to go?

VALERIUS No, I will not. Your own catapult works, doesn't it?

DEMETRIUS It may break down at any moment.

VALERIUS Then it can be repaired in the workshops. Every unit of the army is supposed to be self-sufficient. (*With a grim amusement*) And by the gods, it would seem that the unit at Vindobala is going to be put to the test! Run along, Demetrius. A jaunt to Corbridge is one thing, but an expedition to the ruins of Condercum is quite another. We are holding Vindobala with two hundred men short. I have no intention of being still shorter.

[DEMETRIUS *turns abruptly on his heel, and goes out.*]

RUFUS You had better chain him up.

VALERIUS You don't think he would—— (*He pauses*)

RUFUS These specialists have no control of themselves. We had a doctor once in Pannonia who was curious about—— But I'll tell you that story another time. (*Looking repressively at* CLAUDIUS) It is not suitable for children.

VALERIUS It is no time for stories in any case. I have to tell the men the truth. And the sooner the better, before the stories grow too wild. Though God knows, the facts are—fantastic enough. I still can't believe it. If it were anyone but Marius—— I suppose we should have seen it coming. All our best men helping Albinus play politics in Gaul; pay coming by sea because Headquarters were doubtful of the tribes; massacre of reinforcements on the way up; the arrival of four months pay for the Wall. Yes, we should have seen.

RUFUS And if we had foreseen, what? You can't make soldiers out of juniper bushes.

VALERIUS No; there was not much we could have done. What has to be done lies in front of us. Claudius, parade every man who is not on duty, in the outer courtyard. I shall speak to them there in fifteen minutes.

CLAUDIUS Yes, sir. May I say something, sir?

VALERIUS What is it?

CLAUDIUS Don't think me presumptuous, sir, but do you think York will know about us?

VALERIUS York?

CLAUDIUS Headquarters, sir. If the whole of the Wall has gone, as Marius says, they will not expect to relieve anyone. They will come north to rebuild, of course, but they will take their time about it, and clear up as they come.

VALERIUS (*to* RUFUS, *having digested the point, amused*) I suppose that would have occurred to our great military minds eventually.

RUFUS (*handsomely*) Oh, I have learned from babes in my time.

VALERIUS You are right, Claudius. I shall see to it. Go and parade the men. (*As* CLAUDIUS *lingers*) No, you will not be the one to go to York.

[*Exit* CLAUDIUS.]

RUFUS Whom will you send?

VALERIUS Marius. He is the best we have.

RUFUS Only one?

VALERIUS Oh, no. Julius, too. Separately.

RUFUS Why Julius?

VALERIUS Because a keen scout is better than a moping soldier. Besides, he is a Briton, even if he does not speak the north dialects. The people the tribes are murdering are his people. He has a double stake in the game.

RUFUS (*agreeing*) Sounds good enough.

VALERIUS They may not have to go far. They will no doubt meet the Legion about Catterick. (*Turning to more immediate worries*) I suppose we can expect an attack in force tonight.

RUFUS About dawn tomorrow, I should say.

VALERIUS Where do you think it will come?

RUFUS All four ways at once. They have no science, only numbers.

VALERIUS But what numbers!

RUFUS Yes; we shall be brushing them off the walls like ants.

VALERIUS (*producing a plan of the fort*) Well, look; I suggest that we block up the north, east, and west gates, and leave only the south gate to be guarded. . . .

[*They huddle over the plan as the light fades.*]

FADE OUT

SCENE 2

The Scene is the same; on a morning nearly two weeks later. VALERIUS *is sitting at the table, his head propped in his hands, palms in eye-sockets. The bandage on his forearm is smaller, now; a mere strip.*

Enter, at his leisure, RUFUS, *from the courtyard.*

RUFUS I have a wonderful idea, Valerius. When we—— (*He notices that* VALERIUS *has not stirred, and pauses*)

VALERIUS (*wakening up*) I was not asleep.

RUFUS You ought to be.

VALERIUS I am waiting till it is time to visit the hospital. The orderlies don't like it if I appear before they have tidied up. One would think it was a convalescent home at Ostia instead of a beleagured post on the frontier! What was your plan?

RUFUS When we build the Wall again, we must plant vines the whole length of the south face. Seventy-three miles of them.

VALERIUS (*dryly*) That will be pretty.

RUFUS We shall have a reserve vintage of our own for emergencies. It will taste like ink, but it will be a great deal less sudden on the stomach than that cold well water.

VALERIUS Every day I bless the gods for those two wells. Without them there would have been no hope.

RUFUS Maybe; but next time I shall take care to have a cellar.

VALERIUS (*casting him a half-amused glance for his matter-of-factness*) Next time? (*He rises and begins to move up and down restlessly*) I wish we had a better doctor, Rufus.

RUFUS Yes. I did try to palm little Taminius off on the draft for Gaul. But they demanded Vindex instead.

VALERIUS There are five more men down with fever today. He is quite bewildered. And he bungled that amputation yesterday. Bungled it disgracefully.

RUFUS (*comforting*) The man would have died in any case.

VALERIUS (*turning on him*) Go on! Tell me there were worse losses at Cremona! (*After a pause*) I am sorry, Rufus. I didn't mean to bark at you.

RUFUS (*equably*) Bark away, if it makes you feel better.

VALERIUS (*with a half smile to him*) I strive after your unending calm, but I never achieve it. (*His smile disappearing*) And just now my mind hums and spins and wobbles like a failing top. Nearly two weeks, and not a sign of either of them. Surely one got through! Julius is a good boy enough, but Marius is a genius. If you sent Marius to fetch a hair from Caesar's head he would come back with it. And what is the Legion doing! (*He sounds cross with the Legion*)

RUFUS If I know anything of them, they are solemnly beginning to build the Wall from the Solway end. About the middle of next year they will arrive at Vindobala. Still solemnly building.

VALERIUS Don't, Rufus. I can't make a jest of it. Everything I am, everything I have, everything that I set store by, is bound up in this. My own pride, the lives of my men, my friends, and—— (*he searches for words*) and the survival of something intangible; of an idea. It is some kind of symbol, that Vindobala should not be lost. A sign to the barbarian that Rome is still here; is indestructible.

RUFUS I know what you mean.

VALERIUS (*pleased by his implied agreement*) Do you, Rufus?

RUFUS Don't worry. You are not going to lose Vindobala. But you *are* going to have to deal with the barbarian inside the fort as well as out.

VALERIUS Inside?

RUFUS This time from beyond the Rhine.

VALERIUS Varus!

RUFUS Yes. (*Ruefully*) About two thousand Caledonian arrows have landed in the fort this last week, and not one on Varus!

VALERIUS What is it? Mutiny?

RUFUS Actually, yes. Technically, no. You will be receiving a deputation, I understand.

VALERIUS What is the grievance? The food ration?

RUFUS Yes.

VALERIUS I knew they were grumbling, but I had no idea that they felt strongly about it.

RUFUS They didn't until Varus had worked on them. Even he had several boss-shots before he hit upon their stomachs, so to speak.

VALERIUS For instance?

RUFUS Well, he wasted several days on the theory that Demetrius and his twelve men had reached Condercum alive, and that we should send a party to rescue them. That roused no enthusiasm, I need hardly say. The general view was that if Demetrius had disobeyed orders and sacrificed twelve men, the Caledonians were welcome to him. Then he had a fine scheme for fighting our way to the coast instead of dying by numbers where we stood. That was not very popular either. But the food ration, of course, has proved to be the grievance of his dreams.

VALERIUS How serious is it?

RUFUS Fairly serious.

VALERIUS So!

RUFUS If they were to attack the stores, the Legion would have to arrive pretty soon to do any good.

[*Enter* CLAUDIUS, *with a paper.*]

CLAUDIUS (*laying the paper on the table*) The duty roll, sir. (*Lingering after* VALERIUS *has thanked him*) Valerius, there is a mob of men in the outer courtyard, and they seem to be headed this way.

RUFUS Your deputation, I take it.

CLAUDIUS I don't know if you know, sir, but the men have a grudge about their food.

VALERIUS So I have learned. It seems that Varus has a more devoted following at Vindobala than I have.

CLAUDIUS Oh, no, sir; the men would go through hell for you.

VALERIUS But not tighten their belts.

CLAUDIUS In normal times they would kick Varus in the— from here to Dover. It is just the being-shut-in that upsets them, the oddness of the Wall going, the suspense. They can't reach the Caledonians, so they want a scapegoat. They are a good lot, sir.

VALERIUS (*amused*) Are you recommending my men to me? (*What accent there is, is on ' men '*)

CLAUDIUS (*abashed*) Oh, no, sir. I just didn't want you to think that they were disloyal to you in their hearts.

VALERIUS I see. (*Dismissing him*) Thank you, Claudius.

CLAUDIUS Shall I stay, sir?

VALERIUS No; go back to your duty.

CLAUDIUS But they look—they may be——

VALERIUS I shall not need you, Claudius, thank you. (*The dismissal is unmistakable*)

[*Exit* CLAUDIUS.]

Nor you, Rufus.

RUFUS Oh, come! What did I make this morning call for?

VALERIUS I thought you hadn't come just to talk about vine-planting.

RUFUS You must have someone to stand behind your chair and hold an umbrella over your head. Impress the bastards.

VALERIUS No; you look too like a reinforcement.

RUFUS Besides—they are in a wicked mood.

VALERIUS If they decide to kill me, I don't suppose your presence will deter them. Go away, Rufus.

RUFUS No; I am going to Gaza, who appreciates me, and will give me soup. (*He makes for the inner door*)

VALERIUS Soup is made of swillings these days, but you are welcome to it as long as you keep out of sight.

[*The murmur of the approaching crowd, which has been audible for some time now, changes to the sound of individual voices and laughter as the men approach the door.* VARUS *appears and enters a step or two inside, followed by the simple* CANDIDUS, *the others crowding in the doorway; the front rank leaning back to prevent being pushed into the room and the men too far behind to see well bobbing up and down and moving uneasily from side to side, so that there is a continual small movement in the press.*]

VARUS (*insolently*) We want a few words with you, Valerius Valens.

VALERIUS (*smoothly*) Only that? From the lack of courtesy one would have thought you wanted my head.

VARUS You can keep your head. What we want is justice.

VALERIUS You don't do yourself much justice, do you, Varus?

VARUS (*taken aback*) I?

VALERIUS (*indicating* CANDIDUS) With the whole garrison to choose from, you pick a very odd lieutenant. Pull your tunic down, Candidus. And your belt-buckle is supposed to be worn in the middle of the front. That is better. Yes, Varus, you were saying?

VARUS (*trying not to feel that the wind has been taken out of his sails by this appropriation and valuation of his lieutenant*) I was saying that the garrison of this fort is being starved.

VALERIUS They look remarkably well on it.

VARUS Starved deliberately and for no reason.

VALERIUS That is not possible, surely? If the starvation is deliberate there must be a reason.

VARUS I am not here to bandy words with you. I am here to say to your face that the troops are being starved so that Rufus Sita and his friends can make a pretty penny off the surplus.

VALERIUS That is a grave charge to bring against an officer.

VARUS I make no charges that cannot be upheld. There is food in store for weeks, and you cannot deny it. In a few days at most we shall be relieved, and new stores will arrive. And all that is lying there unused, all that has been kept from starving men, will turn into gold pieces in the officers' pockets. Oh, we know the pretext! We have heard it morning, noon, and night. 'Pull in your belts till the Legion finds us.' That was the watchword two weeks ago, when there were two hundred of us. Since then we have lost nearly fifty men, but is there an extra bean in the ration? No! (*There is a murmur of agreement from the crowd*)

VALERIUS And is there a legion in sight? No, again!

VARUS Any hour now the Legion will be here. Meanwhile men do their guard in the bitter cold on a handful of beans. They die like flies of fever because they have no strength to fight it. We refuse to be exploited any longer. Either we are given our full legal rations or we take them.

VALERIUS And be executed for looting when the Legion comes?

VARUS It is not loot to take possession of one's own property. Army Regulations say that a soldier's ration is so much. There is ample food in store, and yet you keep it from us. It is you, Valerius Valens, not we, who will answer to the Legion.

VALERIUS And who will answer to the men when the last mouthful is eaten and the Legion still delays.

VARUS Why should the Legion delay!

VALERIUS (*with the patient persuasion of a teacher putting a proposition to a dull pupil*) Think, my good Varus, think! You are the General commanding the Sixth. Refugees, from Solway to the North Sea, pour into York crying that the Wall has gone. You take your legion north. By the sea, to protect your flank. Truly the Wall *has* gone. A hundred thousand Caledonians are celebrating the fact all over the landscape. You set a guard against the Caledonians and begin to build. Every day a little further into the heather. By the middle of the spring you arrive at Vindobala—— (*he pauses suggestively*)

VARUS We have only to send messengers to the Sixth.

VALERIUS We have already sent two. Until they find the Sixth and bring it here we have to eat. You agree?

VARUS Of course we have to eat.

VALERIUS And since no one knows when, if ever, a messenger will reach the Legion, it is wise to eat very little. You agree again?

VARUS (*pushed into a corner and rushing wildly out*) No! The heather outside is thick with game.

VALERIUS And who will go hunting it?

VARUS I for one!

VALERIUS But you—forgive me, but are you not the man who went hunting and brought back a coney that had been dead four days?

[*There is a little laugh from the crowd at the door.*]

And I think you would find it difficult to satisfy the Garrison. Especially my friend Patricius (*He refers to a small plump man in the front row of the spectators*) who was known at Caerleon, if I remember rightly, as Come-again Caius, because one helping was never enough for him. (PATRICIUS *disappears discreetly backwards among his amused fellows*) And my good friend Sanctius (*he refers to a tall, thin man also in the front row*), who is so pernickety that he looks on both sides of a cherry before putting it into his mouth. (SANCTIUS *also presses himself backwards to anonymity in the crowd*) And—— (*Catching sight of a red head in the third row*) Well, well, Salvius; are you in the bread queue?

SALVIUS (*disgustedly*) Not me, sir. I'm the opposition.

VALERIUS (*silkily*) Oh? There is an opposition?

SALVIUS Not every man squawks like a calf when his belly is empty.

VALERIUS My brave, silent Salvius! My compliments. Are you here to protest?

SALVIUS No, sir. I am waiting to have a word with Varus.

VALERIUS There have been too many words already, I think. (*His voice growing momentarily harder as he goes on*) Only Varus could have spilled so many in so poor a cause; or worked so hard to weaken the faith of men fighting for their lives. The Rhine still flows wide and deep between you and civilisation, Varus, for all your Roman citizenship. To be civilised is to have a sense of obligation; a will to build rather than to destroy. You took an oath to uphold and defend. What have you ever upheld or defended?

VARUS I defend the rights of the downtrodden.

VALERIUS (*not heeding him*) Where there was courage you mocked it, where there was loyalty you undermined it, where there was faith you destroyed it. You never saw something fine but you wanted to overturn it, nor something peaceful but you wanted to stir it up. You are a blight, a mould, an infection, a canker, among healthy men, and it surprises me that your fellows have been patient with you so long.

VARUS (*furious*) My fellows will bear witness that no one—— (*He flings an arm out to the men behind him, and casts a glance in their direction and stops. From the first moment of* VALERIUS's *speech about ' too many words ' the crowd has begun to melt away, with murmured words to each other; the front ones telling the ones behind the main points of the exchange. So that now there is no one on the veranda but* SALVIUS, *standing large and still.* VARUS *is left with his poor lieutenant*, CANDIDUS.

VALERIUS (*quietly, into* VARUS's *horrified pause*) They are *my* fellows, Varus. And if they had not been sick with doubt and bewilderment, even your talent for trouble-making would have been wasted on them. They are men, Varus. They live by a creed, not a catchword. They have built and defended all their lives, and an oath, in their eyes, is something to be honoured. An obligation. Which you would not understand. Go back to your duty, Varus, and, if possible, hold your tongue for a little.

[VARUS *turns abruptly and goes out, hesitates past* SALVIUS *and disappears.* SALVIUS *turns slowly after him.*]

Salvius. (SALVIUS *pauses*) I don't want any more men in hospital.

SALVIUS (*virtuously*) Oh, no, sir. Not hospital. (*He is evidently going to stop short of that. He disappears*)

CANDIDUS (*standing bewildered and forlorn ; in a small voice*) I am very sorry, sir. I didn't understand about the Legion not coming. And I *was* very hungry, sir.

VALERIUS Run along, Candidus, and have more sense next time. Remember this: when a man tells you how ill-used you are, go away from him into a corner and find out what he is getting out of it.

CANDIDUS (*submissively*) Yes, sir. I am very, very sorry, sir. I just didn't understand.

[*Exit* CANDIDUS.]

[*Enter* RUFUS *from the inner room, a bowl of soup in one hand and one for* VALERIUS *in the other.*]

RUFUS My Demosthenes! My Cicero! 'A blight, a mould, an infection, a—what was it?—a canker!' Who would have thought the simple soldier had such stores of eloquence. Have some bilge-water to clear your throat. It tastes of peat and very dead shell-fish, with a suggestion of tar.

VALERIUS You know, I used to be sorry for that worm. Used to plan how I could cure him by promotion. Make a man of him. Now he makes me even sicker than this stuff. What is it?

RUFUS Gaza's pot-scourings. The fragrance of a thousand memories.

VALERIUS How dared you say my men were in a wicked mood! They were lambs. (*Laughing*) They were also cowards. They faded away at the first shot. Poor Candidus, high and dry. I never thought I would live to see Candidus fighting a lonely rearguard action.

[*They are laughing together over their bowls of soup, standing there drinking in gulps before going to their respective duties.*

[*Enter* CLAUDIUS, *with a pale, shocked face.*]

CLAUDIUS (*in a small voice*) Valerius.

VALERIUS Yes? (*As he sees* CLAUDIUS'S *face, sharply*) What is it?

CLAUDIUS The Caledonians have catapulted something over the wall.

VALERIUS Something? Well? What?

CLAUDIUS A man's head.

VALERIUS (*after a slight pause*) One of Demetrius's party? (*He says this almost in hope*)

CLAUDIUS No, sir.

VALERIUS (*with an effort*) Who?

CLAUDIUS Julius.

VALERIUS (*having put down his bowl of soup slowly*) Poor Julius! He must have done well, or—or it would have happened earlier.

RUFUS (*comforting*) There is still Marius. If Julius got so far, Marius is a certainty.

VALERIUS Yes, there is still Marius. Are you coming to hospital with me?

[*They go out as the light fades.*]

FADE OUT

SCENE 3

The Scene is the same, a fortnight later. A light coating of frost or snow makes a white light in the courtyard that is reflected in the room.

Kneeling on the floor are CANDIDUS *and* AEMILIUS, *the young soldier from Act I, Sc. 2. In front of them is a great heap of moss, which they are busily sorting into two heaps: one of good stuff and one of rough discard. Their equipment is neatly piled on one side: spear, hand-catapult (a square wooden affair a little bigger than a washing-board), shield and helmet and cloak.*

It is morning, about ten.

Before the curtain goes up AEMILIUS *can be heard singing the song from the Loire valley that he has sung on the ramparts.*

He goes on singing while they work, blowing on his hands now and then.

AEMILIUS (*breaking off his song, and picking up a piece that* CANDIDUS *has just contributed to the 'good' pile*) No hard bits, Candidus. (*From his tone he has said this before*)

CANDIDUS I am sorry, Aemilius. I grow muddled as to which is the good heap and which the bad. (*After a pause of work*) How do you think the Caledonians discovered that moss was good for wounds?

AEMILIUS I expect one of the little painted devils cut himself one day and clapped on the first thing that came to hand. It is a wonder to me that they have never tried to sell us the stuff.

CANDIDUS But it grows everywhere.

AEMILIUS That wouldn't stop them. They would try to sell you fresh air if they thought you would buy.

CANDIDUS It is not right that Valerius Valens should risk his life to get dressings for our wounds, is it!

AEMILIUS No; but he is the only one who knows where to get the moss in the dark. I have hunted with Valerius. I think he knows every stone from here to Tava.

CANDIDUS I have still a spare tunic that they could have torn up for bandages.

AEMILIUS You will need that to keep your bones from freezing if we are here much longer. If the last rag had not been used believe me Valerius would not have gone over the Wall. He is not given to empty gestures. It will be my turn to go over the Wall tonight.

CANDIDUS (*surprised*) For moss?

AEMILIUS No; intelligence. If there is no word of Marius by sundown, I am going out with a message to the Sixth.

CANDIDUS (*impressed*) Oh. That is a great honour. (*Naively admiring*) But of course you are very clever, Aemilius.

AEMILIUS Well—I think it is, a little, that he knows my family. His mother comes from Gaul, you know. My grandmother was her nurse when she was young.

CANDIDUS You will be decorated for that—if you come back.

AEMILIUS Oh, I shall come back. By now the Legion will have reached the east end of the Wall. I shall not have to look for them as poor Julius and Marius did. I can do it in a night, at this time of year.

CANDIDUS Well, it will be very nice to have a good meal again. And a fire to warm oneself at.

AEMILIUS (*grimly*) It will be very nice to deal with the barbarian. Five to one, instead of five hundred to one.

CANDIDUS We have not done so badly so far.

AEMILIUS No.

CANDIDUS Why do you think they have stopped the big attacks? Now, when we are so few.

AEMILIUS Me, I think superstition begins to work.

CANDIDUS Superstition?

AEMILIUS They can't understand how we are still alive. All these weeks no food comes to us, and yet we not only live but we throw them off the ramparts by the hundred. They probably think there is a god in the fort.

CANDIDUS Do you think Valerius can be a god, perhaps?

AEMILIUS (*amused*) I had not thought of it.

CANDIDUS But for Valerius we should all be dead. I feel very much ashamed every time I eat my beans. I put back one or two into the pot each time, as a sort of punishment. He didn't punish me, you know; for being second in command of the mutiny.

AEMILIUS (*taken aback*) For what? (*Amused, but hiding it*) Oh, yes.

CANDIDUS He didn't even tell me off. Not that I would have minded. When he curses you he curses very nicely, doesn't he? I have been told off about one thing or another ever since I entered the army, but no one was as nice about it as Valerius.

[*With a sigh and a light fragile clatter an arrow falls on the pavement beyond the veranda.* AEMILIUS *casts a glance round at it and goes on with his work.*]

AEMILIUS An arrow. (*Dryly*) The good point about arrows is that they can be sent back where they came from. A great saving in ammunition.

CANDIDUS (*accepting this praise of arrows doubtfully*) I don't like arrows, to tell you the truth, Aemilius. (*He might be talking of onions*) They are very difficult to get out once they go in. Poor Sanctius was—— (*He pauses in his work preparatory to enlarging on the matter of* SANCTIUS'S *wound*)

AEMILIUS (*indicating his work*) Never mind Sanctius. Let us finish with this. (*Catching sight of his own hands*) My hand hasn't been wrinkled with the wet like that since I tickled trout in the river at home. Three years ago. (*Resuming his work with a small laugh*) When I come back a week from now with six thousand men, I may bring letters too. Are you expecting a letter, Candidus?

CANDIDUS (*not at all sorry for himself; merely stating the fact*) Oh, no. Nobody writes to me. My aunt—she brought me up—she is dead. My cousin writes sometimes to say that she has had another baby and needs money. But I don't think she can be having another one just yet.

[*Enter* VALERIUS. *He has picked up the arrow at the door and deposits it on the table without remark.*]

VALERIUS Well, have you finished? (*He begins to divest himself of his wrappings and sword-belt*)

AEMILIUS Yes, sir. Practically.

VALERIUS That should last us a day or two. And by that time—— You will be ready to go over the Wall tonight, Aemilius, if no word has come?

AEMILIUS I have been ready any time these ten days, sir. (*The two soldiers are busy finishing up the last scraps of the sorting*)

VALERIUS If we had not been so desperately short of men, I would have sent you before now. Don't forget to tell them how short of medical supplies we are.

AEMILIUS I won't, sir.

VALERIUS I don't want the Eagles parading in here with all the pomp of an Emperor's birthday celebrations and not a salve or a bandage between them.

AEMILIUS No, sir. I'll bring a cart-load. (*Standing up and brushing the clinging scraps from his wet fingers*) I think you'll find that all right, sir. It works out a bit less than you'd think. There was a lot of waste stuff.

VALERIUS Yes, I had to take it as it came, in the dark. That looks a good job. (*As they begin to bundle together the two pieces of canvas on which the separate heaps are lying*) Take it to the kitchen, and spread it out to dry. Tell the kitchen people that an orderly will come for it this afternoon. You look cold, Candidus.

CANDIDUS I am not very warm, sir. (*He and* AEMILIUS *put on their equipment. Shield and catapult slung on their backs, their cloaks flung plaid-wise round the shoulder and under the armpit. They pick up their bundles and fling them too on a shoulder. Lastly they collect their spears*)

VALERIUS That will be another thing to remind the Sixth about. Fuel. They will say that they cannot be expected to fight their way to our rescue loaded with firewood. But don't listen to them. If you manage to look miserable enough, Candidus, the cook may be moved to the extent of hot soup. Since it will be largely made of hot water, I don't think it can be considered an infringement of anyone's ration rights.

CANDIDUS Thank you, sir.

AEMILIUS Can we quote you on that, sir?

VALERIUS (*smiling*) There speaks Gaul. Very well, my canny friend; quote away. (*As they are staggering out under their load of moss and equipment*) But I shall expect you both to have rejoined your company fifteen minutes from now.

AEMILIUS *and* CANDIDUS Yes, sir. Thank you, sir.

[*As they go out,* FLAVIUS *appears. His arm is no longer in a sling.*]

FLAVIUS You wanted me, sir?

VALERIUS Yes, Flavius. The cold in the barracks is intense, and very depressing for the men. Now that we are so few, they have not even their neighbours to keep them warm.

FLAVIUS No, sir, it isn't possible even to raise a fug.

VALERIUS I have decided to divide the garrison into two small units, where the men can be warm and close together—and less conscious of the gaps. One here, under me, with Claudius as second. And one in the south Gate House, under Rufus Sita, with you as second.

FLAVIUS Yes, sir.

VALERIUS We ought to be able to manage a brazier of sorts for each place. There is still the furniture in the Tribune's house to be burnt.

FLAVIUS Yes, sir. And I've been thinking: your foraging has been so successful, sir: some of the people in the town used to burn peat. It must be still there, and one load a night would keep us going.

VALERIUS It is a good idea, Flavius; but I hope we won't need it. The town is not my idea of a midnight saunter.

FLAVIUS No, sir, I agree. You can smell it from here even, when the sun is up.

VALERIUS The Tribune's furniture will last us till the Sixth arrive, I hope. I never liked those inlaid chairs, anyhow. Did you?

FLAVIUS Frightful, sir.

VALERIUS I think that is all. You might begin the arrangements this afternoon, in the slack time. We can make the change-over tomorrow, provided things are quiet.

FLAVIUS Yes, sir. (*Lingering*) I wish you would get some sleep, sir.

VALERIUS (*good-humoured*) Why? Am I beginning to fail?

FLAVIUS No, sir. Not a sign of it. But Rufus Sita and I can—— (*He pauses, not knowing how to put it diplomatically*)

VALERIUS (*still good-humoured*) 'Can easily run the post between you if I snored my head off for three consecutive days, and I am an interfering fusser with old-maid tendencies and an inflated idea of my own infallibility.' I agree, but you will have to put up with me.

FLAVIUS (*dismissing this with a smile*) I know the last bit before relief is always the worst, sir. But for the honour of the Second, you can't meet the Sixth looking——

VALERIUS (*interrupting*) Looking like something going to the knacker's yard. I shall sleep this afternoon, I promise you, Flavius. (*As* FLAVIUS *is going out*) How is Sanctius, do you know?

FLAVIUS The doctor thinks he will live, sir.

VALERIUS That is good news. An omen, I hope.

FLAVIUS I hope so, sir.

[*Exit* FLAVIUS.]

[VALERIUS *sits down, by the table, and begins to change his soaking shoes for another pair that have been left ready for him.*

[*Enter* RUFUS. *He comes in slowly, and slowly sits down on the end of the couch. He has always been unhurrying in his movements, but now there is a deliberateness, a control executed by an effort of the will, a care to make no unnecessary gesture.*]

VALERIUS (*casting a glance round at him and going on with his shoe-lacing*) Rufus. I have told Flavius about the changes. He took the prospect of having you as his commanding officer very politely. One of the horrors of a siege is having to lace one's own shoes. Since Gaza became a fighting man, I live a life uncherished and forlorn. Did you see Petronius?

RUFUS No.

VALERIUS (*looking round*) Why? He is—all right, isn't he?

RUFUS Yes, I think so.

VALERIUS (*looking closely at* RUFUS *for the first time; dismayed*) Rufus? Is something wrong? Are you ill?

RUFUS (*sitting upright and still*) I have an arrow in me.

VALERIUS Rufus! No! (*The cry is eloquent; fear, grief, protest, repudiation. He goes to* RUFUS)

RUFUS I broke off the shaft so that the men should not see. (*The end of the broken shaft is visible in the right side of his back, just beyond the curve of the ribs*) No, don't. There is nothing you can do. Pity. I would like to have seen the Eagles marching up the road in column of four.

VALERIUS Keep still. I shall bring the doctor. I won't be a moment.

RUFUS (*gripping* VALERIUS'S *forearm with his left hand*) No. He is busy.

VALERIUS But I must! You can't just sit there——!

RUFUS Valerius! It is not like you to run away from the truth. (VALERIUS *stands there, helpless and lost;* RUFUS *still gripping his arm tightly in his pain*) You won't forget that very handsome tombstone, will you? Outside the Wall. Facing Caledonia. (*He keels over on to the couch.* VALERIUS, *almost beside himself with distress, moves him to a comparatively comfortable position, repeating his name under his breath*) Rufus. Oh, Rufus. (RUFUS *lies still for a moment and then his eyes open. Seeing the grief-stricken face above him, he puts up one hand with a smile*) Cheer up, my friend. There were worse losses at—— (*The hand falls and the eyes close again*)

[*Enter* CLAUDIUS.]

VALERIUS (*passionately*) No, Rufus! No!

[*He turns quickly to go for a doctor and sees* CLAUDIUS.]

What are you doing standing there? What do you want?

CLAUDIUS (*beginning automatically*) I came—— (*He breaks off*) But Rufus, sir! Is he wounded?

VALERIUS Don't stand there asking stupid questions! Go

and fetch the doctor. At once. It doesn't matter what he is doing, he is to come here this moment. (*He makes for the table, where there is the remains of a meal*)

CLAUDIUS (*going, at speed*) Yes, sir.

[*Exit* CLAUDIUS.]

[VALERIUS *unwinds the scarf from his neck, pours water from a jug into a bowl that has held soup, carries it over to the couch, wrings the water out of the scarf and begins to bathe* RUFUS's *face, talking all the time.*]

VALERIUS You can't desert me, Rufus. You can't. Did I leave you for Rome and all its nonsense? Of course I didn't. One afternoon with you on the Wall is worth a thousand nights in Rome. And to go now! (*Rallying*) It is desertion in face of the enemy. How would that look on your very handsome tombstone? (*Unable to keep it up; his voice breaking to a passionate whisper*) No, Rufus. Oh, no. Mithras, God All-powerful, I vow an altar. Seven altars. Listen, Rufus. Help is coming. I know the man is a fool, but he will think of something. You have never turned your back on an enemy, have you? You can't run away now. (*His finger-tips search for a moment for the pulse in* RUFUS's *neck*) Mithras, I vow all I possess, I vow my life. I who have never asked before. Everything, everything for this one request. (*He examines the wound again and goes back to his work with the wet cloth*)

[*Enter, at a run, a small man with a satchel, attended by* CLAUDIUS.]

CLAUDIUS I found the doctor in the street, sir.

[VALERIUS *gives way to the little man. The* DOCTOR's *urgency drops from him as he sees* RUFUS. *He examines him for a moment and straightens again, shaking his head.*]

VALERIUS Nothing! (*Another shake*) Very well. (VALERIUS *is suddenly relaxed and indifferent-seeming*) You may go.

[*Exit the* DOCTOR.]

[CLAUDIUS *stands irresolute.*]

CLAUDIUS (*aware of the tragedy but at a loss*) Is there something I can do, sir?

VALERIUS Tonight, when it is dark, you will help me bury him.

CLAUDIUS In the dark?

[PETRONIUS, *the middle-aged soldier from the second scene of Act I, appears in the doorway.*]

PETRONIUS Beg pardon, sir, but did you want me?

VALERIUS Petronius! Yes, you are the man I want. Though not—for the original reason. (PETRONIUS *takes a step inside the door*) You served with Rufus Sita in Pannonia, didn't you?

PETRONIUS I did, sir.

VALERIUS Tonight, you will help Claudius and me to bury him.

PETRONIUS (*taken aback*) Oh. (*Controlled again*) Yes, sir.

VALERIUS Outside the Wall.

PETRONIUS Outside, sir?

VALERIUS Facing Caledonia.

PETRONIUS Very good, sir.

VALERIUS Say nothing to the others. Report to me here at eleven. That is all.

PETRONIUS Yes, sir. I am sorry about Rufus Sita, sir. He was a fine officer.

[*Exit* PETRONIUS.]

VALERIUS (*to* CLAUDIUS) What did you come to see me about?

CLAUDIUS (*hesitating*) I wish it were not now that——

VALERIUS I said: what did you come to see me about?

CLAUDIUS I came to give you an armlet that the Caledonians have thrown over the wall. (*He offers it*)

VALERIUS An armlet!

CLAUDIUS Do you recognise it, sir?

VALERIUS Yes, it belonged to Marius. He won it for being first into the stockade at Culter. Well, it seems that Aemilius must go after all. (*He puts the armlet down on the table*)

CLAUDIUS Isn't it odd, sir, that the Caledonians would part with that? I mean, when they could send—anything.

VALERIUS Yes. Yes, I suppose it is. (*There is a rising inflection of interest in his voice*)

CLAUDIUS It is more like a token than a—a sneer. You don't suppose that Marius himself could have sent it?

VALERIUS Why should he send an armlet? Unless—— (*he snatches up the armlet and begins to examine it closely, first on the outside and then on the inside; excited now*) unless there is some kind of message. (*Catching sight of a word on the inner surface*)

'Legion'! Yes! There is a message! 'York' (*Twisting the armlet in an endeavour to read it*) 'There is' (*deciphering with difficulty*) 'There is no—legion at York. The town—is—burnt out.' (*Before the last two words his head comes up so that his eyes meet those of* CLAUDIUS. *They stare at each other while the full implication of the message grows clear to them. Very slowly* VALERIUS *puts the armlet down on the table; delicately, as if it would break.*)

SLOW FADE

SCENE 4

The Scene is the same. The time a little before dawn on a late February morning, some ten weeks later. The room is a living-room for all the men left in the unit occupying the principia. Most of the floor space is taken up with straw mattresses. The larger table has gone, and only the small lower one remains. The thick curtain covers the doorway. The only light is from the brazier in the middle of the room.

On the couch, up R., is a wounded man, PATRICIUS. *Lying parallel with the couch, between it and the door, the unoccupied mattress of a man on guard. Below the couch on the R. side are four mattresses, head to wall, and feet to the centre of the room. The first is occupied by a sleeping man, the second is occupied by* VARUS, *the third is empty, and the fourth occupied by* SALVIUS. *Down from the last, in the corner of the room,* GAZA *is curled up like an animal. Up L., parallel to the back wall, and between the main door and the one to the inner room, is a mattress with a sleeping man. Below the door to the inner room are four mattresses, head to wall. The first is occupied by a soldier,* LOSSIO, *who is kneeling on the far side of it facing the wall and building an altar of small pieces of stone which he has stolen from the catapult ammunition. The second is* VALERIUS'S, *empty at the moment, with the small table at the end; his 'mattress' is actually a camp-bed as high as a low stool. The third is* CLAUDIUS'S; *empty too. The fourth is occupied by* AEMILIUS.

Two empty mattresses lie parallel with the front edge of the stage. One belongs to CANDIDUS, *who is attending to the wounded man, up R. The equipment of each man is piled neatly beside the head of each mattress.*

Before the curtain goes up, AEMILIUS *can be heard singing his song of the Loire. He is sitting propped up against the wall, knees under his chin, and feet on mattress, and is accompanying himself on a primitive one-string instrument. He is singing very softly.*

VARUS (*after a moment*) Stop making that row.

SALVIUS (*who has been lying with hands behind his head, listening*) Let him sing if he wants to. When we were well off, you did nothing but whine. If he can sing, now that we are sunk, let him.

AEMILIUS We are not sunk yet, Salvius.

SALVIUS Sing, boy. Your voice is better than your judgment.

[AEMILIUS *resumes his song, and presently the curtain is pulled aside to admit* CLAUDIUS, *followed by* PETRONIUS, *both muffled to the ears.*

[PETRONIUS *comes down to the mattress between* SALVIUS *and* VARUS, *sits down and begins to take off his wrappings.* CLAUDIUS *casts an anxious glance round as he comes in, and notes* VALERIUS'S *still empty berth.*]

CLAUDIUS (*standing by the end of his own mattress and beginning to take off his things half-heartedly, as if he feels that he must go out again rather than take them off; to* AEMILIUS) Has Valerius not come back?

AEMILIUS No, sir.

CLAUDIUS (*worried*) But it will soon be dawn!

AEMILIUS (*comforting*) He'll be back, sir. He always is. What I would like to know is when Valerius Valens sleeps.

CLAUDIUS I don't know myself, Aemilius. I can't remember when I last saw him with his eyes closed.

VARUS It doesn't take all night to empty a few traps. I expect he curls himself up in a snug shelter and snoozes till it is time to come back.

[SALVIUS *is about to get to his feet when he catches* CLAUDIUS'S *eye and desists. He has to be content with words.*]

SALVIUS In weather so cold that your spear freezes to your hand if you lift it without a glove! (*He makes an eloquent sound of spitting*)

PETRONIUS Are you hungry, Varus?

VARUS Isn't everyone hungry?

PETRONIUS Then you will be glad to eat the food tha Valerius risks his life for?

SALVIUS You watch him!

CLAUDIUS (*having watched the absorption of the man who is makin the little altar; to* AEMILIUS) What is Lossio doing?

AEMILIUS He is building a new altar. He has a new goc today.

CLAUDIUS What, another? Which is it this time?

AEMILIUS Silvanus, I think, sir. He has decided tha Coventina was no use.

CLAUDIUS (*having watched again the man's moving lips and obviou strangeness*) Do you think he is fit to do his guard?

AEMILIUS Oh, yes, sir. He may change his gods daily bu his views on Caledonians are constant enough.

CANDIDUS (*as the wounded man restlessly flings off the covers he ha just arranged*) Oh, no! Patricius! Just when I have tucke you up so nicely!

CLAUDIUS (*crossing to look*) How is he, Candidus?

CANDIDUS I think he must be the only man in Vindobal who is too warm, sir.

[*Enter* VALERIUS.]

[*There is a general movement of satisfaction and expectation The sleeping men gradually become awake and join in the ne interest.*]

CLAUDIUS You are back!

SALVIUS What did you get, sir?

VALERIUS (*beginning to peel off his coverings*) Two hares. On for Flavius's lot and one for us. I gave them to the cook befor I went the rounds. They should be eatable by now, I think Candidus, you might go for our share.

CANDIDUS (*coming down and picking his cloak and sword-belt u from his mattress*) Yes, sir.

[*Exit* CANDIDUS.

[VALERIUS'S *eye, automatically exploring, lights on* LOSSIO. *H exchanges a glance with* CLAUDIUS, *who lifts an expressi shoulder.*

[VALERIUS *turns to the man on the couch.*]

VALERIUS How goes it, Patricius? (*The man turns his hea wearily in his fever*) You will feel better when you have ha some food. There will even be enough for one of your famou cond helpings, I think. (*He watches a moment longer, and turns way, vaguely discouraged, to warm himself at the brazier*)

AEMILIUS (*after a pregnant pause*) Sir, there is something we ould like to say. We have been discussing it among ourselves.

VALERIUS Yes? What is it?

AEMILIUS All the winter we have held Vindobala; and we ave kept the barbarian out. But every day we grow a little ss able to fight. You know that, sir. Soon a day will come hen we can no longer lift our swords. We shall be meat for e barbarians. We don't want to wait for that, sir.

VALERIUS What do you want?

AEMILIUS To go out, all together—today, tomorrow, or the xt day—and die in the open, fighting.

VALERIUS No!

AEMILIUS That way we take our price before we die. We n't die with their heels on our throats, like sick animals.

VALERIUS No!

SALVIUS (*exhibiting his enormous right arm*) I want to use that m while it is still strong enough to take five barbarians with e, sir.

VALERIUS Our orders are to hold the post, and we will hold I will not have it said, by Caledonian or Roman, that y men opened the gates to an enemy for any reason. Even so strong a one as Salvius's right arm. And what had you anned to do with our wounded? (*As this provokes no answer*) hey have as much right to live as you have to die profitably. o, my friends. We work out our contract. A day will come en the barbarian is too strong for us. That is obvious. t they will have to come inside the walls to prove it. And it is side the walls that we die. (*Into the silence*) And if it is any nsolation to you, I think that is going to happen before you e too enfeebled. There was a stirring in the darkness to the th. A sound I have not heard since the big attack last nth. (*Enter* CANDIDUS, *carrying a dixie of soup*) So eat arty, my friends, for I may not hunt for you again.

[CANDIDUS *goes the rounds, filling with a dipper the bowl that each man holds out to him. The man who has been sleeping next to* PATRICIUS *finds the sick man's cup and sees that it is filled. He begins to feed the wounded man before taking his own.*]

ALVIUS We wouldn't be alive now if it wasn't for you, sir. uess you have a right to say how we die.

VALERIUS I have a right because I am still your commandin officer. Though you always had the greatest difficulty i remembering it, Salvius.

AEMILIUS (*trying to make amends*) We had not planned to brin your achievement to a bad end, sir. It is just that we did wa to die—profitably, as you said, sir.

VALERIUS However we die, it will not have been profitles For four months Vindobala has stood among the barbarian A wonder and a warning. A portent. An example. A sma fragile thing that was greater than all their hosts. Somethir that they wanted, that was there for the taking, and that the could not take.

SALVIUS (*as if realising it for the first time*) Come to think of i we must have been a smell under their noses these last fo months.

VALERIUS (*relaxing to a smile*) As you say, my Salvius, a stir in their nostrils. And what is much worse, a small fear at th back of their minds. This is not the end, you know. Oth men will come.

AEMILIUS (*supplicating, not challenging*) How do you know the will come, sir? It is not ten years since we abandoned all th country north of the Wall.

VALERIUS We had no contract to keep it. We campaigne in Caledonia, but we had never said to the people: 'Give u your arms and we will give you protection.' But Britain Rome, and Rome looks after her own. Ultimately. (*There is small laugh, since they share the feeling that makes the last word so dr*

[CANDIDUS *has been trying to rouse* GAZA *to an interest in foo but he stays curled up on the floor, like a dog that is ill and sel pitying.*]

VALERIUS Let him be, Candidus. Gaza has his own way dealing with the hour. (*He regards the bundle on the opposite si of the room with a half contemptuous, half affectionate interest*)

[LOSSIO, *busy at his altar, has refused to take any notice* CANDIDUS *and his dixie, but the man on the mattress L. of t door has found his bowl for him and having had it filled leaves by his side.*]

PETRONIUS What eats me, sir, is that no one will ever kno of the stand we made.

VALERIUS The Caledonians will.

PETRONIUS But they have no history, sir.

VALERIUS No, but they make songs. And a song lives longer han any of your records-of-the-campaign by the General's rother-in-law. If I know anything of the Caledonian it will ose nothing in the telling. A hundred years from now they will ing of the thousand thousand times they attacked Vindobala efore their final triumph.

SALVIUS The lying bastards.

VALERIUS All the more glory to you, Salvius.

SALVIUS I don't need my glory handed to me in a song. Especially by a black-hearted little coward who never stood up o me unless there were ten of him.

AEMILIUS Could we not write something for the men who ome after us, sir? Write something and bury it. We want ur own men to know.

VALERIUS There is Rufus Sita's stone in the heather. (*There a moment's silence*) When they come to build the Wall they vill find that. And last night, in the short moonlight, I found ; and wrote on the side of it the date and the names of all the nen in the fort. Rufus will bear witness.

AEMILIUS (*drawing a pleased breath*) Ah. That is what I vanted. Not to die for nothing.

VALERIUS You are very quiet, Claudius. What are you hinking?

CLAUDIUS I was thinking: that when I cursed the gods for paring me, I thought it was a punishment; now I know that it vas a privilege.

[GAZA *moves suddenly into a half-kneeling position, with the swift arrested movement of a dog who has been wakened from sleep by hearing his master call. The men nearest him glance at him and look away again uninterested. After a moment he gets slowly to his feet, making no sound. Everyone is watching him now. After another pause of immobility he moves swiftly to* VALERIUS *and catches him by the arm, his face blazing with some inner and incommunicable excitement. He shakes the arm he is holding impatiently, as if trying to call* VALERIUS's *attention to a phenomenon which he is failing to perceive.*]

VALERIUS What is it, Gaza?

[*With a queer high cry* GAZA *flees out of the room.* VALERIUS *looks after him soberly.*]

VALERIUS If Gaza is going mad someone else will have to—— can't do it.

CLAUDIUS I am afraid Gaza is not the only one, Valerius.

[VALERIUS *turns his head to look at the absorbed* LOSSIO.

[*Far away, outside the walls of the fort altogether, a bugle-call sounds. Thin, delicate, and clear.*

[*Every vestige of movement in the room ceases. Whatever a man has been doing, he pauses with the action half spent. Only their eyes move, doubtingly, to each other.*]

AEMILIUS (*after a long silence, in a whisper*) Did you hear that?

[*They go on listening, immobile.*

[*Then in the distance, on the ramparts, a man's voice is heard shouting, wild with surprise and glory:* The Eagles! The Eagles!]

SALVIUS (*slowly*) The Eagles. Gods and gods, they have come!

[*In the distance the sound of cheering begins, and men's laughing voices calling. At that, the spell that holds the room motionless breaks.*

[VARUS *is first out of the door, leaving the curtain open so that on can see the pale dawn outside; the others bundle out close on hi heels.*]

VALERIUS Are you going to meet them like a crowd of ill bred children running to an overturned fruit stall! (*But the have gone, leaving him with* CLAUDIUS) Oh, well, what does i matter? They will not expect a guard of honour. (*He i suddenly unutterably weary*)

CLAUDIUS I think you underrate Aemilius. I shall be sur prised if the south gate is not lined in the most correct manner And anyhow, Flavius is there.

VALERIUS I wish it were not such a pig-sty to receive a nic shiny General in. (*He refers to the room*)

[*The shock is still so great that only small things will come to thei minds.*]

CLAUDIUS At least our equipment is polished and our chin shaved. We have not gone native.

VALERIUS (*in a far-away voice*) I have the oddest feeling c having come unwound.

CLAUDIUS You must be terribly tired, sir. I didn't know

that any man could carry a whole garrison on his shoulders as you have done.

VALERIUS No man ever had a better lieutenant.

CLAUDIUS Thank you, sir. There will be sleep for us all now.

VALERIUS Sleep. Yes. I wish Rufus could have been here. He always said that we would not lose Vindobala.

[*The sound of approaching footsteps and voices can be heard.*]

CLAUDIUS I wonder who they are. Odd to think we don't even know who is Emperor.

VALERIUS That is nothing new!

[*Enter* FLAVIUS, *showing in a General and his aide. The General is* VIRIUS LUPUS.]

FLAVIUS Our relief has arrived, sir.

VIRIUS Valerius Valens?

VALERIUS Yes, sir.

VIRIUS I am Virius Lupus, Governor of Britain under the emperor Severus.

VALERIUS Severus!

VIRIUS Yes. Albinus lost the game he was playing in Gaul. We were busy rebuilding York when a small Caledonian trader came to say that up in the north one of our forts was still holding out.

VALERIUS Cogi!

VIRIUS We thought it was a trap, but he insisted that you were a personal friend of his. So we risked it, and came. To say that I am glad is not to express my feelings at all. We are dazzled by your achievement. Now that we are here in force, we shall stay, and make Vindobala the base for rebuilding the Wall. Is the handful of men I saw your whole garrison?

VALERIUS These are all, sir.

VIRIUS Then I suggest that you and they go back to York now with the convoy that will be leaving this morning.

VALERIUS My men will go, sir, and my wounded; but I stay here.

CLAUDIUS (*unable to contain himself*) You what!

VALERIUS I stay to build the Wall. (*Already his speech is fighting with his sleep*)

CLAUDIUS But Valerius, that is madness. Think! Wine, beds, warmth, clean linen, houses! You can't stay in this desolation; it must have gone to your head.

VALERIUS (*wryly*) Yes. Yes, I think that in a way it has. I hate the place so much that I love it.

VIRIUS (*who has been watching him; in his unofficial voice*) I think I understand that. But go down to York now, for a rest. You have earned so much.

VALERIUS If I did that, I should never come back.

VIRIUS (*appreciative*) Presently, young man, I shall give you a legion.

VALERIUS (*unimpressed*) I shall need it.

VIRIUS (*surprised and a little amused*) Oh? You take it for granted that you are in command on the Border.

VALERIUS Of course. The Wall is mine. (*His eyes begin to close as he stands. He sinks gently on to the end of his bed, which is behind him*) I stay to build the Wall. (*His arms go out across the little table in front of him and his right cheek is pillowed on them. As he falls asleep a murmur comes from him that sounds like :*) A Wall with vines all the way.

CURTAIN

DICKON

CHARACTERS

EDWARD IV, *King of England*
ELIZABETH WOODVILLE, *his Queen*
PRINCE EDWARD, *his son*
PRINCESS ELIZABETH, *his daughter*
RICHARD, DUKE OF GLOUCESTER, *afterwards Richard III*
ANNE NEVILLE, *his wife*
HENRY, DUKE OF BUCKINGHAM
FRANCIS, LORD LOVELL
WILLIAM, LORD HASTINGS
ANTHONY, LORD RIVERS, *the brother of the Queen*
SIR RICHARD GREY, *her son by her first marriage*
JOHN MORTON, *Bishop of Ely*
THOMAS, LORD STANLEY
ROTHERHAM, ARCHBISHOP OF YORK
CLEMENT, *a page and squire*
MARK, *a squire*
BOB THACKER }
BEN WILLETT } *Guildsmen of Gloucester*
ROGER KEMP }

Characters who do not speak

THE PRINCESS CECILY, *fourteen-year-old daughter of Edward IV*
YATES, *his servant*
PAYNTER, *Richard's servant*
AN INNKEEPER
A MONK
THREE FURNITURE REMOVERS
THREE MEN-AT-ARMS

ACT I

SCENE I

A small room in the KING'S *palace of Westminster, on a night early in January,* 1483. *It is the* KING'S *private apartment: rich, beautiful, hot with the light of many candles and of a blazing fire, and stuffy with the fumes of supper. R. is the large fireplace, centre the supper-table, and up L. the door to the corridor. Above the fireplace is a smaller door to the bedroom. The remains of the last course are still on the table (fruit and wine and sweetmeats) and round it are grouped the occupants of the room.*

With his back to the audience, half kneeling on his stool and leaning over the table, is EDWARD, PRINCE OF WALES, *a boy of twelve, good-looking but young for his age. He is pursuing small ivory counters (like the modern tiddleywinks) among the debris of supper and spurting them into a shallow ivory cup. This being his latest craze and his chief occupation for the past week, he is very good at it. The others are watching his performance with amused interest.*

L. of the table, his father, EDWARD IV, *is sitting, his chair turned a little front. He is six feet and some inches tall, and until lately has been the handsomest man in Europe; but now his beauty has run to seed, lost in puffiness.*

Behind his chair is the QUEEN'S *brother,* ANTHONY, LORD RIVERS. *He is a man of forty with a passion for the dramatic and the limelight. In his active days he showed forth his prowess in the lists; now that he is the* PRINCE EDWARD'S *governor and lives a quieter life at Ludlow Castle he makes life dramatic for himself by going on lengthy pilgrimages (in great comfort and luxury), and keeps himself in the public eye by writing translations and original poems for the latest sensation: book printing by Caxton.*

Next him is his nephew, SIR RICHARD GREY, *the* QUEEN'S *son by her first marriage; a young man whose clothes are more striking than his personality.*

There is a slight gap between these three and the other two men. On the up side of the table, but towards the R., is the KING'S *cousin,* HENRY, DUKE OF BUCKINGHAM. *He is about thirty-two, full of surface graces which hide the fact that, fundamentally, he is a child still; acquisitive, egotistical, spoiled.*

On the R. of the table is WILLIAM, LORD HASTINGS, *the* KING'S *intimate friend. He is older than the others, about fifty; and his chief claim to fame is his loyal furthering of* EDWARD'S *interests whatever they may be: battle, bed, or borrowing.*

When the curtain goes up the group round the table have the stillness of a tableau, except for the squirming movements of the PRINCE *as he goes the round of the counters. They are quite genuinely anxious to see whether young* EDWARD *can achieve a 'possible'; that is, eight counters in the cup at eight tries. As he does it, they relax with a murmur of admiration and laughter.*

PRINCE There! I told you I could do it.

GREY Well done, Edward.

RIVERS You really have a wonderful eye, Edward. I wouldn't have believed it possible.

EDWARD (*dry but good-humoured*) You know, Rivers, if you feed him *too* much flattery he may lose his taste for it.

RIVERS That would be no bad thing, surely. (*The unheeding* PRINCE *is busy putting out the counters again*)

EDWARD Don't mortgage the future. How can a man fish for favour if there is no more bait?

PRINCE (*having laid out the counters in a circle again*) I can do it again, quite easily. Who will play against me? Lord Hastings?

HASTINGS I give you best, sir.

PRINCE My cousin Buckingham?

BUCKINGHAM I may be your cousin, sir, but not your match at playing with counters.

PRINCE Then you, Richard. (*He pronounces the name French-fashion, to avoid any confusion with Gloucester in the audience's mind*)

GREY It might be lese-majesté to defeat one's half-brother.

PRINCE What nonsense!

RIVERS (*without conviction*) Perhaps it is time that you went to bed.

PRINCE Oh, not yet, uncle, not yet! (*He begins to play with the counters by himself*)

EDWARD Talking of bed—— (*He looks across at* HASTINGS *with a raised eyebrow and a quizzical expression*)

HASTINGS (*before he can say anything; too quickly*) It is a malicious lie! (*The others laugh at the too-hasty defence*)

EDWARD What a pity! It was such a good story. Then you didn't escape through a window.

HASTINGS No!

EDWARD Nor fall into a rain-water barrel?

HASTINGS Certainly not.

EDWARD And you didn't—— (*He pauses*)

HASTINGS I don't even know the lady.

EDWARD (*airily*) Who makes up these stories?

HASTINGS At a guess, I should say an invalid roué who wants vicarious excitement.

EDWARD (*accepting the barb, lazily*) If I didn't love you, William, I would cut you in little bits for that.

BUCKINGHAM You must never make fun of Hastings. Even his loves are serious. He treats them as Rivers does his soul: a burden to be enjoyed.

RIVERS (*without heat*) My soul, however unsatisfactory it may be, is my own affair.

BUCKINGHAM Ah, no. That is just my fault with it. It is such a very public soul. If you are not writing poems about it, you are exhibiting it to the populace. (*After the manner of a child's questionnaire*) 'What is that magnificent procession wending o'er the lee? Can it be an emperor who goes to greet his bride?' 'Ah, no, my child, that is merely my Lord Rivers who goes on pilgrimage.' (*To* EDWARD) You know, the Pope told the French ambassador that he had never met a pilgrim with finer plate.

PRINCE (*catching at the word French*) When we go to war with the French, may I go with the Army?

EDWARD No, you may not. You will go back to Ludlow and improve your Latin.

PRINCE Latin will not make me a great general.

EDWARD No, but it will help you to argue with the Church, which you will find almost as useful.

HASTINGS How many troops will it take to beat Louis?

EDWARD About—— Oh, I don't know. Ask Richard. He knows all the details.

RIVERS Are we taking artillery?

EDWARD Richard did suggest about twenty pieces.

HASTINGS These things will always be more trouble than they are worth.

RIVERS Is it wise to waste transport on so doubtful an advantage?

EDWARD If Richard says so, it is.

GREY You will give me a command, won't you, sir? Even a small one.

EDWARD Did I promise your mother that I would?

GREY She says you did.

EDWARD Then we must find you something.

HASTINGS (*who hates the* QUEEN'S *family*) I should be delighted to have your step-son as my master of Horse.

GREY (*amiably*) That sounds too like a threat, my lord Hastings.

[*Enter from the corridor, a page.*]

PAGE (*announcing informally*) The Duke of Gloucester, sir.

[*Enter* RICHARD, DUKE OF GLOUCESTER.

[*He is quite young; only thirty. Smallish, slight but wiry. He has a short face with hollow cheeks, long grey eyes set close under the brows, a bold nose, a thin mobile mouth. His eyes are lively, his expression gentle, his manner controlled and quiet. His hair is pale brown, in contrast to his brother's flaxen. His only obvious charm is in his voice, which is very attractive.*

[*The ill-health from which he suffered as a child has left its mark on his face and body (in repose his face still looks as if he were in pain) but the face is vigorous and the body tough. He has won renown both on the battlefield and at the council table. In any gathering that contained both Edward IV and his brother, it is to the King that attention would go immediately. But it is to Richard that attention would come back.*

[*At the moment he is wearing a coat of velvet over a doublet and hose, and is carrying his velvet cap under his arm. In the other hand he has a book.*]

RICHARD (*getting the full blast of the hot little room after the icy corridors*) Whew! What a heat. (*He slips off the loose coat, which the page takes and goes*)

EDWARD (*from his chair*) Oh, there you are, Dickon. We had given you up.

RICHARD I am sorry to be so late. I was going over those estimates. (*Coming down to them*) Good evening, gentlemen. (*Touching* BUCKINGHAM *lightly on the shoulder as he passes him on his way to the* KING) How are you, Harry?

PRINCE Good evening, Uncle Richard!

RICHARD What! Do babes come to carousal these days?

PRINCE (*not too pleased*) I am not a babe!

RICHARD (*dropping the book lightly on the table in front of the* KING) I have brought you a present.

EDWARD (*picking it up*) A new book from Caxton! Richard, you dog; and he promised me the next one! *I* was going to give it to *you*. Did he not tell you?

RICHARD No. I looked in, in passing, and the book was ready and I thought you would like it.

EDWARD (*mock indignant*) Am I the fellow's patron or am I not? (BUCKINGHAM *proffers wine but* RICHARD *refuses*)

HASTINGS You may know how to coax a woman, sir, but Richard has only to crook his little finger and men jump over precipices for him.

RICHARD I must try that some time. So far, I produce a coin and they give me a book.

PRINCE (*coaxing*) *You* play against me, Uncle Gloucester. (*He is longing for another victim*)

RICHARD (*examining the lay-out of counters*) What is it?

EDWARD (*glancing up from the cover of the book which he is examining*) It is an invention of the devil that his aunt sent to him from Burgundy. (*Having seen the title-page of the book*) Ah! Not by Rivers this time!

RICHARD So I observed. That must be the only pie in England that no Woodville has a finger in. You are slipping, Anthony.

RIVERS (*taking this as amiably as it is said*) Even without my talents it is a very charming little volume.

EDWARD Yes. He is improving, don't you think? (*They go on examining it*)

PRINCE You have to get all eight counters into the cup in eight shots.

RICHARD (*taking the ninth counter and beginning the operation in a casual and half-absent-minded fashion*) I see. (*He continues the process in irregular spasms while he talks*)

BUCKINGHAM What have you been up to all day, Richard? I tried to see you this morning but you were busy.

RICHARD I have been uncovering scandal.

[*They all prick up their ears, and look at* RICHARD, *unaware and busy with the counters*.]

EDWARD Hopton's wife and the Dean?

HASTINGS Roger's trip to Calais?

RIVERS The Dacre affair?

GREY Dacre has three affairs! (*They wait breathless*)

RICHARD (*after a pause to flip a counter into the cup*) Have you any notion how many people are sleeping away their days in the civil service in this country?

[*The others relax and laugh a little at this typically* RICHARD *interest.*]

EDWARD Dickon on the war-path!

RICHARD The Privy Seal's office is nothing but a home for indigent gentry. Or at least for such as can afford the original bribe. I haven't yet discovered what they all do. One signs his name, a second dries the signature, and a third rolls up the document.

BUCKINGHAM And the fourth?

RICHARD The fourth records the transaction, of course.

EDWARD Why worry? Thanks to my low gift for trade, we have the money to pay them.

RICHARD It is not your pocket I am worrying about. It is the little clerk who has sweated all his life, honestly, at his desk, only to see the place he has hoped for go to some new-comer who has the price of a bribe.

EDWARD Yes. That is not so good.

RICHARD It is quite damnable. And very bad for the country. Six, seven, eight. (*He finishes off the counters*)

PRINCE (*in a wail*) Oh, you've done it in eight!

RICHARD (*surprised*) That was the idea, wasn't it?

EDWARD (*delighted*) Have you beaten him? Dickon, I am your servant for life. He has been crowing over that hellish piece of nonsense all the evening.

RICHARD (*sorry, to the boy*) I'm sorry, Edward. I didn't realise that I was stealing your thunder.

PRINCE (*recovering his good manners*) Oh, that is all right. If I had known you were so good, I shouldn't have asked you to play.

[*Enter the page.*]

PAGE (*announcing informally*) The Queen's grace, sir.

[*Exit page.*]

[*Enter the* QUEEN, ELIZABETH WOODVILLE.]

[*When* EDWARD THE FOURTH *scandalised the kingdom by marrying a subject, she was already a widow with two small sons (now the Earl of Dorset and* SIR RICHARD GREY). *Since then she has had ten children, and she still is radiantly beautiful, vital and attractive. She is not very tall, very fair (her 'gilt' hair is famous and very fashionable). The tall hennin, the 'foolscap' head-dress always associated with the reign of Edward, is already old-fashioned, and she is wearing the short round cap (like a truncated hennin) set back on her head and covered with a wisp of veil.*

[*Her entry has the effect of a breeze. One feels that the suction created by her vitality would set dead leaves dancing in her wake.*]

QUEEN Just as I thought! A gambling hell, and my son in the middle of it. (*To* RIVERS) Anthony, I am surprised at you.

RIVERS My good sister, it is still Christmas holidays. When we go back to Ludlow I promise you he shall work like any Eton boy.

QUEEN If he does not go to bed now and then he will not survive to go back to Ludlow. (*She is in high good humour all the same*)

PRINCE A prince is not subject to female governance after he is seven.

QUEEN Perhaps not, but a mother is free to box her son's ears until she is seventy. Say good-night to the company.

PRINCE (*appealing to* EDWARD) Father, speak for me. You are the King.

EDWARD (*washing his hands*) Rivers is your governor, and your mother is your mother.

PRINCE (*bitterly*) When I am King I shall have no women in the kingdom at all.

QUEEN (*with a glance at her husband*) That will be a change in royal policy.

HASTINGS What will you do with them, sir?

PRINCE I shall banish them all to Ireland.

BUCKINGHAM Even Ireland has not deserved that!

QUEEN (*seeing the book*) A new book! (*She picks it up*)

EDWARD Yes; Richard brought it in from Caxton just now.

[*The* PRINCE, *seeing his mother's attention held, goes back to his counters.* RICHARD, *standing by the table, picks up a counter idly and joins him.* BUCKINGHAM *looks on.*]

QUEEN How delightful! The very first copy of a new book is exciting. Is it dedicated to anyone? (*Seeing the title-page*) Oh, not by Anthony this time!

HASTINGS No; Mr Caxton is tired of ballads against the seven deadly sins.

QUEEN (*as if she has seen him for the first time*) Oh, good evening, Lord Hastings. (HASTINGS *finds this peculiarly shattering. Her attention going back to the others as if he had not spoken*) Of course it has ceased to be fashionable, hasn't it? (*She says that without irony*) Soon every fishmonger will own a book. Then they will be of no more importance.

RICHARD No more than the plague. (*He goes on flipping the counters with the* PRINCE)

QUEEN Oh, come! of what importance can a book be if everyone has one?

RICHARD My heart faints when I think of the power in that little bundle of inky paper. It will make and mar dynasties, scatter nations, alter the very face of the earth.

QUEEN Oh, my good sober Richard, you are worse than my tiring-woman. When she was dressing me for the party tonight she informed me that printing was an invention of the devil, and that Mr Caxton will be found one morning changed into a bat with the feet of a goat, and his printing shop withered by a fiery blast.

EDWARD I see Dickon's point, all the same. Did you enjoy the party?

QUEEN (*with a doubtful lift of a shoulder*) Yes. That odious wife of Stanley's was there. No woman should have a nose as long as that.

EDWARD I don't suppose Stanley minds. When you marry the heir of all the Lancasters, you take the nose with the pedigree.

QUEEN You are too kind to Stanley, I think. That woman is a Lancaster even in bed, if I know anything about women.

GREY I shouldn't have said that seduction was Lady Stanleys's strong point.

QUEEN No, but ambition burns her like a fever.

EDWARD Poor Stanley! How uncomfortable.

RIVERS (*who has been watching with a jealous eye the* PRINCE'S *rapprochement with* RICHARD, *unable to bear it a moment longer; to* EDWARD) With your permission, sir; it is bed time, I think. Edward!

PRINCE (*groaning*) Oh! (*He begins to gather up his counters*)

QUEEN You had better leave these behind.

PRINCE (*protesting*) Oh, no! One of the pages might find them and practise with them.

QUEEN What harm?

PRINCE Then I might not be able to beat them any more. (*To* EDWARD) Good-night, sir. (*He turns to his mother*)

QUEEN I shall come in later to see that you are in bed.

PRINCE Good-night, gentlemen.

GREY (*as* RIVERS *and the* PRINCE *go towards the door; to* EDWARD) If you will allow me, sir, I shall go with my uncle and brother. Good-night, sir. (*Dropping an airy kiss on the* QUEEN'S *cheek*) Madam my mother! The new head-dress is very becoming. Tell me who made it for you.

QUEEN So that one of your mistresses may have a replica? Oh, no! Where is your brother tonight?

GREY Dorset? I understand that he is calling on Mistress Jane Shore.

QUEEN (*to* EDWARD) Does Your Grace permit Mistress Shore to entertain the rips of the town?

EDWARD Good madam, if your son enjoys Jane's company, it is a sign of grace in him that I should be the last to discourage.

GREY (*going out, laughing*) Good-night, sir. Good-night, gentlemen.

[*Exit, after* RIVERS *and* PRINCE.]

[RICHARD *offers wine to the* QUEEN.]

QUEEN No, thank you, Richard, I have not come to stay. I hope the wool trade has been good this year, Edward. We shall have a great deal of entertaining to do for this Parliament. All the pedigrees and the parsons, up from the country. Clothes smelling of cupboards and much talk of crops. I hear that Parliament is going to thank you for your services in Scotland, Richard.

RICHARD (*lightly*) Good madam, I have earned so much. Only God who made them can explain the existence of the Scots.

EDWARD (*smiling in lazy affection at his brother*) I used to think I was a great soldier because I was the only man to beat Warwick. But Richard is the only man in history to invade Scotland and bring back both an army and a peace treaty.

RICHARD Don't forget Stanley's share. He sat in front of Berwick looking so fierce that not a Scot had the courage to lift a golf club.

QUEEN How like Lord Stanley to achieve something by doing nothing! I think I must go. I have a strange conviction that Edward is playing leapfrog in the corridor.

BUCKINGHAM It is time for us to go too. May we escort you, madam?

QUEEN If Lord Hastings can put up with me for the length of the corridor.

HASTINGS Madam, against such beauty even disapproval is helpless.

QUEEN (*looking at him*) Mutual disapproval might be a great bond, I think. Good-night, Edward. Richard.

RICHARD (*kissing her hand*) Good-night, madam. (*To* BUCKINGHAM, *who is the last to go out after taking leave, as he reaches the door*) I am sorry you missed me this morning, Harry. Will you dine tomorrow?

BUCKINGHAM I should be delighted. I have several couples of hounds to show you.

RICHARD Good.

[*Exit* BUCKINGHAM.]

EDWARD (*in a mild half-inquiring tone*) You are very good friends with Buckingham.

RICHARD (*a little surprised*) Surely. So are you.

EDWARD Oh, I am friendly with everyone. (*He means that his friendliness is a habit more than a conviction*) You won't forget his Lancaster streak, will you? (*It is said lightly, but with an underlying anxiety*)

RICHARD (*with a disapproving headshake*) That prejudice dies hard.

EDWARD Moreover, he was brought up by his grandmother. Always beware men who are brought up by their grandmothers. They expect the earth as a brooch for their bonnet.

RICHARD (*smiling*) You talk a deal of nonsense.

EDWARD (*still lightly but still with the undercurrent of warning*) You know, Dickon, the difference between us is that you expect men to be honest and are furious when they turn out to be knaves, while I expect men to be knaves and am vastly gratified when they prove—as they occasionally do—to be honest. (*He reaches for the wine to pour it into his cup.* RICHARD *puts his hand over the mouth of the cup. Flaring*) Is that reproof?

RICHARD (*quietly; not removing the hand*) No, sir; petition. (*As* EDWARD *relaxes*) I should hate to have to deal with a country run by your wife's relations.

EDWARD I see your point. But you need not worry. I have no intention of dying for a long time to come. Between us we shall manage England for thirty years yet. We are a distinguished pair, Dickon. (*He is just a very little drunk*)

RICHARD By virtue of what?

EDWARD By the mere fact of our survival. After twenty years of battle, murder, and sudden death we are not only alive but prosperous. To be alive might be a matter of luck, but to be also prosperous savours of genius.

RICHARD And to be popular as well? I suppose that is a gift from God.

EDWARD Ah, that is the York charm. The Lancasters never had any. A bleak and uncouth race. What Lancaster could not do with a pocket full of money, York could do with a handful of charm. It will be the death of us, too, that charm.

RICHARD What?

EDWARD A family whose motto is 'Live and Let Live' is bound to be *out*lived by a family whose motto is 'Kill Just In Case'. There was a courier from Yorkshire, I hear. How is Anne?

RICHARD Better, I think. She writes a little dolefully. Complains that I am never at home.

EDWARD (*with compunction*) That is my fault, isn't it? You do two men's work and I get the credit. Ever since the days when we sat in the rain at Flushing and wondered where our next meal was coming from, it has been like that. You're an odd creature, Dickon. Why do you do it?

RICHARD When I was seven, you were my god. When I was fourteen, you were my hero.

EDWARD (*well aware how far he has fallen from heroic standards*) And now?

RICHARD You are my brother. (*Feeling that too much emotion is seeping into his voice, going on lightly*) Who eats too much, drinks too much, and is rapidly losing his looks. A little campaigning would do you no harm.

EDWARD (*who has no intention of doing any such thing*) I shall probably go to France with the army.

RICHARD (*after a slight pause*) Is your heart set on this French war?

EDWARD (*regarding him in great astonishment*) Don't tell me that Richard of Gloucester has fallen in love with the French!

RICHARD Hardly.

EDWARD Then, what in God's name?

RICHARD (*searching for the words*) When we had a good reason for going to war, you took a pension from the French not to. The loss of that pension hardly seems an adequate reason for a new war.

EDWARD But it was a deliberate insult on Louis' part to stop that pension.

RICHARD It was a greater insult to offer it.

EDWARD I should have thought that a successful general would be glad of a new chance to show off his talents.

RICHARD (*dryly*) I *have* other interests.

EDWARD And it will be a very popular war.

RICHARD But expensive. (*As* EDWARD *opens and shuts his mouth looking for words*) Why not spend the money on improving your son's inheritance?

EDWARD On England? What do you suggest? A college every six miles?

RICHARD (*good-humoured*) Oh, come! I have founded only two colleges in the whole of my estates.

EDWARD What then?

RICHARD Oh—fewer footpads and more roads. You might with advantage spend more on the Navy.

EDWARD Oh, that's it, is it? Touting for your ships.

RICHARD No. You can teach Louis a better lesson in the Channel than ever you could in Picardy, and lose nothing in doing it. When I was small, living in the Paston's lodgings—— (*He breaks off*) You used to come every day to see us.

EDWARD (*also smiling; they are friends again*) I remember.

RICHARD I found a political pamphlet in rhyme. The kind they sell in the street. It was very long, but I have always remembered two lines:

> 'Cherish merchandise, keep admiralty,
> That we be masters of the narrow sea.'

As a merchant, you should appreciate that.

EDWARD How many King's ships have we?

RICHARD Seven. For the price of a French war, you could have seventy.

[*There is a small knock on the door, and* ELIZABETH, *the* KING'S *eldest daughter, puts her head in. Seeing that her father is alone except for* RICHARD, *she comes in.*

[*She is sixteen, still growing, with a slender coltish grace. Very fair, and, if not a beauty like her mother, sufficiently lovely. Her manner is a mixture of schoolroom directness and just-remembered good manners. Utterly unaffected and unself-conscious.*]

ELIZABETH. Oh. I thought you were alone. It was so quiet.

EDWARD (*scandalised*) Elizabeth!

ELIZABETH (*smiling at* RICHARD) But it is only Uncle Richard. (RICHARD *greets her*)

EDWARD Elizabeth, what are you doing, prowling about the palace alone at this time of night! And walking in—— Is that page of mine asleep again!

ELIZABETH No. No, I don't think so. Perhaps a little drowsy. (*As her father is about to rise in wrath, lifting an admonitory palm*) Now, don't be angry, don't be angry.

EDWARD And why not, pray?

ELIZABETH It does terrible things to one. Ties knots in one's liver, or changes one's bowels to scorpions, or something equally frightful.

EDWARD Will you stop talking nonsense and tell me what brings you?

ELIZABETH Well, it is like this—— (*breaking off to look at him*) It is no good if you are angry.

EDWARD I am not angry.

ELIZABETH Well—now that there is going to be a Parliament, everyone will be coming to town, and I have no fit gown to wear, and mother says that I may not have another. I have had no new gown since Aunt Margaret came from Burgundy.

EDWARD What about the blue velvet? That is very fine, isn't it?

ELIZABETH Oh, that! It is so old it is white at the seams. Mother is having three new gowns.

EDWARD Or the lilac silk?

ELIZABETH I have grown out of it. My arms stick out of the sleeves like frying-pans.

EDWARD Or the white with the pearls?

ELIZABETH Mother gave that to the nuns of St Leonard's to make an altar-cloth. (*As her father seems to have dried up; prompting bitterly*) You have forgotten my tawny satin. (*Mollified by their laughter*) That is the worst of a father who notices what women wear! Please, father; how can you dance with your eldest daughter if she looks like Mother Cobbe, the midwife?

EDWARD Oh, well, I suppose you had better not disgrace me before the whole country. You may have your gown.

ELIZABETH (*pressing with advantage*) A gown with fur on it?

EDWARD With fur.

ELIZABETH And nothing scrimped?

EDWARD Nothing scrimped.

ELIZABETH Oh, father, you are the greatest King since David!

EDWARD (*who is very proud and very fond of his daughter*) Poor

David. He too was plagued by women. We must get you married, miss.

ELIZABETH Unless you find me someone as nice as Uncle Richard, I shall take me to a nunnery.

RICHARD (*promising*) We will find you the perfect knight, Elizabeth.

EDWARD On the contrary, we shall find someone who will beat you twice a week and give you a gown every third Christmas.

ELIZABETH (*not with pride but as one recounting a matter of mild interest*) Old Bridget who tells fortunes says that I am to be a Queen.

EDWARD (*dryly*) Perhaps she has not heard that the Dauphin has jilted you.

ELIZABETH (*equably*) Oh, yes. All the world knows that.

EDWARD (*raising his eyebrows*) In that case, next time she has visions tell her that the King would be glad to know where such an advantageous match may be found.

ELIZABETH No, I like Uncle Richard's plan for me better. (*To* RICHARD) There was a courier from Middleham. I hope everyone is well?

RICHARD Wonderfully well, thank you. (*Feeling in his doublet*) There was a letter for you.

ELIZABETH For me?

RICHARD (*producing the letter and reading the superscription*) 'For my cousin Elizabeth.'

ELIZABETH (*affection and amusement welling up in her voice*) Oh, from Edward! (*She takes it, and with a glance at her father for permission, opens it. Reading slowly*) 'My sweet Elizabeth, I have shot a deer. This is a picture of it.' (*Deciphering with greater difficulty the sentence below the drawing*) 'Legs are difficult, so I have stood him in heather.' (*Handing it over to* RICHARD, *as they all laugh*) My sweet Edward!

EDWARD (*leaning over* RICHARD's *elbow to see*) My nephew may be a good shot but he is no artist.

RICHARD (*smiling affectionately at his son's work*) I am afraid not. (*He looks a little longer, and presently drops it on the table*)

ELIZABETH (*examining the contents of the supper table; to* EDWARD) Were you going to eat any more tonight?

EDWARD No. Why?

ELIZABETH In that case—— (*She tilts the contents of a silver sweet-dish into her pocket*)

EDWARD Elizabeth!

ELIZABETH (*tranquilly*) Cecily said that I wasn't to come back empty-handed.

EDWARD Has your sister not had supper?

ELIZABETH Oh, yes. But she has a very large stomach. And she said if I was going to have a gown the least I could do would be to bring her something off the supper table.

EDWARD To listen to them, one would think my family were naked and starving paupers!

ELIZABETH I shall go back to bed now. You have made me so happy that I don't know how to thank you.

RICHARD Perhaps I had better protect you from the bogles in the corridor.

ELIZABETH Oh, would you? I don't mind the dark places, but your being with me would make it more official.

RICHARD (*picking the letter from the table and offering it to her*) Do you want this?

ELIZABETH (*about to take it, but changing her mind; smiling at him*) I expect you want it more. You have a sweet son, Uncle Richard. Would he were old enough for me to marry! (*Sweeping her father a curtsey at the door*) Good-night, sir. You will be very proud of me, I promise you.

RICHARD (*also taking his leave*) Good-night, sir. Think over what I said about being 'master of the narrow sea'.

EDWARD Louis, too, could build ships.

RICHARD Yes; hundreds of them. But only England breeds the men for them. (*Pausing at the door for a parting shot*) And a sea voyage is just as good for the liver as a land campaign.

EDWARD Good-night, Dickon. What would I do without you?

RICHARD A little more work!

[*Exit* RICHARD.]

[EDWARD, *after a few moments sunk in thought, calls for his servant.*]

EDWARD Yates! (*After a moment, louder*) Yates!

[*Enter from the door up L.,* YATES; *a shadow from the shadows. He is carrying a furred robe and slippers. Without remark from his master, he changes the* KING'S *doublet and shoes for the garments he has brought.*]

EDWARD (*submitting automatically to his ministrations*) Dickon is right, you know. I ought to take more care. (*Regarding his hands*) Getting puffy. Getting fat. (*His speech is growing lethargic already as the swift sleep of the half-drunk overtakes him)* Ought to pull up in time. Yes. But what is one to do when women are lovely and wine like perfume in the throat? That is the problem, Yates. That is the problem. (*Relaxing still further*) A problem I have no intention of solving.

SLOW CURTAIN

SCENE 2

A small room in Middleham Castle, in Yorkshire. In comparison with the room in the previous scene it is a homely place. It is pleasant, and everything in it is the best or most beautiful of its kind, but it is a room that has been used by generations, each one contributing its share; it is not fashionable; it is, in fact, a home.

There are two windows; one looking out through the outer wall to the countryside, and the other looking down on the courtyard; and one door. By the outer window, ANNE, RICHARD'S *wife, is sitting sewing. Near the other, but not so near that he can see out of it,* RICHARD *is idling over a large book of accounts; it is an inspection not methodical but absorbing.*

ANNE NEVILLE *is twenty-six; tallish, with all the good looks of the Nevilles and much of their character; but it is a fragile beauty she possesses, without health or stamina. Her clothes are dullish, not because they are poor or unbeautiful, but because dressing is not a daily excitement for her.*

Her face is that of a kind woman; dignified, honest, a little narrow in judgment but not allowing her prejudices to govern her conduct. She has been brought up to respect conduct above most things. She has had an adventurous life (there is a story that she was rescued by Richard from a kitchen-maid's work during one of her forced flights) and, like her husband, has an experience of common straits and common people not usual in one of her class and period.

The time is the second week in April, 1483*; that is to say, about three months after the previous scene.*

ANNE (*breaking the comfortable silence; in the unaccented tones of one continuing a desultory conversation*) I think I shall use the satin you brought me to make a new cap. You will like that? (*It is only half a question; she is still sewing*)

RICHARD (*without looking up*) Very pretty.

ANNE Kendal shall bring me some buckram next time he goes to York. (*Without malice, as a matter of interest*) I suppose Elizabeth dresses as extravagantly as ever.

RICHARD (*considering it absent-mindedly*) Fewer jewels, I think.

ANNE Why?

RICHARD Edward's conscience is less troublesome lately.

ANNE (*marvelling for the thousandth time*) How can she be so light-hearted about it! She is virtuous herself; how can she wear her shame so happily? Has she no pride!

RICHARD She is not a Neville, my dear. What took Holroyd to York on the twenty-fifth?

ANNE Holroyd? Oh; to fetch the Gascony wine. You will find the entry further down. Nine shillings and eightpence the dozen gallons. (*Glancing at him with a faint amusement*) Why do you pore over the account book? You know very well that if Dimmock were a farthing out he would chase it from here to Thirsk.

RICHARD I am patching the holes in my life.

ANNE The holes?

RICHARD All the stuff of Middleham is here. All that I have missed.

ANNE But I write the news to you most faithfully.

RICHARD Of course. But you don't tell me that—that Betsy has been shod, that there is a new lock on the little east gate, that the dairy window was broken, that Kemp has had a boil on his neck——

ANNE Has he?

RICHARD 'To the herb-woman, for the boil on Kemp's neck, four pence.' I expect Kemp thought it was cheap. (*Indicating the book*) That is Middleham. If I cannot live it, I can at least look at the picture.

ANNE Now that Scotland is quiet, and Parliament over, and no war yet with France, perhaps you will have more time to be at home.

RICHARD Perhaps. (*Looking up from the book and considering her*) Things have not changed much since this was our schoolroom, have they? You with your needle, and I with a book. You were a very prim little girl.

ANNE And you were always stuffing Utrecht down my throat.

RICHARD Utrecht?

ANNE Yes. You had been abroad, and I hadn't. 'The sun

is bigger than the moon, and I should know because I have been in Holland!'

RICHARD (*amused*) Poor Anne! (*Going back to the book*) I thank God every day that my life has fallen in such pleasant places.

ANNE (*simply*) I too. If it were not that I cannot—— (*After a pause*) Do you think if I were to go on a pilgrimage to——

RICHARD (*rallying her*) Oh, you are worse than Rivers. If his tooth aches, he must needs fly to a shrine.

ANNE It is not my tooth that aches.

RICHARD (*touched but still rallying her*) Bind up your heart, Anne. God has given us one son. The finest boy north of Trent. That is riches enough.

ANNE (*with a glance at the window; without anxiety*) It is time that he was back. It will soon be dark. Lovell ought to have more sense. By the way, must Edward go to Coverham on Monday?

RICHARD That was the plan, wasn't it?

ANNE Yes, but now that you are home he will be heart-broken to go.

RICHARD Perhaps, but he had better go. (*Answering her silent protest*) You would not have him grow up like Edward's boy, would you?

ANNE (*dryly*) There is no fear of that. He was bred differently. I don't think you realise how much your being here means to him. You are his hero, you know. He is always boasting about you. I heard him telling Holroyd the other day that you were the greatest soldier since Caesar.

RICHARD He must learn not to boast. And I don't know that it is a good thing to have a hero.

ANNE Oh, surely! Didn't you?

RICHARD Yes. (*There is a slight pause before the word, and a slight silence afterwards, so that the monosyllable, unaccented as it is, is heavy with meaning*) Well, we shall see. I may ride over and pay the good monks a visit myself. Give them the gossip of London. They have a passion for gossip and the oddest ideas about London.

ANNE I have been thinking that when the King's health is better, I might go to London for a little.

RICHARD (*pleased*) Would you like to, Anne? Yes, of course. You have always been so reluctant, I—— (*did not want to press it, he means*)

ANNE (*defending her reluctance*) I feel so—so *grey* among all these bright-coloured women.

RICHARD (*amused*) Now I perceive that even a Neville may be a woman.

ANNE But I at least can wear my jewels without shame.

RICHARD (*delighted*) Doubly a woman! (*Going back to her suggestion*) Going back to London will be almost like a holiday if you are with me. Perhaps Edward might come too.

ANNE (*tentatively*) The atmosphere would not be very good for him, would it?

RICHARD Perhaps not. It is damp in that house by the river.

ANNE I did not mean that kind of atmosphere.

RICHARD My dear, he must learn some day that women are frail and that men are dishonest.

ANNE Yes. But I hope he will be like his father, and never quite believe it.

RICHARD (*astonished and resentful*) You and Edward make me sound like an idiot!

ANNE (*surprised*) Did Edward say that?

RICHARD (*getting up in a sort of testy embarrassment and moving to the inner window*) Something of the sort.

ANNE (*softly*) He is clever, Edward; very clever. Did you—— (*She breaks off as she looks up and sees the expression on her husband's face. He is watching something in the courtyard below. She studies him for an appreciable moment before he speaks, but she knows what it is that he is watching*)

RICHARD They are back.

[*She rises without haste and joins him at the window. Together they watch.*]

RICHARD (*with careful detachment*) He manages that mare very well.

ANNE Yes. (*She lets him have all the pleasure of praise, knowing that praise is rationed*)

[RICHARD *lifts his hand in salute to the boy, who has seen and waved to him.*]

ANNE (*as they turn away*) Lovell should not have kept him out so long. A whole day is too much.

RICHARD If I know anything about it, it was Edward who did the keeping. Well, I suppose it will soon be supper time. (*It is not worth while settling down to the book again, but he is reluctant*

to leave it. He leans on his hands on the table, glancing down the pages)
'To Hobb's daughter, to provide her with wings, six pence.'

ANNE She was an archangel. In the miracle play, you know.

RICHARD Tomorrow is the steward's court. I must put in an appearance and renew my acquaintance with the local scalliwags.

ANNE (*beginning to arrange her sewing for putting away*) Old Tom at the Ford has learned that you have been home ten days without going to see him. He is very indignant.

RICHARD I shall look in tomorrow. Last time, he reproved me for what he called my London ways. That is the worst of living in the place where you grew up. (*He dearly loves it*) No one has any reverence for you.

[*Enter* LOVELL.]

Well, Francis.

[FRANCIS, LORD LOVELL, *is about eighteen months younger than* RICHARD, *and has been* RICHARD'S *companion since boyhood. He is pleasant to look at, friendly, quietly gay, forthright, honest.*]

LOVELL I hope supper is in the offing? (*Slapping his stomach*) I am as toom as a sookit grosset, as a Scot once remarked to me. (*In awe*) What a language!

ANNE And what is a—sookit grosset?

LOVELL In the tongue of civilised man, it is a sucked gooseberry. I could eat a dragon.

ANNE Have you not eaten since this morning?

LOVELL Oh, yes. We dined at the Scropes'. Edward was very firm about that. It seems that their cook makes——

ANNE (*interrupting and saying the word with him, amused*) I know. Syllabub. So does ours; but other people's food always tastes better, when one is small.

RICHARD You have had a long day. Did you ride far?

LOVELL You may not believe it, but I have been to Edinburgh and back. Yes. I have also explored the Western Marches, and a large part of Gloucestershire. In fact, I have been all through your campaigns, Dickon. I know the exact gesture with which you refused the bribe of the French king (*he burlesques it*), just how thick the mist was at Barnet, how many corpses lay round you at Tewkesbury, and how you took Berwick from the Scots. I was in the Berwick affair myself, but it seemed effrontery to mention the fact.

RICHARD Really, the boy must learn not to be a bore.

Where is he? (*The question is a desire for information, not the preliminary to any lecture for* EDWARD)

LOVELL He said that he had to see his horse stabled. (*To* ANNE) Is it a rule?

ANNE No. But he once heard his father say that it was the proper thing. (*All three laugh a little at this further revelation*)

LOVELL (*approving*) He'll do. He is so stiff that he creaks, but there he went, staggering off to the stables. I wish I had a son. (*He says it matter-of-factly, without self-pity*)

RICHARD (*referring to the paper with which* LOVELL *has been gesticulating*) Is that a letter?

LOVELL (*remembering*) Oh, yes. 'For the most noble duke of Gloucester, utterly secret and in frantic haste.' (*This is said in mockery of all the unimportant letters which are so franked*) From London, I think.

RICHARD (*in a tone that is a groan*) Edward has had a new idea. (*Breaking open the seal*) If he takes me from Middleham now—— (*He reads. There is silence. He does not move*)

ANNE Is something wrong, Richard?

LOVELL (*tentatively*) Sir? (*Something in* RICHARD's *face makes his unconscious attitude one of service, so that he uses the more formal address unaware*)

RICHARD (*dully*) He is dead. (*He holds out the paper to them with an uncoordinated gesture, like a child showing in bewilderment a broken toy*)

LOVELL (*taking it; in a whisper*) Edward?

RICHARD (*in a burst; furious*) The fool! The selfish fool! He would deny himself nothing. What was England at the mercy of a child compared with another cup of wine! (*Pulling himself together, and considering it more quietly*) God in Heaven, what a mess!

LOVELL (*still dazed*) But it is unbelievable. He was a young man.

ANNE Does this mean that you are Lord Protector?

RICHARD According to Edward's will, yes. The saints be good to me!

LOVELL (*giving his allegiance after his fashion*) If the Lord Protector should need protection, he will not forget that Francis Lovell has a sword arm?

RICHARD I am more likely to need physic to keep me sane. (*Touching* LOVELL's *arm in acknowledgement*) Make me laugh sometimes, Francis, and I shall quit you of other service. Edward always said that I did not laugh enough.

LOVELL (*as the sound of horses' feet comes up from the courtyard*) Horses. (*He looks from the window*) New arrivals. Were you expecting company?

RICHARD No.

LOVELL It looks like Buckingham.

RICHARD Harry? It can't be. He is in the Midlands.

LOVELL If he was in the Midlands, he must have heard the news before we did.

RICHARD (*at the window*) Yes, but why ride—— Go down, Francis, and bid him welcome for me.

LOVELL (*going*) Shall I bring him here?

RICHARD Yes.

[*Exit* LOVELL.]

ANNE (*into the silence*) Odd, what a little minute can do.

RICHARD Do you remember what he was like at twenty?

ANNE Yes. So beautiful.

RICHARD The most magnificent person I have ever known. The courage of a lion; radiant; generous and——

ANNE (*as his voice dies away; with no malicious intention, merely remembering the man she knew*) And self-willed.

RICHARD (*resenting it furiously*) What of it? Do you expect a man to—— (*Realising that he is almost shouting; horrified*) I am sorry. (*She touches his hand in understanding*)

ANNE Do you want to start out at once?

RICHARD There is no need. Rivers will bring the boy from Ludlow to London. (*Beginning to organise*) We must have a requiem mass at York. And everyone of consequence in the North shall swear allegiance to the boy in public.

ANNE The Woodvilles will not like the loss of their governorship.

RICHARD (*his mind on greater matters, not much interested*) No. But they would have lost it in any case when the boy was fourteen.

ANNE You don't think they will make trouble?

RICHARD Why should they? They have had the picking of England for twenty years, and their loot is safe. Even Nero would be satisfied with such booty.

ANNE (*doubtful; reflective*) Men are very vain.

RICHARD (*with a glance for what he considers the ineptitude of her remark*) And women are not.

ANNE Not that way. A woman would take the cash in hand, and be happy. But men want glory. More men will sell their souls for power than for money, I think.

RICHARD Rivers is too enamoured of his soul to sell it for anything. It is his chief interest in life.

[*Enter* LOVELL *with* BUCKINGHAM.]

It is good to see you, Harry. (*They greet each other*)

BUCKINGHAM (*greeting* ANNE) Anne, my dear. How are you? You look better.

ANNE Yes, yes; I am very well.

RICHARD I take it that you did not ride all the way to Yorkshire on impulse.

BUCKINGHAM No. There is trouble.

RICHARD (*flicking the open letter on the table*) More trouble than this?

BUCKINGHAM Yes.

RICHARD (*after a moment's pause*) Who?

BUCKINGHAM Rivers.

RICHARD (*astounded*) Rivers!

BUCKINGHAM And company. The whole Woodville clan. They have sent two thousand men to escort the boy from Ludlow.

LOVELL Two thousand!

BUCKINGHAM They wanted to send more, but the Council put its foot down.

RICHARD But why? What are they afraid of?

BUCKINGHAM They are not afraid of anything. They plan to rule England.

RICHARD (*with quick scorn*) The Woodvilles! (*Quietly, with unconscious assurance*) England is my business.

BUCKINGHAM They have fixed the Coronation for the 4th of May.

RICHARD It is not for them to fix dates. And the 4th of May is absurd. There are endless things to be done first. Parliament to be summoned, foreign countries notified, guests invited —a thousand matters to be seen to.

BUCKINGHAM Nevertheless there is nothing to hinder them from crowning him on the 4th of May, as soon as he arrives in London. And I need hardly remind you that there is precedent for his choosing his own councillors once he is crowned King.

RICHARD (*considering it, detachedly*) Well, it was a bold play. We are having a requiem mass at York. Will you stay for it, and go south with me later——

BUCKINGHAM You mean that you are not going to set out at once!

RICHARD There is no need.

BUCKINGHAM No need! When Rivers will have left Ludlow by now on his way to London, and the whole future of England is at stake!

RICHARD If you had as much experience as I have of moving two thousand men from one place to another, you would know that a snail is fast in comparison. That was a blunder. I told you the Woodvilles had no talent for the larger game. Petty intrigue is their limit. Tomorrow I shall send out a summons to the northern gentry to meet at York and take the oath of allegiance to the boy. Then, having secured my rear—always secure your rear, Harry—I shall go south to join the Woodville procession. I hope you will give me the pleasure of your company. It was good of you to warn me. I shall not forget it. Meanwhile you must be tired and dusty, and supper is due. Let us go down. (*He takes an arm of* BUCKINGHAM *and* LOVELL, *and moves to the door*) We shall join you at table, Anne.

ANNE Yes. (*She seems to want to say something, and* RICHARD *pauses in the doorway as the other two move on*) I am going to London with you, Richard.

RICHARD Of course, my dear. You shall follow me.

ANNE Not ride with you?

RICHARD No. I have some important business to discuss with Rivers.

[*Exit* RICHARD.]

[ANNE *looks at the empty room, thinking of their so suddenly shattered plans. She moves over to the account book, runs her hand over the page in a caressing movement, and slowly shuts the book. Middleham is not to be* RICHARD'S *portion.*]

CURTAIN

SCENE 3

The main room of an inn in Stoney Stratford, on the morning of the last day of April. Trestle tables and benches, and such rude comfort as might be expected. PRINCE EDWARD (*who, though now King, will continue for clarity's sake to be referred to as* PRINCE) *is standing in the middle of the floor, smoothing his short coat nervously. He has the air of one dressed for an occasion. To his L. is the door to the passage. To his R.* RIVERS *is standing, dressed in very fine mourning.*

PRINCE (*anxiously*) Do I look properly king-like?

RIVERS The coat is very fine, I think.

PRINCE My uncle Gloucester is a very great lord. I would not have him think me of little account.

RIVERS He is hardly likely to think that, sir.

PRINCE (*breaking in, not listening*) Shall I stand, do you think? Or should I sit?

RIVERS Whichever Your Grace pleases.

PRINCE (*his attention coming back to* RIVERS *for a moment*) Are you never going to call me Edward any more?

RIVERS It would not be fitting, sir.

PRINCE I command you to call me Edward when we are alone. (*Pleased with this small despotism*) I can command you, you see. (*His mind going back to the more urgent matter*) I think I shall sit. Then I can rise to receive him. That will be more gracious. I wish now that we had waited to receive him at Northampton, instead of coming on to Stoney Stratford. The castle would have been a more fitting place than this inn.

RIVERS As I have said, sir, time is precious if you are to be crowned on the 4th as we arranged.

[*Enter* RICHARD GREY, *in a flustered condition.*]

GREY They are here. (RIVERS, *with a quick movement of annoyance, warns him to disguise his excitement*)

PRINCE My uncle?

RIVERS How many are with him?

GREY Troops? About three hundred.

RIVERS And lords?

GREY A score, I should say. Enough to behead us, anyhow.

PRINCE (*at a loss*) Behead you?

RIVERS Your brother is being playful. He means: enough to compose a jury of one's peers. (*He withers* GREY *with a glance*)

PRINCE (*impatient*) Well? Well? Let him come in. I am ready. (*As* GREY *goes out, to* RIVERS) You know, I never much liked my uncle Gloucester. It is odd that I should covet his good opinion, isn't it?

[*Enter* GREY, *with* RICHARD, BUCKINGHAM, *and* LOVELL. *Each of the newcomers kneels in turn to kiss the boy's hand.*]

PRINCE My good uncle.

RICHARD (*with emotion and sincerity*) I am your very loyal servant, sir.

PRINCE My cousin Buckingham, you are welcome.

BUCKINGHAM Your Grace has my most faithful duty.

PRINCE And you, Lord Lovell. I am glad to see you all.

RICHARD We had hoped to meet you at Northampton, sir.

PRINCE Yes. It was not possible to linger, with my Coronation only four days away. But I knew that you would overtake us.

RICHARD Four days? It would hardly be possible, sir, that you should be crowned so soon.

PRINCE (*equably*) But it is all arranged.

RICHARD (*choosing instinctively an argument that might appeal to the boy*) Even your clothes could not be ready by then.

PRINCE (*his attention arrested*) Clothes?

RICHARD Suitably fine robes must be made. And what of the forty squires whom you are to make Knights of the Bath, according to custom? They must be summoned from far and wide.

PRINCE (*doubtfully*) I had not thought of these things.

RIVERS (*hastily*) A nation with a king uncrowned is at sixes and sevens. His Grace is sensible of that, and wishes to make the difficult period as short as possible.

PRINCE (*warned by* RIVERS' *tone, and glad to fall back on decision after his brief glance into speculation*) Yes. Yes. Rivers is right. With Canterbury to put the crown on my head, with you to hold one hand and Rivers the other, what more is necessary?

RICHARD Lord Rivers will not be present at your Coronation, sir.

PRINCE Not present? But he must!

RICHARD At Northampton yesterday a council of his peers judged it safer for the realm that Lord Rivers should not be at liberty for the next few weeks.

PRINCE No! No! I forbid it.

RIVERS You dare to arrest me!

RICHARD (*dryly*) I had not thought of it as daring.

RIVERS Are you aware that I have two thousand men?

RICHARD That, my lord, is remarkable enough to be obvious.

PRINCE (*answering the accusation in the tone*) They are my guard!

RICHARD Against what, sir?

PRINCE My guard of honour.

RICHARD Two thousand of them? (*As the* PRINCE *finds no ready answer*) And all the armour in your baggage? Is that for two thousand more men to do you honour?

PRINCE (*at a loss*) Armour?

GREY How did you know that?

RIVERS (*to* GREY, *sotto voce*) You fool!

RICHARD You have equipment with you for an army, sir.

PRINCE (*turning to* RIVERS) But——

RIVERS The King's person is precious. At a time like this it is best to take no chances.

PRINCE You cannot arrest anyone for that. There is no law against carrying spare equipment.

RICHARD No, but there are excellent laws against disturbing the peace.

RIVERS You make me sound like a drunken brawler!

PRINCE Who is disturbing the peace?

RICHARD It looks sadly as if your mother's relations were doing their best, sir. Your——

PRINCE I don't believe it. I won't believe it.

RICHARD —brother Dorset has broken into the royal treasury and has used the money for further war-like preparations.

PRINCE (*staggered*) Dorset!

RICHARD One can hardly conclude that such an extravagance of conduct arises out of a simple desire to do you honour, sir.

PRINCE I do not know what my brother Dorset may have done, but I do not believe that my uncle Rivers or my brother Grey have done any wrong. You have no right to——

RICHARD (*producing a parchment and handing it to the* PRINCE) Do you know what this is, sir? (*As the boy looks blankly at it*) It is a tax demand. Or rather, a commission to collect tax. If you read it you will see that it is issued in the names of Rivers and Dorset, by virtue of their relationship to you. No mention is made of the Lord Protector of England, or of your other councillors, the Duke of Buckingham, Lord Hastings, Lord Stanley and the rest. That document has appeared throughout all the southern counties. Do you still think that Lord Rivers' haste to have you crowned, his show of armed men, his tax demands are honourable proceedings such as a young king has the right to expect from those who are nearest to——

RIVERS My lord Duke, you waste your time. You cannot wean my nephew from me by words, and you cannot arrest me with a handful of men.

RICHARD My lord Rivers, I am arresting you with two men; your peers, Buckingham and Lovell.

RIVERS And what of my two thousand?

RICHARD They are already being told of your detention, and the reason for it.

RIVERS And you think that two thousand men, well paid and well armed, will succumb to a little argument?

RICHARD They will do more. They will follow me to London, every man of them, with the King. There was one weapon that you lacked in your armoury, Rivers.

RIVERS (*in spite of himself*) What was that?

RICHARD Reputation. I have trodden on some toes in my time, but I have never collected other men's shoes. You dangle with them, like a market huckster. Your two thousand will remember those shoes when they are asked to choose between the Queen's brother and the King's uncle.

[RIVERS, *in an involuntary movement, takes his sword a short way from its sheath, but is stopped by the scorn in* RICHARD'S *eyes. Only* LOVELL, *of the three, has moved at all, and he only to a posture of readiness.*]

RICHARD (*as* RIVERS *stands irresolute, his hand still on his slightly drawn sword, with quiet scorn*) That would be the only disservice that you have not already done him. (*To brawl in the boy's presence, he means.* RIVERS *lets the sword go back slowly*) I have no desire to destroy you, Rivers. The safety of England and of my brother's son is my only concern. If you have the grace to give up intrigue and live quietly in the North, under surveillance, until this crisis is over, neither you, nor your family, nor your estates, shall suffer at my hands.

RIVERS (*after a long pause*) Who goes with me?

RICHARD Grey, and Vaughan, and Hawte.

PRINCE No! Not my brother too.

GREY On the same conditions?

RICHARD On the same conditions. No more intrigue on your part, no retribution.

GREY Very well. But don't send me to Middleham. It is a boring place. (*He is greatly relieved to find that the crisis is over and that he is still alive*)

PRINCE What is this, a plot? You are taking all my friends away from me. I forbid you!

RICHARD No, Edward, no. (*In his genuine sorrow for the boy, the name comes first to his lips*) The others stay with you. There is no evidence that any of them have served you other than well. Will you go with Lovell, my lords? He will arrange an escort for your journey. Take farewell of the King now.

PRINCE No, oh no.

RIVERS Courage, sir. We shall go hawking together yet. I hope you will be a credit to me at your Coronation.

GREY (*taking his leave*) I shall send you all the news of Yorkshire, sir. Fairs, and country dances, and calvings.

BUCKINGHAM (*as* RIVERS *passes him going to the door*) Goodbye, my lord. May I offer my congratulations?

RIVERS On what?

BUCKINGHAM On escaping your deserts.

RIVERS We shall meet again, Buckingham.

BUCKINGHAM I wonder. (*In answer to* RIVERS' *raised eyebrow*) Your taste for intrigue amounts to a vice. I doubt if even the prospect of losing your head can cure you. If that happens, I promise to pray for that very expensive soul of yours.

[RIVERS *and* GREY *go out with* LOVELL.]

[*The* PRINCE *begins to sob angrily, without covering his face.*]

PRINCE I don't believe it! It is a trick. Rivers would not plot to make war.

RICHARD What more evidence do you want, sir?

PRINCE I don't want evidence. I don't want explanations, or accusations, or examinations! I just want people to stop quarrelling and live at peace with each other!

RICHARD Alas, sir! Men have cried for that ever since they were turned out of Eden. I am going to have a second breakfast. We rode out of Northampton at dawn. Will you join me?

PRINCE (*making for the door*) No! I hate you. You come into my life and make everything hateful. A few minutes ago we were all happy. I was glad that you were coming. I planned how I should receive you. I wore my best doublet for you. And now you have ruined everything. You have taken my friends away from me and told lies about them. I hate you.

[*Exit in a breeze of emotion.*]

[RICHARD *looks suddenly tired. He props himself against one of the trestle tables.*]

RICHARD It is going to be difficult, Harry.

BUCKINGHAM You knew that. Don't worry. He'll come round. His tutor will talk to him. Shall I see about breakfast for you?

RICHARD Thank you, it is ordered. (*His thoughts going back to* EDWARD) His mind is so solid with Woodville teaching that not an independent thought stirs in it. (*With a wry smile*) Poor Edward! Poor me! Poor England!

BUCKINGHAM (*watching him*) There may be a speedier deliverance than you expect.

RICHARD (*his mind still on the boy*) He is probably wretched. He was devoted to his father.

BUCKINGHAM Tell me, Richard, did you ever know Edward refuse a plea for mercy?

RICHARD (*coming out of his abstraction to consider it*) Yes. Once.

BUCKINGHAM Clarence.

RICHARD (*shortly*) Yes.

BUCKINGHAM Why no mercy for Clarence?

RICHARD (*repressive*) He was a traitor three times over.

BUCKINGHAM Nevertheless you pleaded for him.

RICHARD He was my brother.

BUCKINGHAM He was Edward's brother. Why did the soft-hearted Edward not soften to Clarence? What had he done? What did he know?

RICHARD Know? (*Stiffly*) I don't like your suggestion, Harry.

BUCKINGHAM (*amiably*) Don't snub me. Clarence was drunk five days out of seven. A dangerous creature to have stumble on to a secret. His tongue went like a bell-clapper——

RICHARD (*bored and a little angry*) You are very heavy-footed sometimes, Harry. What possible reason have you for suggesting that there was any secret!

BUCKINGHAM Only that old Stillington is waiting in London now to tell you one, and I suspect that it is the same secret.

RICHARD Stillington? The Bishop of Bath?

BUCKINGHAM So my gossips tell me.

RICHARD You love sensation, don't you, Harry? May I remind you that my brother Clarence was condemned to death by Parliament for repeated treason. As for the good Bishop's secret, it is probably some scandal in his diocese that troubles his conscience.

BUCKINGHAM Scandal, yes: but not in his diocese. (RICHARD *looks enquiring*)

[*Enter mine host with laden tray.*]

CURTAIN

SCENE 4

A room in the part of Westminster Abbey devoted to those seeking sanctuary; three days later. The room is bare and entirely without furnishing, but several rich chests, some open and spilling their contents, various bundles and boxes, and mounds of rich stuffs, make an incongruous brilliance on the cold stone floor. The QUEEN *is in the process of establishing herself in sanctuary.*

As the curtain goes up a man is putting down still another small chest and bundle. He goes out, R., through the door that is open to the continual traffic from the passage without. The QUEEN *is rummaging among the stuffs; L., sitting on a pile of rolled-up rugs, is* ELIZABETH, *looking detached; at the back* CECILY, *aged fourteen, is mooning about among the collection, industriously sucking a stick of barley-sugar. They are all dressed in sober mourning, but the* QUEEN, *incorrigibly fashionable, manages to make it look like a gala dress.*

QUEEN What have they done with my fur coverlet? And where are the purple hangings from my closet? (*Calling*) Clement! Where is the creature? Not half of our things are here. (*Enter, with difficulty, two men bearing on their shoulder a rolled-up carpet*) Oh, my carpet. There is no room to put anything in this miserable cavern of a place. Leave it lying in the passage for the moment. (*They withdraw with more difficulty*) Elizabeth, have you seen my little standing mirror anywhere?

ELIZABETH What does one want a mirror for in sanctuary?

QUEEN Your uncle Rivers brought that mirror to me from Italy. I would not lose it for the world—poor Anthony. It is worth a small fortune.

ELIZABETH I don't know why we are in sanctuary at all. What is there to be afraid of?

QUEEN What is there? With your uncle and your half-brother arrested, and the King your brother in Gloucester's clutches?

ELIZABETH You talk as if he were a crab. I think it is all very silly.

[*Enter* CLEMENT, *who is the page from the first scene.*]

QUEEN Oh, there you are, Clement. Where have you been?

CLEMENT Madam, I regret to say that the cypress cupboard

is too large to come through the gate between the palace and the Abbey. They have tried it every way.

QUEEN Then tell them to break down the wall.

CLEMENT Breach the wall, madam?

QUEEN Certainly. It can be mended again—when my belongings are on the right side of it.

CLEMENT Yes, madam. (*Producing a book*) This is the Princess Elizabeth's book of romances. I thought that she might miss it.

ELIZABETH Oh, thank you, Clement. That was kind.

[*Exit* CLEMENT.]

QUEEN The silly creature spends half his life inventing ways of doing you service. I wish he was as inventive about my cupboard! Cecily, for the love of God stop pulling that sweet in and out of your mouth. Do you want to ruin the shape of it—and the best complexion in Europe at the same time? Go and see what the children are doing in the next room, and tell them not to. (*Calling to a monk who is passing beyond the open door*) Oh, brother! Express my duty to my lord Abbot, and say to him that I must have better quarters. I know that I am merely a helpless widow, and that furnishing is not part of sanctuary custom, but I have a family of children who need a little sun if the marrow is not to freeze in their bones. Three rooms on the sunny side of the courtyard would be pleasant. No doubt my lord Abbot can arrange that. (*The monk bows and disappears as a man comes in carrying several bundles of stuffs*) Oh, there are the purple hangings! And my fur coverlet. (*The man puts them down and backs out*) Now when they get the bigger things through the wall we shall have everything.

ELIZABETH We have forgotten the door-handles.

QUEEN Elizabeth!

ELIZABETH (*brittle*) They are quite valuable. Beaten silver.

QUEEN Elizabeth, I should have thought that at a time like this I could count on your help—your understanding.

ELIZABETH There is a great deal that I don't understand. If we have done nothing wrong, why have we run away?

QUEEN (*indignantly*) I have never run away in my life! To take sanctuary is mere prudence. No one knows what may happen next.

ELIZABETH Nothing will happen to anyone who has not done anything.

QUEEN You really must learn to express yourself.

ELIZABETH (*beginning to put into tentative words the fear that, behind her brave exterior, has been gnawing at her heart*) Mother, you did not know what Uncle Rivers was plan——

[*Enter* CLEMENT.]

CLEMENT Madam, the Bishop of Ely is here. He asks if you would be so gracious as to receive him.

QUEEN Ely? John Morton? What brings him? Is he a messenger from someone?

CLEMENT He did not say, madam.

QUEEN Yes, I shall see him.

CLEMENT Here, madam?

QUEEN Yes, here. (*As* CLEMENT *goes*) If the Queen of England can sit on the floor, so can John Morton. Get up, Elizabeth, and let me sit there.

ELIZABETH (*rising from her seat on the pile of rugs*) Wouldn't you look more dignified on one of the chests?

QUEEN Yes, but not so appealing.

ELIZABETH You can't appeal to someone who has no heart. The Bishop of Ely is only a brain, a pair of ears, and a pocket.

QUEEN Let us hope that the ears have heard of something to our advantage.

[*Enter* CLEMENT, *showing in the* BISHOP. *Exit* CLEMENT.]

[JOHN MORTON *was a lawyer before he was a churchman, and he is still, at sixty-three, more lawyer than priest. Not the lean meticulous type; but, rather, the type which today is a successful defender in criminal cases: large, vain, showy, clever, insensitive, coaxing or bullying as it suits his purpose. Rich, good-living, one of the greatest pluralists on record.*]

QUEEN My lord Bishop. (*She gives him her hand*)

MORTON Your Grace. I am distressed to find you in such wise.

QUEEN This visit cheers me greatly, my lord.

MORTON I should be glad to think so, madam.

QUEEN My situation cannot be so parlous if John Morton finds me worthy of remembrance.

MORTON Alas, madam; if it were not so parlous, I should not be here.

QUEEN (*her complacency gone*) What now? My son——

MORTON The King is well, I am glad to say. He and the Duke of Gloucester are expected to enter London tomorrow. London, I understand, has prepared a magnificent welcome.

QUEEN (*bitterly*) They will be glad, the Londoners. They never liked my family. Then, what——? Does Gloucester plan some—humiliation for me?

MORTON Not Gloucester. (*Giving the devil his due*) It would not occur to him.

QUEEN Then—who?

MORTON A colleague of mine, who was your husband's Lord Chancellor. The Bishop of Bath.

QUEEN (*in quick alarm*) Stillington? (*Restraining herself*) But he was always loyal to Edward, always faithful.

MORTON Unfortunately, he has a conscience.

QUEEN Elizabeth, you may join Cecily and the others.

ELIZABETH (*protesting*) But I want to hear——

QUEEN Elizabeth!

ELIZABETH (*sweeping her mother an obeisance*) Very good, madam. (*With another to* MORTON) My lord.

[*Exit* ELIZABETH.]

QUEEN And what burdens Stillington's conscience, my lord?

MORTON That twenty years ago he witnessed a contract of marriage, and kept silent when he should have published the fact.

QUEEN Marriage between whom?

MORTON Between the King of England and the Earl of Shrewsbury's daughter, Lady Eleanor Butler. (*As the* QUEEN *says nothing*) Tomorrow, madam, Stillington will tell Gloucester that the King was never legally married to Elizabeth Woodville.

QUEEN He can be stopped, surely?

MORTON He might. But I am afraid that in the excitement of the last few days the story has become known to more than Stillington. To me, for one. And I suspect that my lord Duke of Buckingham has a working knowledge of it.

QUEEN (*in an agony*) But why now? Why does he speak now?

MORTON While the King lived there was no need to speak. Lady Eleanor was dead; no wrong was being done to anyone. Now that there is a question of a bastard succeeding to——

QUEEN (*furious*) My lord Bishop, you are blunt!

MORTON (*unabashed*) Madam, if we are to achieve anything, it will not be by soft phrases.

QUEEN (*catching at the word*) Achieve? Do you plan achievement in the face of so much defeat? I envy your courage.

MORTON Your Grace, a woman who, being a commoner, has the courage to marry a King, and thereafter to find land, fortune, and titles for every one of her many relations in face of a jealous and powerful nobility, has the courage to achieve anything.

QUEEN The courage perhaps, but not the means. My many-titled family is in full flight, my lord. And what friends has a fallen climber?

MORTON What friends has a man suddenly placed far above his fellows?

QUEEN Gloucester? There is nothing that Gloucester's friends would not do for him. They would die for him.

MORTON They have never had to crook a knee to him. It is wonderful how sensitive the knee-joint becomes upon such an occasion. (*As the* QUEEN *offers no comment*) If the sons of Edward the Fourth are not to succeed, then Richard of Gloucester has a crown, and you, madam, new friends. But the crown is not on his head yet. I have with me at the moment Lord Hastings, who hopes that you may receive him.

QUEEN (*quickly*) Hastings! He is no friend of mine.

MORTON I said, madam: new friends. He was a faithful servant to your husband.

QUEEN (*slightly scornful*) He was Edward's devoted slave for twenty years, but that does not make him mine. I shall be as blunt with you, my lord, as you have been with me. I distrust this visit. John Morton is not apt to interest himself in a cause as frail as mine. You are a priest, and Richard is a good son of Holy Church; what ails you at his new glory?

MORTON The Duke of Gloucester disapproves of me. I have too many livings, it appears.

QUEEN How many?

MORTON To be honest, madam, I have no idea. And I had hoped—— (*He pauses artistically*) The fen country is bad for my rheumatism——

QUEEN (*following his drift quite easily*) You had hoped for a change to Canterbury? (*Marvelling*) And you would gamble your life against that!

MORTON No, madam. Against a cardinal's hat.

QUEEN (*after a pause, appreciative, capitulating*) My lord, I think we can do business.

[*With a bow,* MORTON *goes to the door and summons* HASTINGS.]

MORTON Lord Hastings!

[*Enter* HASTINGS, *looking worn and troubled. He greets the* QUEEN'S *offered hand.*]

QUEEN So the long secret is out, my lord.

HASTINGS (*surprised*) You know, madam?

QUEEN Oh yes, I know. There was nothing about Edward that I did not know. (*Kindly*) It has been a shock to you?

HASTINGS It has been a great grief. (*Rage rising in him*) And I will not stand by and let Gloucester make bastards of those innocent children!

QUEEN (*dryly*) Edward did that, my lord. (*Half pitying, half contemptuous*) You always saw him through a mist of banners.

HASTINGS I loved him.

QUEEN (*to her own thought more than to him*) Richard saw him whole and loved him too.

HASTINGS (*quickly*) Did Richard know of this?

QUEEN No. He was barely eleven.

HASTINGS But afterwards?

QUEEN (*shaking her head*) Edward cared more for Richard's good opinion than you would believe possible.

HASTINGS (*dry and angry*) I believe it! Even when he was a boy of sixteen the King would listen to his advice while old campaigners stood by with their tongues tied. Many a time I sat outside a tent door while Edward listened to Richard. It didn't matter what it was: disposing troops at Barnet or victualling a ship at Flushing, the first word was Richard's.

QUEEN (*a slight edge in her voice*) But the last is to be yours? I thought you were Richard's friend.

HASTINGS (*sullenly*) I will not see him King!

QUEEN (*amused*) Poor Richard! How little he guessed, when he was handing out ships' stores in Holland, the future he was storing up for himself. Well, my lords, what is your plan?

MORTON First, we must stop Parliament from meeting. He will do nothing without Parliament. We shall send out an order cancelling his summons. That will give us time.

QUEEN Time for what?

MORTON To get in touch with Rivers, and the rest of your family; to plan an opposition; to suppress the Stillington story if possible, and if not, to deal with Gloucester.

QUEEN And how do you plan to deal with him?

HASTINGS That we must leave to circumstances. Our need at the moment is time.

QUEEN (*coolly*) Richard and I have always been on opposite

sides politically, but I have never had anything but kindness at his hands. I will not be a party to his murder.

MORTON (*indignant*) Madam, you horrify me.

QUEEN (*unimpressed*) What horrifies you? My squeamishness?

MORTON (*stiffly*) We are here to help you, madam, not to be subjected to——

QUEEN God love you, we are three knaves together. Let us make no bones about it. But let there be a limit to our knavery. Will you come, my lords, and see the children? I don't know about you, my lord Bishop, but Hastings is very fond of them—even if they were his rivals in Edward's affection.

[*She leads the way out.* MORTON *and* HASTINGS *consult each other's eyes, find mutual understanding, and follow her through the door.*]

CURTAIN

SCENE 5

A council chamber in the Tower of London, before noon on June 13th. Round the council table are seats for eight, but only five are occupied. At the head of the table, facing the audience, is the PRINCE, *now* EDWARD V. GLOUCESTER'S *place immediately to his R. is unoccupied, but the place on his L. is filled by* ROTHERHAM, ARCHBISHOP OF YORK, *a benevolent creature with his hands clasped comfortably over his gently heaving person; it is very hot this June morning and he is more than half asleep. The place down from him is empty, and below that is* HASTINGS. *On the other side of the table, the two places below* GLOUCESTER'S *empty chair are occupied by, first,* MORTON, *and below him,* LORD STANLEY: *a tall, thin, dreary person, with a long thin face, a deprecating manner, and a cautious soul. The chair at the bottom of the table is empty. Door R. back.*

The PRINCE *is sitting sideways in his chair, in a listless attitude. Conversation is going on between the Councillors, but in a desultory fashion.*

HASTINGS We could, of course, increase the grant as a temporary measure.

MORTON Yes, we could do that. How much do you suggest?

PRINCE I am very tired of listening to you talk.

MORTON (*deferentially*) If your Grace is weary there is no need to wait. No papers can be signed unless the Lord Protector is here to add his signature to your Grace's.

PRINCE Is my uncle Gloucester not coming to council today?

HASTINGS We have been expecting him every moment for the last three hours, your Grace.

PRINCE He comes less and less, it seems. Why is that?

HASTINGS He calls it leaving us free, sir.

PRINCE Free for what?

HASTINGS For—discussion, I take it.

PRINCE (*pausing on his way to the door*) When he comes, say that I would be glad if he could persuade the Queen my mother to let my small brother join me here. It is very boring to do lessons alone, and I have no one to beat at games.

[*Exit* PRINCE.]

HASTINGS (*into the subsequent silence, gloomily, as they resume their seats*) Even the boy thinks it odd.

MORTON What?

HASTINGS That he leaves us so much alone.

MORTON Oh, come! Why should four distinguished members of the Council—(*He enumerates them with a wave of his hand*)—The Archbishop of York, Lord Hastings, Lord Stanley, and the Bishop of Ely, be held to require supervision? You fret, Hastings, you fret. We should be thankful that things go so smoothly.

HASTINGS You think so? When you have campaigned as long as I have, you can *smell* trouble. Many a time I have looked at a countryside where not a leaf was stirring, and smelt the ambush in it.

STANLEY I agree with Hastings, I think.

MORTON (*protesting*) Oh, my cautious Stanley!

STANLEY I have my family to think of. He has been in London for a month, and he is still only Protector. Why? Stillington went to him on the night of his arrival; it is not possible that he doesn't know; but he has done nothing! Why? The Coronation is only ten days away, the guests have been summoned, the clothes are being made, the very cooks are busy. Parliament is to be asked to confirm Gloucester as Protector. Why?

HASTINGS And there is Parliament. He found out about those cancelling notices. But was there any inquiry? Not a murmur! And that from Gloucester, who hates a piece of trickery like the devil.

STANLEY And then he leaves us alone while he spends hours with Buckingham and Lovell and the others at Crosby's Place. Why?

MORTON Perhaps the Archbishop of York, who seems to be asleep, can make a suggestion.

ROTHERHAM (*waking from his doze with a start at the mention of his name*) Hm?

STANLEY Why does Gloucester not want to know what goes on in his absence?

ROTHERHAM (*placidly*) I can only suggest that he does. Very warm today, isn't it?

HASTINGS How could he!

ROTHERHAM (*his eyes closing again*) One of us is no doubt a traitor. (*The others involuntarily turn to look at each other*) The Tower is always very stuffy in summer. It is the reflection from the river, they say. (*He refolds his hands comfortably*)

STANLEY (*dismally*) I wish it were tomorrow and all well.

HASTINGS Does Rivers know his part?

STANLEY Yes. Two hundred of my men will free him as soon as the news reaches them, and with the rest he will take York before anyone stirs a foot to defend it.

HASTINGS With York ours, even Gloucester's adoring North will be loath to try conclusions.

STANLEY Even if they do, we have men enough. It is not the fighting that troubles me. It is this—— (*He pauses*)

HASTINGS This feeling of ambush. I know.

MORTON (*smooth and positive*) And now shall we count our good fortune? By some miracle, specially designed for our benefit, no word has been said of the Stillington story. England therefore is wholly devoted to the boy, and unaware that there is any bar to his succession. Good. By tomorrow Stillington will be in no position to tell that story, and Hastings will be Lord Protector of England.

HASTINGS It sounds very pretty. (*Brooding*) Not a leaf stirring, and the whole place one bristling ambush. Many a time I have known it. You could smell it.

MORTON You always enjoyed making yourself miserable, my lord.

HASTINGS I want to know why he did nothing about Stillington!

It wasn't a piece of information Stillington gave him, it was a crown! A crown!

STANLEY Was the story not true, perhaps?

MORTON (*with contemptuous amusement*) The good Bishop of Bath would not lie even to compliment a woman on her looks. Besides, he has witnesses. It is no doubt the gathering of evidence that has occupied them these past weeks. Gloucester has a passion for constitutional methods. For which we must whole-heartedly bless him!

[*The door opens to admit* BUCKINGHAM, *very fine, very friendly, very confident. He comes into the stagnant air of the council chamber like a waft of fresh air.*]

BUCKINGHAM Bless whom, my lord, and for what?

MORTON Ah, Buckingham!

BUCKINGHAM (*making for his seat between* ROTHERHAM *and* HASTINGS) Good morning, my lords.

HASTINGS It is nearly afternoon.

BUCKINGHAM And the heat is bad for Hastings' spleen. You should wear cooler colours, my lord.

MORTON Is the Lord Protector coming?

BUCKINGHAM He will be here in a moment.

STANLEY You have had heavy business at Crosby's Place?

BUCKINGHAM Yes. The Lord Protector has decided to summon men from Yorkshire.

HASTINGS Summon them to London! Why?

BUCKINGHAM To ensure that the peace is kept.

MORTON But everything is going so smoothly!

BUCKINGHAM There are always fools who fish in troubled waters.

MORTON Why fools?

BUCKINGHAM They drown, mostly. They catch things they never dreamed of.

ROTHERHAM (*into the little silence that succeeds* BUCKINGHAM'S *light remark*) It is very hot today.

BUCKINGHAM It is going to be much hotter.

[*Another slight silence is interrupted by the opening of the door and the entry of* GLOUCESTER, *followed by* LOVELL. *They stand up to receive him.*]

GLOUCESTER (*amiably*) Good morning, my lords. (*He moves to his place at the R. of the* PRINCE'S *chair, but does not sit.* LOVELL *remains standing to his R. and a little behind him*) I am sorry to be so laggard in sharing your labours. Please sit down. I hope your morning has been productive of benefits for England.

MORTON We hope so, your Grace.

STANLEY (*in the same breath*) The matter of a few grants, sir.

RICHARD It is nearly dinner time, but I hope that you will bear with me for a moment. I have journeyed from Crosby's Place on purpose to express my gratitude to you.

HASTINGS Your gratitude, sir?

RICHARD I was tempted to a great wrong, and you saved me from it.

MORTON Wrong to whom, sir?

RICHARD To my conscience, my lord Bishop. I loved my brother Edward, my lords; and I served him well, I think; but it was not until he was dead that I was ever tempted to compromise my soul for him. That happened when it was shown to me that owing to my brother's irregular marriage his sons must be barred from the throne. It shocked me that Edward's children should fail to succeed him. It seemed no great wrong to keep the truth back and to let his line go on. My own line was a frail one and his was lusty; and if my talents for kingship were adequate, my interest was elsewhere. My mind played delightedly with the crown—to rule England is the unique glory of the world—but my heart was not engaged, my heart was in the North. I planned to stay Protector, I planned to prop a bastard on the throne of England, to lie and cheat and bribe if necessary to keep him there. You prevented me from that, my lords. I had hoped to save England for my brother's son, but you taught me that if England is to be saved at all, it will not be by any Protectorship. For the last month I have watched you, his councillors, his father's friends, his liege men, behaving like ill-bred children round a sweetmeat booth that has been overturned. What thought had you for the boy? For England? None! England to you was a place to loot, and the boy a means to an end; and you were ready to risk civil war to achieve that end. There will be no loot for you, my lords. Only your deserts; to each according to his degree.

HASTINGS (*on his feet*) Degree of what?

RICHARD Of guilt. You, my lord, will be tried by your peers for treason and attempted assassination.

HASTINGS It is a lie! You have no proof!

RICHARD (*marvelling*) What madness took you, Hastings, after so long a life of service? You who fought that rear-guard action, who starved with us, and wandered with us, and——

HASTINGS I will not be patronised by an upstart usurper, and I will not be arrested by anyone. (*Taking out his sword he leaps to* STANLEY'S *side of the table and makes for the door*) Out of my way, there. Come on, Stanley, draw. Let us make an end of the business now! (LOVELL *comes in front of* RICHARD *to engage him*) Stanley, take Buckingham. (STANLEY *half draws his sword, but looks at* BUCKINGHAM *waiting for him with his hand on his sword-hilt, at the watching* RICHARD, *and changes his mind.* HASTINGS, *fighting with his back to* STANLEY, *becomes aware that no second conflict is materialising*) Stanley, you damned coward, draw! (*The door opens to reveal men-at-arms with drawn swords.* HASTINGS, *startled, is momentarily off his guard, and* LOVELL *strikes the sword from his grasp. The guards seize him*) God curse you, Stanley, you chicken-hearted traitor.

RICHARD Give him his sword. (LOVELL *retrieves it and hands it to* HASTINGS) I could forgive your treachery to me, Hastings, but not your playing traitor to your country. If I had died tonight as you expected, twenty thousand men would have sprung to arms tomorrow to avenge me. Was that the England you had planned? Or had you not planned—beyond tonight? Take him away.

[*Exit* LOVELL *and guards with* HASTINGS.]

[RICHARD *turns to* ROTHERHAM, *who is looking dazed.*]

My lord Archbishop, I think it unwise that you should continue as Chancellor, but I cannot believe that any great harm stirs in that unhurried mind. You will find ample scope for your talents in your diocese. Good morning to you!

ROTHERHAM (*stammering*) Your Grace, such generosity——I have not deserved——

RICHARD Good morning to you!

[*Exit* ROTHERHAM.]

Your talents, Morton, are not suitable to any diocese. I am not sure whether you should be ruling a province or running games of chance at a fair. Thanks to your gift for self-preservation, there is no evidence that will send you to the block with Hastings, though you richly deserve it. On the other hand, you can hardly be exhibited as a pattern of Christian virtue in any of your livings. I have decided to give you into the Duke of Buckingham's custody. You will find that both comfortable and constant, and you will have leisure to write that history of our times that you have so often planned. I shudder to think how I shall appear in it.

MORTON At least you will not be neglected, sir.

RICHARD Thank you.

[*Exit* BUCKINGHAM *with* MORTON.]

Stanley, my brother raised you from obscurity to great wealth and position, and you served him well. I know that it must be difficult to have Lancaster in your bed and York in your heart. You do have York in your heart?

STANLEY How can you doubt it, sir?

RICHARD (*dryly*) There are various small indications that make me wonder. But the country has been torn too long by that old quarrel. If I am to govern England I need help from both sides of the house. If I promise to forget your part in this conspiracy, can I count on faithful service in return?

STANLEY Your Grace, what can I say? Such generosity shames me. Give me the chance and I shall show you in deeds rather than in words how grateful I am for your clemency.

RICHARD You speak for your wife too? I find her Lancaster persistence more frightening than your Stanley backsliding.

STANLEY I stand surety for my wife. She finds it difficult to forget that she is the heir of all the Lancasters. And because Henry Tudor is her only child, and in exile, she is apt to make him a hero. But she too will be moved by your Grace's greatness of heart.

RICHARD By England's need, I hope. Goodbye, my lord. I shall expect both you and your wife to take leading parts at my Coronation. There is to be no faction in the country any more.

[*Exit* STANLEY *as* BUCKINGHAM *returns.*]

BUCKINGHAM Stanley looks like someone who has fallen over a precipice and can't believe that he is alive. Is all forgiven?

RICHARD I have forgiven his part in the plot. I can't forgive him for not backing Hastings. I shall never be able to forget that. Have you handed over Morton to the guards?

BUCKINGHAM With unction. (*Looking at the empty room*) A clean sweep, your Grace. When you sit with your own council here, the atmosphere will be sweeter. (*Looking at* RICHARD *sideways*) So I am to crook my knee to you, Richard! (*The tone is bantering but faintly tinged with envy*)

RICHARD (*without emphasis or consideration*) No. To the crown as usual.

BUCKINGHAM Ah, well; the Hastings estates will come in very useful at the beginning of a reign.

RICHARD (*his attention arrested*) For what?

BUCKINGHAM (*lightly*) Rewards and retainers.

RICHARD (*coldly*) Because I step on a snake there is no need to lay waste a hillside.

BUCKINGHAM (*puzzled*) You mean—you are not going to confiscate Hastings' lands?

RICHARD No, nor his goods, nor his fortune, nor the wardship of his children, nor anything else that was his. I do not make war on innocent people. Had *you* expected——

BUCKINGHAM (*breaking in hastily*) No, of course not. (*But the disclaimer is too hasty.* RICHARD *stares at him curiously*) And Rivers?

RICHARD Rivers will lose his head. I see no reason why his wife should lose goods as well as husband. (*Reluctantly facing an unpleasant duty*) Now, I suppose, I must see the boy.

BUCKINGHAM To tell him?

RICHARD No. I have asked his tutor to break it to him. He is very fond of Alcock. He must be lonely here. Perhaps Elizabeth can be persuaded to let his brother join him, now that he is of no more value as a pawn. He will take this badly, I'm afraid.

BUCKINGHAM Well, the country will not regret him, God knows. They will be delighted to have a man they know and like instead of a child, who might turn out to be anything. (*With a sideways glance at* RICHARD) They would be still more delighted perhaps if you were to seal the peace between York and Lancaster by alliance.

RICHARD Alliance? There is no one to ally.

BUCKINGHAM There is your son and my daughter. After Lady Stanley I *am* the next Lancaster.

RICHARD (*remembering*) Yes, of course. Edward's 'streak of Lancaster'. (*Pigeon-holing it*) Well, it is a good suggestion.

BUCKINGHAM (*eagerly*) You like it?

RICHARD (*his mind already on other matters, looking at the future with a smile*) There are so many good suggestions in my mind, Harry, they boil up and spill over. Life will not be long enough for all I have to do in England. A thousand years from now, I promise you, men will say: There was no better reign in our history than that of Richard the Third.

CURTAIN

ACT II

SCENE I

A room in Gloucester on a morning at the beginning of August, 1483. *The room is a small ante-chamber with no furnishing to speak of beyond a small table and a couple of chairs. Doors Centre R. and Centre L.*

CLEMENT, *the squire, transferred from* EDWARD'S *service to* RICHARD'S, *is lounging by the table composing verse—presumably to that* PRINCESS ELIZABETH *still in sanctuary.*

CLEMENT (*murmuring*) 'My lady she doth wear
The sunlight in her hair,
And all the dews of morning
In her eyes.' (*Considering his screed*)
Morning. Dawning. Morning. . . . Virtue. . . . Virtue. . . .

[*Enter a second squire,* MARK. *If* CLEMENT *reminds one irresistibly of a faithful sheep-dog,* MARK *is like nothing so much as an ill-bred household pet 'on the make' round a dining-table. That he is in the royal household at all is due no doubt to* RICHARD'S *well-known passion for requiting service; his father was probably a good friend to* RICHARD *and withal a worthy man who did not at all deserve a son like* MARK.]

MARK (*bustling in*) Go away, Clement, and write your love-sick poems somewhere else. This room is needed.

CLEMENT (*still in a dream*) Mark, is there a rhyme for 'virtue'?

MARK Virtue? What is that? Run away, my Clement, and make room for your betters.

CLEMENT (*coming out of his dream*) Listen, Mark, last time you said a room was needed, you wanted it yourself for some low scheme that you had——

MARK Will you be quiet and look what is following me down the corridor.

CLEMENT (*having peered over* MARK'S *shoulder*) Oh. (*He begins to put away his poem*)

MARK All the majesty of the city of Gloucester, bless its parochial heart.

CLEMENT I fly. I don't suppose there is a rhyme to virtue.

[*Exit* CLEMENT *L.*]

MARK (*ushering in the approaching deputation*) If you will be so kind as to wait here, gentlemen, the King will come to you in a few moments. He begs you to forgive him for any delay. He has had a great press of business since his arrival in Gloucester.

[*Exit* MARK *L., after* CLEMENT.]

[*The deputation consists of three men, each a leading man in his own trade guild and chosen by lot to represent together all the trade guilds of the city. They are resplendent in the distinguishing robes of each guild, and hung about with impressive chains. The up-stage one of the three is little* BEN WILLETT, *the shoemaker, chief of the Cordwainers: small, timid, well-meaning. The down-stage one is* ROGER KEMP, *chief of the Drapers: tall, thin, vain and dreary. The middle one is* BOB THACKER, *chief of the Loriners (bridle-makers): a colossal man, six feet tall and broad in proportion; jovial, prosperous, a bit of a bore after the third drink. All three are middle-aged.*

[BEN WILLETT *is bearing on a cushion in front of him a casket filled with gold pieces.* THACKER *is clutching the rolled parchment on which is written the ' address '.*]

THACKER (*looking after the retreating* MARK *disgustedly*) Whipper-snapper!

[*The three stand facing the door through which* MARK *has disappeared. They are left alone in a silence which can be felt.* WILLETT *clears his throat timidly and seems alarmed at the presumption.* THACKER *stretches his neck in his collar.* KEMP *surreptitiously wipes a palm on his robe.*]

WILLETT (*breaking the silence, in a very small voice*) Do you think I might put this down for a moment? (*He indicates the table which is to his L.*)

THACKER No, you can't.

WILLETT It is very heavy; and my hands are beginning to shake.

KEMP I said at the time that he was a most unsuitable choice.

WILLETT (*miserably*) I didn't want the honour, you know that. They chose me by lot.

THACKER (*squashing him*) Don't fuss him. (*To* WILLETT, *kindly*) You're not afraid of meeting Dickon, are you? Why, man alive, he's just a creature like ourselves. Who should know if not me? Didn't I——

KEMP (*interrupting in a bored drawl*) We know! You fought alongside him at Tewkesbury.

THACKER Alongside! Shoulder to shoulder. Except that his shoulder only came to my elbow. ' Get out of my way, you ox,' says he, ' and give me room to use my sword arm! ' (*With admiring affection*) Little cock-sparrow! Fighting on foot like any commoner, and laying about him like a giant. Eighteen, he was. Looked as if you could break him between your finger and thumb. But all steel wire, take it from me. I fought at his elbow.

KEMP (*cold and jealous*) About five thousand other men fought at Tewkesbury.

THACKER (*laying his finger on the sore spot*) But not Roger Kemp. What were you doing that day, Roger? Measuring out bits of stuff for women to make wimples of, belike. You don't know what it was like to have Somerset's men round you so close you could hardly breathe. Like being caught in a press of bullocks on market-day; and every bullock out for your blood. Fighting for life and for breath at the same time. And then (*He is telling it all in a reminiscent drawl, quite unexcited*) when we were all near dead, we felt them give. ' Thank God,' says I. ' Now we can rest.' ' Rest be damned,' says Dickon, ' now we charge them.' ' But we're half-dead with fighting,' says I. ' And *they* are half-dead with fear,' says Dickon. ' Come on! ' And that's the way we had them. Because Dickon didn't believe in breathing-spaces.

KEMP Any man can fight well when he is excited.

THACKER You were eager enough to come and do him reverence, I notice.

KEMP I don't revere him for anything he did in a battle; but for the things he has done since he became King.

THACKER (*agreeing*) Ah. (*His ' Ah ' means yes. With satisfaction, contemplating it*) No more common lands snitched to make hunting forests for the court. No more buying of jurymen's votes at a shilling a time. No more sitting in prison while your business goes to ruin because you can't get bail. That's a King for you!

WILLETT My sister in London saw the Coronation procession.

THACKER (*kindly*) Did she, Ben?

WILLETT She says it was the best attended Coronation on record. People came from the ends of England to it. Yes, and from Wales, too. The only thing she didn't like, she said, was that Buckingham had finer clothes than the King.

THACKER Ah. He wants watching, that one.

WILLETT I wish he would come. This is really very heavy.

[*The door, L., is thrown open and* MARK *announces the* KING.]

MARK Gentlemen, the King's Grace.

[*Enter* RICHARD, *attended by* LOVELL, BUCKINGHAM, *and* STANLEY.]

RICHARD Good day to you, gentlemen. I am truly sorry to have kept you waiting. So many people have come to offer their good wishes that it is difficult to arrange for them all. I hope you will forgive me.

[THACKER, *recovering from his deep bow, unrolls the parchment and begins to read. But his confidence has left him. After all his glib talk of* DICKON *he finds that it is a King he is facing, a King supported by very great and magnificent nobles. The hand holding the upper edge of the parchment is trembling obviously, and he stammers now and then over his words.*]

THACKER (*reading the address*) 'May it please your Grace, we, the members of all the trade guilds of your loyal city of Gloucester, being desirous of expressing to your Grace our fealty, and our satisfaction in your Grace's late elevation to the throne and present condescension in visiting us, would be gratified by your Grace's acceptance of a small gift at our hands. It is with great——

RICHARD (*who has been looking in a puzzled fashion at as much as he can see of* BOB THACKER *over the document; in the slow tones of one confirming a suspicion, as* THACKER *reaches his first period*) Bob Thacker!

THACKER (*agreeing*) Yes, sir. (*He has raised his eyes automatically and now searches frantically for his place*) It is with—— It is with—— Oh, now I have lost my place.

RICHARD (*taking the parchment gently from him*) Never mind the rest of it. I shall read all the kind things for myself presently. (*Shaking hands with him*) How are you, Bob? I am delighted to see you. You have put on weight, haven't you? (*He pokes a finger at* THACKER'S *waist*)

THACKER I expect I am a bit heavier, sir. I am glad to see your Grace looking so well, that I am! No extra flesh on you, sir.

RICHARD No. I worry it off, they tell me.

THACKER Who'd have thought you'd know me, sir, this long time!

RICHARD Why not? Did you not save my life twice over? Once with your battle-axe and once with food. Do you remember that march? Twenty-eight miles without food or water. And then we sat under a hedge together and shared bread and meat. I could have eaten a horse!

THACKER Well, now that it won't do any harm, sir, I don't mind telling you that it was horse.

RICHARD It was ambrosia. I can taste it yet. It is very good to see you again, Bob; so well and prosperous. Are these friends of yours?

THACKER This is Roger Kemp of the Drapers' Guild, your Grace. And this is Ben Willett, who makes the best shoes in Gloucester.

RICHARD Perhaps he will make a pair for me.

WILLETT (*too stunned by this condescension to make proper rejoinder, seizing his chance*) May it please your Grace, on behalf of all the trade guilds of Gloucester, we ask your—we pray your acceptance—your Grace's acceptance of this small gift, as a mark of our affection and loyalty.

RICHARD (*opening the lid of the casket and seeing the contents*) But this is a very great sum of money.

THACKER (*proudly*) A thousand pounds, your Grace.

RICHARD So much! That is indeed a princely gift. You will not take it amiss, I hope, if I say that while I have your hearts I have no need of gold. Let me keep the casket, which is beautiful, and I shall leave the gold to the Guilds of Gloucester to spend as it seems good to them on my behalf. (*Aware that little* WILLETT *is longing to set it down somewhere*) Perhaps you would like to put it down here meanwhile. Do not think me churlish to refuse so brave a gift. I shall never forget that you offered it to me, and my heart will never cease to warm at the recollection.

THACKER If your Grace ever needs it, you know where to come for the money.

RICHARD Thank you, Bob Thacker. I shall remember. And now——

THACKER The Blacksmiths' Guild are giving a play in your honour in the courtyard, sir, and they hope that you will grace it with your presence.

RICHARD Yes, certainly we must see the play. When does it begin?

THACKER When your Grace and the Court are ready.

RICHARD Stanley, go and warn the Court that there is entertainment forward.

[*Exit* STANLEY, *L.*]

And Lovell, perhaps you would see that my friends have something to eat and drink before the play? (LOVELL *leads the way out after they have taken leave of* RICHARD) Have you children, Bob?

THACKER (*pausing on the threshold*) Three children and a grandchild, sir.

RICHARD I should like to meet them before I leave Gloucester. Perhaps you would bring them one day.

THACKER (*overcome*) That's very kind of your Grace. They will be greatly honoured. (*Tentatively*) My wife too, sir?

RICHARD Your wife, too.

THACKER I don't mean to presume, but she'd never let me hear the end of it if she wasn't included, you see, sir. Thank you, sir. God save your Grace.

[*Exit* THACKER.]

RICHARD (*looking after him, smiling*) The salt of the earth.

BUCKINGHAM (*running his fingers through the gold pieces in the coffer*) A thousand pounds! Are you mad, Richard? All that for a gesture!

RICHARD What makes you think that it was a gesture?

BUCKINGHAM Well, wasn't it? What was it but buying their goodwill?

RICHARD I have no need to buy their loyalty.

BUCKINGHAM It was the same at Reading, at Oxford, at Woodstock. So—so *superfluous*! They *expect* to pay the expenses of a royal progress.

RICHARD I should have to be very poor before I taxed my people for the pleasure of my presence.

BUCKINGHAM That sounds noble, but actually it is very selfish. If you have no personal need of the money, your followers might be glad of it.

RICHARD There is not a man in England who ever gave me as much as a shoe-latch that has not been amply rewarded these last months.

BUCKINGHAM True; but your nobles have heavy expenses in gracing your progress, and no offerings to balance the cost.

RICHARD Henry, Duke of Buckingham, lord of all the

manors, lordships, and lands of De Bohun, Constable of England, Chief Justice and Chamberlain of North and South Wales, steward of the royal manors in England and governor of all the royal castles of Wales.

BUCKINGHAM (*half defensive, half defiant*) Well?

RICHARD And you grudge a few tradesmen their little heap of gold! (*As* BUCKINGHAM *merely looks mulish and angry*) What ails you, Harry, that you grin like a child needing physic? It is not like you to be so ungracious. (*With a faint smile*) Have the rigours of the progress been too much for you?

BUCKINGHAM (*not relaxing*) I confess it is a little tedious to listen to your virtues read from so many different parchments in identical phrases.

RICHARD Change your mind about going to Brecon, and come on with us to Warwick. It will be gay there.

BUCKINGHAM But I have to take Morton to Wales.

RICHARD The good Bishop can help to entertain the ambassadors when they arrive in Warwick. He is an impressive old knave, and if he is allowed to meet France, Spain, and Burgundy only at meals, he can impress without achieving any knavery to speak of. I am hoping great things of the Spanish visit.

BUCKINGHAM (*still a little sulky*) A treaty?

RICHARD Better still; an alliance. A whisper reached me privately that they are going to propose a marriage between the eldest girl and Edward.

BUCKINGHAM Your son!

RICHARD Yes. (*He takes* BUCKINGHAM'S *horror to be astonishment*)

BUCKINGHAM But you would not consider it!

RICHARD Consider it! I should be delighted. Apart from other advantages it would be a bulwark against France.

BUCKINGHAM (*almost wordless with emotion*) But you said—you promised that Edward should marry my daughter.

RICHARD (*astonished*) I? My dear Harry, you made the suggestion once. Twice, now I remember. But we have never even discussed the matter. How could you have——

BUCKINGHAM (*desperately*) But, Richard, a foreign alliance would mean new entanglements.

RICHARD New security, rather; new prestige; new trade. It will be of enormous value to England if we bring it to pass.

BUCKINGHAM It may never happen.

RICHARD I hope very much that it will.

BUCKINGHAM (*realising that it is hopeless*) So your boasted desire to reconcile York and Lancaster fades as soon as a foreign gew-gaw is dangled in front of your nose.

RICHARD (*with superhuman restraint*) I think you overrate your importance to the House of Lancaster, Harry. And I don't like your tone. We are old friends, certainly, but——

BUCKINGHAM (*all his jealousy and frustration rising to the surface, losing all control*) But you are King of England, and I must not forget it. As if one could! As if the air were not thick with hosannas day and night, the whole country gone crazy with flung caps and daft creatures singing your praises, silly towns-people bringing you gifts and silly countrymen running to open gates so that the coin you give them can be passed down to their children's children like a holy emblem. When we acclaimed you at Westminster do you think it was to watch you play the Pope in England, the righteous, the infallible, the benevolent godhead! It makes me sick to watch your graces and your posturings, and when I remember how I shouted for you when they put the crown on your head I could cut my tongue out!

RICHARD (*as* BUCKINGHAM *stops for breath, contemplating him, cold with shock, withdrawn*) My brother had his faults but he was an extraordinarily clever man.

BUCKINGHAM (*surprised by his quiet and by the unexpected remark*) Edward?

RICHARD He said that you would want the earth. (*The emphasis is on* '*said*') As a brooch for your bonnet, I think he said.

BUCKINGHAM (*roughly*) I don't know what you are talking about.

RICHARD (*ignoring him*) I gave you so much of England that it is hardly a butterfly's journey from one piece of Stafford land to the next. I gave you separate honours for each piece. And all the time you were sick with envy of the only thing that I could not give you: the thin gold circle round my head. (*Going*) It will be quiet at Brecon. In Morton's company you will have no one to sing my praises in your ears. Perhaps the respite from that exasperating sound may induce a change of heart. I hope so. It may not be in your power to serve me with pleasure but you can at least serve England with efficiency. That is still our mutual interest.

[*Exit* RICHARD.]

[BUCKINGHAM *is left glaring at the coffer of gold and contemplating the almost unbearable prospect of not being the father of the Queen of England.*

[*Enter R.* MORTON, *crossing to the other door L. He is carrying a book and some manuscript. He pauses by the coffer.*

MORTON Charming. Quite charming.

BUCKINGHAM (*rudely*) The coffer or the gold?

MORTON (*smoothly*) So much gold in so fine a coffer. Are you not going to see the play, my lord.

BUCKINGHAM No. Since I am not King, I do not have to endure the mummery.

MORTON (*instantly aware of the atmosphere*) It you will forgive the impertinence, I am surprised that you endure so much.

BUCKINGHAM (*taken aback*) I?

MORTON It has long amazed me that a man of your brilliance should be content to play the obedient shadow.

BUCKINGHAM (*dismissing it angrily*) What do you suggest that I do? (*The accent is on suggest*) There is room for only one King in England.

MORTON (*reasonably*) Only one at a time, of course.

BUCKINGHAM (*having eyed him, coldly*) I have no pretensions to a throne.

MORTON Oh, my good lord Duke, any fool with the right blood in him can sit on a throne. It takes talent to stand behind one.

BUCKINGHAM There is no room behind Richard's throne for even a lost farthing.

MORTON (*without emphasis*) Why Richard's? (*As* BUCKINGHAM *absorbs this*) Because Warwick is dead, are there to be no more king-makers?

BUCKINGHAM For a prisoner, my lord Bishop, you are extraordinarily free with your tongue.

MORTON That is the only freedom left to a prisoner. Besides, it is delightful to talk treason on a bright August afternoon. One partakes of that sharp joy with which women deceive their husbands. The nearness of the axe makes the sunlight more intense.

BUCKINGHAM (*his lack of interest in the* BISHOP'S *moralising leaving his mind free again for his own wrongs, blurting it out, half unaware, half looking like a child for any sympathy that may be handy*) He is going to marry Edward to one of the Spanish princesses.

MORTON (*aware of the capitulation, but interested in the history*)

Ah. A shrewd move. (*Giving the devil his due*) Constructive, as always.

BUCKINGHAM (*not looking at him*) My daughter was to have—— (*The enormity of it overcomes him*)

MORTON I see. A sad blow. Of course, if the boy ceased to be Prince of Wales, that would be very sad, in turn, for the Spanish princess.

BUCKINGHAM (*in a don't-be-a-fool tone*) My lord; you have made this progress with us, you have seen Richard with the people, you know as well as I do that they dote on him.

MORTON In any country there is always the Disaffected Fourth. The square pegs in round holes, the lazy, the greedy, the restless, the (*with a side-glance at* BUCKINGHAM) envious, the misunderstood, the mischief-makers. A wonderful instrument, the Disaffected Fourth. Failing them, there is always Kent.

BUCKINGHAM Kent?

MORTON You have only to ride through Kent crying: 'Unfair! Unfair!' and by the end of the day you will have five thousand men all burning to redress a wrong.

BUCKINGHAM I have only to ride through Wales jingling a money-bag to have an army. Much good that would be without a cause. Where is the rallying cry!

MORTON Why a cry? A whisper is more effective than a shout. You can destroy an empire with a whisper.

BUCKINGHAM Perhaps. You can't lead an army with one. An army wants to fight for someone.

MORTON There are still Edward's sons.

BUCKINGHAM No one is interested any longer in the existence of two illegitimate brats.

MORTON They might be highly interested in their non-existence. (*Meeting* BUCKINGHAM'S *eyes with their growing surmise*) A whisper, only. Nothing more. A question, a light wondering. 'Why have the children not been seen lately?'

BUCKINGHAM And when it becomes obvious that they are busy doing Latin versions in the Tower? What then?

MORTON By that time a new king is on the throne, and no one in authority has ever heard of those odd and quite baseless rumours.

BUCKINGHAM A new King? (*His attention is really arrested now*)

MORTON (*as one picking from a wide choice*) There is Henry Tudor.

BUCKINGHAM (*in instant scorn*) Against *Richard*?

MORTON (*smoothly*) Against a discredited Richard.

BUCKINGHAM Tudor is in France. No one has ever seen him. And the English are tired of the Lancaster claim.

MORTON You forget that he is Welsh as well as Lancastrian. I understand that he is the descendant of a thousand kings—including Arthur—and his pedigree goes back into the mists of time. Noah appears about half-way down. The Welsh would be charmed with the idea of Henry. With the Welsh, the Disaffected Fourth, Kent—— (*he is ticking them off on his thick fingers*)

[*Enter* LORD STANLEY, *and* MORTON *sees him over* BUCKINGHAM'S *shoulder.*]

—and the Stanley family, how could one fail?

BUCKINGHAM (*unaware of* STANLEY'S *entrance*) The Stanleys?

STANLEY Someone is making very free with my name.

MORTON (*before* BUCKINGHAM *can say anything*) We are discussing your step-son's invasion of England.

STANLEY What!

BUCKINGHAM (*in the same breath, horrified*) My lord!

MORTON (*going on, as if he were discussing the cut of a coat*) Provided that you personally were involved in no danger, you have no objection, I take it, to your wife's son making a bid for a throne?

STANLEY I think the jest is in poor taste, my lord. I am a loyal subject of King Richard (*he raises his voice unconsciously, as if to assure both himself and any stray listener*), and I cannot imagine how—how—— (*He looks from* BUCKINGHAM *to* MORTON *at a loss*)

MORTON How the lion and the lamb are lying down together.

BUCKINGHAM (*half suspicious, half beginning to enjoy the enormity of it*) Am I the sheep?

MORTON Oh, no, sir; the English lion.

STANLEY I say again that——

MORTON (*interrupting*) That you are a good servant of the King and doing very well. But it would be pleasant to feel safe, wouldn't it?

STANLEY Safe?

MORTON With Henry Tudor you would not have to wonder.

STANLEY Wonder what, my lord?

MORTON When someone is going to play the informer.

STANLEY I don't follow you. (*He sounds cold and frightened*)

MORTON Any hour, any moment, someone or other—bored

with prison, shall we say?—may be moved to buy his freedom by talking. And then what becomes of those Stanley estates, those thousands of retainers—who would fight so excellently for Henry.

STANLEY I will not listen to you. It is treason. It is a trap. I have my family to think of. (*This last is quite automatic*)

MORTON (*in the same unaccented voice, like counsel wearing down a witness*) Buckingham has large interests in Wales, both personal and political. You have a Welsh step-son, and lands on the Welsh border. You have also Lady Stanley. With such a combination you could shake England to its foundations.

BUCKINGHAM Stanley shakes in his shoes at the very thought.

STANLEY (*stung*) That is not true. I have as much courage as the next man. I have my family to think of.

BUCKINGHAM Long live the Stanleys! And may they die in their beds.

MORTON It could not be, could it, that Lady Stanley might be moved to inspect the beauties of Brecon this fine weather?

STANLEY What my wife does is her own affair. How long are you to be in Brecon?

BUCKINGHAM (*catching* MORTON'S *glance with ironic amusement*) Until my prisoner sees the error of his ways.

[*Enter* MARK, *who looks oddly and shrewdly at the grouping.*]

MARK (*on his way from the door L. to the door R.*) I am commanded to say that the play is about to begin, my lords.

[*Exit* MARK *R.*]

MORTON (*to* BUCKINGHAM) Do you feel more inclined to support the mummery now, my lord?

BUCKINGHAM (*cheerfully*) By all means let us see the play. (*He leads the way out*) Let us hope that the invention is as brilliant as the Bishop of Ely's.

MORTON My lord, you do me too much honour.

STANLEY (*at their heels*) Remember, I know nothing of all this. Nothing whatever. I have my family to think of.

CURTAIN

SCENE 2

A room in Salisbury, on the morning of the 2nd of November, 1483. The plan of the room is the same as the previous one, with two exceptions: down from the door R. is a window looking down on a courtyard (it is a first-floor room), and the door L. is several feet above floor level, so that anyone entering comes first on to a small platform and turns sideways to descend the few steps to the room. From the edge of the platform rises a tall screen of carved wood which serves the double purpose of breaking the draught from the door and of preventing accidents. The upper part of the screen is fretted, so that one can see the room through it.

It is not a room that has been lived in, and the furnishings are even barer than those normal to the period. On a seat, down L., CLEMENT *is once more discovered at work on a poem.*

CLEMENT ' No days-eye pied
Has ever vied ' No. That is unworthy.

' No days-eye sweet
Beneath her feet
Shall bend its head
So light her tread.' So light her tread.

[*Enter* MARK *at speed, and much excited. He comes in at the R. door, crosses to* CLEMENT *to jog him physically into awareness and without stopping makes for the window.*]

MARK Clement! Clement, they have arrived. Come and see. (*As* CLEMENT *is slow as always in accepting the world of reality*) They are here, I tell you!

CLEMENT (*not moving*) Who are?

MARK (*at the window, looking down on the courtyard*) The escort from Shrewsbury with the prisoner.

CLEMENT Buckingham? (*He gets to his feet*)

MARK Yes, Buckingham. Come and see.

CLEMENT (*at the window*) I don't see anyone who looks like—— (*Having found* BUCKINGHAM *he stops incredulously*)

MARK (*answering the astonished pause*) Yes. A change in wardrobe, isn't there!

CLEMENT Is that——! (*He can hardly believe it*) He looks like a pedlar, a vagabond.

MARK So would you if you had been rained on for ten days and then dried off in a cottar's cupboard.

CLEMENT Is that where they found him?

MARK Yes. Dragged out like a cur that has taken refuge from a beating. Constable of England! Not much of the courtier left, is there?

CLEMENT You need not gloat over him.

MARK Are you preparing to sob?

CLEMENT (*coldly*) I shed no tears over a traitor; but that is no reason I should be happy over a man's downfall. (*Looking at* MARK *curiously*) You are *pleased* about it, aren't you?

MARK I hate a fool and I despise a failure.

CLEMENT But you might fail, yourself, some day.

MARK Never. If there was an earthquake I would come out of it sitting on top of a newly uncovered vein of gold. (*His attention going back to the courtyard*) Well, he pinned his faith to the Welsh, and lost even the pin, poor fool! I must go. I am on duty in the ante-room. You can pretend you are on duty too if you want a closer look at him.

CLEMENT (*with something like passion*) No! I don't want to see him any more at all!

MARK Oh, very well. There is no accounting for tastes. But clear out of here before Stanley brings him up.

[*Exit* MARK *R.*]

CLEMENT (*gathering up his manuscript from the seat*) Ah, my lady, it is a poor world the real one.

[*Exit* CLEMENT *up the steps L.*]

[*Enter L.* BUCKINGHAM *in charge of* STANLEY. *He is still wearing the soft leather jerkin that he wore under his armour. It is stiff and discoloured with rain and patterned over with marks from rusty armour and stain from wet soil. He is not muddy or unwashed (there has been no deliberate attempt to humiliate him) and his hair is combed; but his face is haggard, and shadowed with a three-days' beard, his boots are broken, and his hose pulled by briars. His bearing is nonchalant, and gives no hint of the seething cauldron of emotion underneath.*]

BUCKINGHAM You know, my dear Stanley, the righteous look on your face is the only amusing thing that has come my way for ten days. Is Richard developing a sense of humour when he made you my gaoler? Or is it that he still has no nose for treachery?

STANLEY Oh, please, my lord, not so loud!

BUCKINGHAM I used to despise you, Stanley, for a damnable

sitter on fences. But, by the saints, I begin to admire you. Your talent for having your cake and eating it must be unique. Well, when do I see the King? You might at least lend me a better tunic to appear in. What with the gale and the floods and the rain this is not so much a garment as a map. A diary, in fact. That (*a stain on his sleeve*) was a ditch at Weobley, and that (*a tear on the other sleeve*) was a briar in the Forest of Dean, and that (*a dark patch on one hip*) a mouldy haystack in Shropshire—and (*his voice suddenly slackening and some of the bitterness seeping to the surface*) not a bloodstain in the lot!

STANLEY My lord, you have been unfortunate. I hope you will not drag others down with you into misfortune.

BUCKINGHAM Are you going to tell me that you have a family to think of? By the way, is your wife in prison?

STANLEY No. No, she is at home, so far. I am hoping that no evidence will—er—— That is why I suggest that you say as little as possible that may——

[*Enter* LOVELL, *L.* STANLEY, *who is facing him, breaks off as he comes down the steps, bows slightly in reply to* LOVELL'S *movement of dismissal, and goes abruptly.*]

I shall hope to see you again, my lord.

[*Exit* STANLEY.]

[BUCKINGHAM, *aware that someone has come in, turns quickly, makes two impetuous steps forward, and then sees who it is.*]

BUCKINGHAM (*disappointed but pleasant*) Oh, it is you, Lovell. I thought it was Richard.

LOVELL No. I am commanded to receive you. There have been commissions that I liked better. (*His tone is unaccented but somehow forbidding and scornful. To the loyal* LOVELL, BUCKINGHAM *is scarcely human; some lower form of life whose cerebrations if any are beyond the understanding of man*) So neither the weather nor the Welsh would fight for you.

BUCKINGHAM Not even the saints, it appears. Perhaps Morton has the monopoly. I hear that he is safe in France. And Henry Tudor never landed at all. Stanley should appreciate so cautious a step-son! But you, my kind Lovell, can do something for me. Give me some clothes to take the place of these. I can hardly exercise my charm on Richard with a torn tunic and a three-days' beard. Some of your own things might fit me.

LOVELL You are not going to speak with the King, my lord.

BUCKINGHAM Not——! But I must.

LOVELL He refuses to see you.

BUCKINGHAM But I must talk to Richard! (*Looking round for argument*) I am a condemned man. He cannot refuse to grant me a last interview. That is my right!

LOVELL You have no rights, my lord. You are a traitor, caught red-handed in your treason.

BUCKINGHAM He can afford to be generous, surely? There can never have been a more contemptible rebellion. Washed away in floods of water. Not a wound, not a tear, not a banner. Nothing but floods and flight. If I am to die for so sorry a piece of mischief, he can surely spare me a few moments of his time?

LOVELL That is the message, my lord: he will not see you.

BUCKINGHAM You speak for me, Francis. He loves you. Tell him what I have said, that he can afford to be generous, and plead with him for me.

[RICHARD *appears L. and stands watching through the screen.*]

LOVELL (*without heat*) I never liked you, Harry Stafford, and I would not petition the Queen of Heaven for you. You had the chance to serve the best King this country has ever known. You could have had a life of honour and achievement. But you could never bear to come second, even in a game.

BUCKINGHAM Oh, come, Francis, because you have a passion for service——

LOVELL If it had not been for an accident of weather, you would at this moment be waging civil war over the face of England—and then you ask me to plead for you with the man whose very heart is England!

BUCKINGHAM Oh, Lovell, have some pity. If I am not to be allowed a plea for mercy, surely I can at least ask his forgiveness before I die! Two little minutes is all I ask, two little minutes out of all the time he has in store. Speak to him again. Say that I pray, as my last request on earth, that I may see him face to face just once more. Let him refuse the forgiveness if he must, but don't deny me the chance of asking for it!

LOVELL (*his calm glance sliding down from* BUCKINGHAM'S *face to his belt*) When they took your dagger from you, why did they leave the sheath?

BUCKINGHAM (*taken aback*) I had no dagger. I lost it—in a hay-rick where I slept.

[LOVELL *takes a leisurely step forward, and then with a quick movement seizes* BUCKINGHAM'S *right arm below the elbow with his left. His right arm, on its way to explore* BUCKINGHAM'S *sleeve, is caught by* BUCKINGHAM'S *left, and in the sudden short struggle the dagger drops from* BUCKINGHAM'S *right sleeve to the floor.* LOVELL *puts his foot on it.*]

BUCKINGHAM God curse you, Lovell!

LOVELL So that was the plan, assassin!

BUCKINGHAM I had lived for that these ten days.

LOVELL A pretty business for a Stafford. No, leave it!

BUCKINGHAM Dreamed day and night of the moment when I would achieve it, when I would be alone with him, and could put an end for ever to his glory! Did you really think that I was going snivelling to Richard for mercy? Forgiveness? I would count my life well lost if I took his reign with me. And now I shall have to die and leave him in possession! Leave him in the full tide of his magnificence. God curse you, Lovell, you miserable watch-dog, why did you do it?

LOVELL On the water-front in London you can buy assassins at two shillings a time. They die a horrid death when they are caught. If your Stafford blood does not revolt at the cheapness of your company, you ought at least to be glad of the block that waits you this afternoon. It is a more comfortable death than you deserve. Guard! (*The door R. opens to admit the Captain of the Guard and two soldiers*) I am handing you over to the Captain of the King's Guard. Any further petitions you have to make will be made through him.

BUCKINGHAM (*quiet now*) I shall be cursing you with my last breath, Francis.

LOVELL And I shall always be gratified to have earned your curses, my lord.

[*Exit* BUCKINGHAM, *guarded.*]

[LOVELL *picks up the dagger from the floor.*]

[RICHARD *comes down from the platform and walks slowly across to the window.*]

RICHARD (*as* LOVELL *makes an attempt to hide the dagger he is holding; looking neither at* LOVELL *nor the dagger; quietly*) You need not hide it. (*He stands by the window waiting for* BUCKINGHAM *and his guard to appear in the courtyard. When they do he watches them. With a contempt too deep for hatred*) Poor Harry! If he could have brought himself to eat cottar's food like a man, he would be free now. But he needs must have dainties, even under a thatch roof. And so they caught him. (*Turning as* BUCKINGHAM *goes out of sight*) I want Kendal to write to the Duchess of Buckingham. The estates are forfeit, of course. But tell her that I shall pay her husband's debts. That will astonish poor Harry's unaccustomed ghost. And that I shall give her an adequate pension. She is not to be distressed about money. It cannot be very pleasant for her in Wales just now. If she wants to be near her sister in London, say that I will give her safe-conduct for herself, her children, and her household.

LOVELL (*in a burst*) Christ, Dickon! I love you like a brother, but I shall never understand you, never! (*Pulling himself together*) Lord Stanley says that you want to see him, sir.

RICHARD Oh, yes. Send him in.

LOVELL (*indicating the dagger, tentatively*) What shall I do with this?

RICHARD I understand that the well in the courtyard is the deepest in England.

LOVELL (*going*) Yes, sir.

[STANLEY *is waiting at the door and is ushered in as* LOVELL *goes.*]

STANLEY (*very nervous*) You wanted to see me, sir.

RICHARD Yes. Perhaps you can guess the business on hand.

STANLEY No, sir; no.

RICHARD I want you to succeed Buckingham as Constable of England.

STANLEY (*utterly flummoxed*) Your Grace! (*His mouth opens and shuts vainly*)

RICHARD (*half amused*) That, I take it, is acceptance. I want you to know now that I had enough evidence of your part in the Hastings conspiracy to have ruined you. I didn't use it—partly because you had served Edward well, and partly because England's need for capable men is very great. Your loyalty in this sorry business has been my justification. There is, of course, the matter of your wife. Lady Stanley's part in this rebellion has been so riotously public that I shall have great difficulty in saving her from the block. Parliament is not generous to those who make civil war. However, I can promise that it will not come to that. Imprisonment, of course, there must be, but I cannot expect you to serve England with a light heart if your wife is rotting in a dungeon. I think the solution is to give her into the keeping of the Constable of England.

STANLEY Your Grace, that is generous.

RICHARD To be shut up securely in one of her own castles,

with every comfort but without communication. You promised once before to be responsible for her.

STANLEY (*penitently*) Yes, sir. It is not easy.

RICHARD (*dryly*) Knowing Lady Stanley, I believe that. This time it will be no affair of a light promise. It will be your security against hers.

STANLEY I accept that, sir.

RICHARD Only the ring-leaders in this business will pay the penalty. The little men must be free to settle back in safety. There is to be no legacy of bitterness if I can help it. At the beginning of the year we shall have a Parliament. When that is over, and the first benefits begin to show in England, we must come to some permanent understanding with Scotland. And then, who knows, with France. Or is that too wild a dream?

STANLEY (*considering the happy prospect*) It will be odd to have no enemy across the Channel.

RICHARD It will be very awkward for your step-son. The French are his only friends. (*Giving him his hand to kiss*) I shall see you at dinner, my lord. If we have no appetite we can at least make the gesture. (*As* STANLEY *is going out*) I am hoping that Edward's wife may be persuaded to leave sanctuary soon.

STANLEY (*poised in departure*, *tentatively*) But—I understood that she was involved in this affair.

RICHARD Yes. But that is over. She is a sensible woman. She will take the bird-in-hand. It is very uncomfortable in sanctuary.

[STANLEY *bows and goes.*]

[RICHARD *moves over to the window again and stands looking down on the courtyard.*]

CURTAIN

SCENE 3

A room in Nottingham Castle, in the second week of April 1484. *It is a small withdrawing-room, up the steps from the main hall, and has the same lived-in look that the room at Middleham had. There is a comfortable settle down stage, and a small table up R. The only door is a small one up L. Cushions, footstools, books, a growing plant, and such evidences of familiar occupation.*

On the settle, very much at home, is a squire; and once more he is busy with pen and paper. But one is astounded to find that it is not CLEMENT *but* MARK. *He goes through all the motions of a poet in the throes: the shut eye, the distant gaze, the reference to the paper, the tilted head, the recorded inspiration. One is amazed that the materialistic Mark can have succumbed to so tender a passion. Presently his mutterings become audible.*

MARK Five shillings for keeping my eyes shut on the 20th. Ten shillings on the 23rd for keeping my eyes open. A shilling for finding out where Lady Dacre got that green satin. Four and sixpence for bearing a letter to Tanner's mistress. (*He adds these items up with what has gone before, and considers the total*) Not enough, my boy. You must get yourself some new connections.

[*Enter* LORD STANLEY. MARK *scrambles hastily to his feet and disposes of his book-keeping.*]

MARK My lord.

STANLEY (*in the quick lowered voice of the surreptitious*) The horses came from Cheshire this morning.

MARK Yes, my lord.

STANLEY There was a letter for me?

MARK No, my lord. Lady Stanley said that nothing must be put in writing.

STANLEY But your cousin was entrusted with a message? (*As* MARK *nods*) And you received it?

MARK Yes, my lord. Lady——

STANLEY Leave that name out of it.

MARK Yes, my lord. There is word from the Continent. There will be no peace with France. The French plan an invasion next spring. Morton is in good standing there, and has great influence.

STANLEY And—Henry Tudor?

MARK The French will put him on the throne if the invasion succeeds.

STANLEY (*giving him a coin*) You understand that I am not condoning treason. One must know what is liable to happen. I have a family to think of. (*He is justifying his conduct more to himself than to the squire*)

MARK Thank you very much, my lord.

[*As* STANLEY *goes, enter* CLEMENT *bearing a tray with a silver jug of spiced wine and three cups. He bows over them to* STANLEY *and then deposits them on the small table, up R.*]

CLEMENT Another new coat! How do you do it, Mark? I thought your parents were as poor as mine.

MARK My talent for making money is mercifully greater than my parents' was.

CLEMENT Are you going into Lord Stanley's service?

MARK (*genuinely horrified*) You think I would leave the royal household!

CLEMENT He seems to have taken a liking to you.

MARK It is only that I have a cousin in Lady Stanley's service.

CLEMENT (*with loathing*) *That* woman!

MARK Her table is better than most. (*Indicating the wine*) I suppose that is not for mere squires.

CLEMENT No. It is for the Queen. Supper is over, and she will be coming to rest for a little. (*Distressed*) She is looking very ill, isn't she?

MARK (*with a shrug*) She will go the way her sister did.

CLEMENT Oh, no!

MARK A decline, they called it. But it is so rapid they might as well say a precipice.

CLEMENT I hate you sometimes, Mark. (*As the sound of women's laughing voices is heard outside*) Here they are.

[*They stand on either side of the door as the* QUEEN *comes in, followed by the* PRINCESS ELIZABETH. *She is looking tired but happy, and is smiling at something* ELIZABETH *has said. They are both in party attire.*]

ANNE (*amused*) You are a forward child, Elizabeth. You must curb your tongue if you are going to stay at Court. (*She has come down to establish herself on the settle*) Have you heard from your mother lately?

ELIZABETH Yes. She is well, but she is very tired of living in the country. She hopes that the King will let her come to Court again one of these days.

ANNE (*reassuring*) I expect he will.

ELIZABETH You look tired, Aunt Anne. Let me get you some hippocras. (*Going to the table*) Is the party too much for you?

ANNE No; oh, no. I am very well.

ELIZABETH (*busy with the wine*) It is these boring ambassadors.

Are all ambassadors odd? Or is it only Scots ones who are queer? That little man who sat next me, the one with the pink beard——

ANNE Red. That is Scots red.

ELIZABETH Well, with the Scots-red beard; he said: 'You have a grand King now, lassie.' (*She imitates his broad accent*) 'I hear that he gave you the best Parliament since Edward the First.' I asked him if they had parliaments in Scotland, and he said: 'Whiles.' (*She has poured out two cups of wine and now brings one down to the* QUEEN) What does that mean?

ANNE It means: as often as they can trust each other under one roof. (*Sipping her wine*) Ah, that is very good. Go back now, Elizabeth dear. You want to dance, I know.

ELIZABETH No, I want some hippocras. (*She goes to collect the second cup from the table*) And I like being here with you. It was kind of you to give me the beautiful gown—to comfort me for being a bastard.

ANNE My dear, you must not let that rankle.

ELIZABETH (*cheerfully*) Oh, I don't. I don't really mind at all. (*Bringing her drink down to the settle*) All the best people are bastards. Shall I tell you a secret? I am hoping that, now that no one will want to marry me for my rank, I may find someone who will want to marry me for my eyelashes.

ANNE We shall find you someone nice, Elizabeth. Someone who will give you a thousand beautiful gowns so that you may shine at parties as you are shining tonight.

ELIZABETH You don't really like parties, do you?

ANNE To be honest, I never see a laden table but I think of the washing-up.

ELIZABETH (*after an astonished pause*) Did you *really* wash dishes in a kitchen!

ANNE At a low estimate I should say several hundred million.

ELIZABETH I thought that was just a tale! How dreadful! The grease, and the smells.

ANNE And the loneliness.

ELIZABETH Yes, no one to talk to.

ANNE I had no standing, you see. I was imported labour, and of no account whatever. There is very strong class feeling in kitchens.

ELIZABETH (*surprised at this topsy-turvy world*) Oh. And did Uncle Richard really rescue you?

ANNE He did. (*Her thoughts going back to it*) I knew he

would. It had been like that when we were small. Richard always solved my difficulties for me.

ELIZABETH (*fascinated by the romance*) Did you know each other again?

ANNE Oh, yes. It was only five years, after all.

ELIZABETH What did *you* say?

ANNE (*expelling her breath in a soundless laugh*) I began to cry all of a sudden because my hands were red. It had not seemed to matter until then.

ELIZABETH And what did *he* say?

ANNE He said: 'You've grown, Anne.' It was such an absurd thing to say after all the exiles, and the battles, and the persecutions, that we both began to laugh.

ELIZABETH And did he marry you then and there?

ANNE Oh, no. Richard always does the correct thing. He took me to sanctuary at St Martin's.

ELIZABETH And then asked the King for your hand? (*As* ANNE *nods*) How wonderful! It is just like a tale from the romances. I wish something like that would happen to me.

ANNE (*amused*) I hope not!

[*Enter* CLEMENT *with two letters.*]

CLEMENT A letter for the Queen's grace.

ANNE (*examining the superscription*) Oh; from Jane Collins at Middleham.

CLEMENT There is also one for the King, madam.

ANNE You may leave it here. The King will be coming presently.

[*Exit* CLEMENT.]

Edward is too old for Jane's ministrations now, but she still writes to me about him. (*She is smiling at the unopened letter*) How the new feather looks in his cap, and the clever thing he said a week last Thursday. Find the King, Elizabeth, and whisper that there is a letter for him from Middleham.

ELIZABETH (*resuming, half in play, her court manner*) Yes, madam. At my best speed. (*Pausing on her way to the door*) About that marriage of mine—— I don't want anyone with a pink beard.

ANNE I promise you that the beard shall not be pink.

ELIZABETH No beard at all.

ANNE No beard.

[*Exit* ELIZABETH *with a sweeping obeisance.*]

[ANNE, *having postponed the moment a little longer, resigns herself to the pleasure of opening the letter. She reads, makes a half motion to get up as she sees the contents of the letter, but is unable to, and reads the letter to the end. Very slowly the paper is lowered to her lap, her eyes staying where the words have been as if she could still read them in the air.*

[*After a long pause, enter* RICHARD, *pleased with life and as gay as it is in his natural quietness to be.*]

RICHARD Well, they seem to be enjoying themselves. A simple race, the Scots. They need only two things to be happy, drink and argument. There has been a courier from Middleham, I hear. (*He crosses to the little table and pours out some wine*) I hope you are not tired, Anne? (*He casts a glance at her back*)

ANNE No. No. (*The difficult monosyllables sound merely indifferent*)

RICHARD Light conversation is not their best point. But at least we have the treaty. I wish I could come to as friendly an understanding with those light conversationalists, the French. (*Bringing the drink down and putting it on the tall stool to* ANNE'S *L., where the letter to him is lying*) I am beginning to dream, of nights, about that French peace treaty. It is the one thing we need now for security. (*He puts out his hand to pick up the letter, but she covers his hand with her own*)

ANNE (*involuntarily*) Don't open it.

RICHARD (*surprised*) What is this? (*Seeing her face; wary but not yet alarmed*) Is something wrong?

ANNE (*after a fruitless effort to make her lips form the words at the first attempt; quietly*) We have lost our son, Dickon.

RICHARD (*after a silence, not moving, meaninglessly*) When?

ANNE On the 9th, she says.

[RICHARD *takes the open letter from her lap, and reads.*]

ANNE He was all I had. You have England. You have your work, and your crown, and your treaties. Your battles, your victories. (*Dry sobs are beginning to come up through her words*) I have nothing like that. I had only Edward. He was my life. (*As he comes to the end of the letter; putting out a hand to touch his, as if in apology, controlling herself*) That is not true. He was your life too.

RICHARD Security, I said. Where is there security?

[ANNE *gives way entirely, putting her elbows on her knees, and her face in her hands, and rocking herself in an agony of weeping. He sits down beside her on the settle.*]

RICHARD Don't, Anne. (*She turns to him, burying her face in his lap, and he holds her, comforting her like a child*) Don't, my dear.

ANNE (*muffled in sobs*) Why? Oh, why, why, why? We have been good, haven't we? We have never wronged anyone.

RICHARD (*to himself more than to her*) Perhaps I was glad in my heart about Edward's children. Perhaps I was.

ANNE (*presently; more quietly*) I shall not mind dying so much now.

RICHARD Anne, what are you saying?

ANNE It was always Edward that I was afraid to leave. You did not need me so much. Now you can have other sons.

RICHARD I sometimes think that there is no cruelty like that of a kind woman.

ANNE (*raising her head*) I do not mean to be cruel, Dickon. You know the truth as well as I do. It is not like you to avoid the truth.

RICHARD Anne, have mercy. (*His arms go out desperately to enclose her. She lies sobbing gently on his shoulder, while he stares into desolation*)

[*Enter* ELIZABETH, *on wings, full of confidence and happiness. What she has come to say dies on her lips. She stands poised, unseen, aghast. She moves backwards uncertainly, and goes.*]

CURTAIN

SCENE 4

The Scene is the same as the first of the play: the room in Westminster Palace. It is shortly before Easter, 1485. *The room is no longer the scene of a party, and it has lost its air of fashion, though it is still beautiful. What was the supper-table is now a writing-table piled with documents, at which* RICHARD, *on the up side of the table, is working. It is late afternoon, and only the fire in the hearth to his L. makes a spot of cheer in the scene.*

Having worked through a document, RICHARD *signs it, and adds it to a pile. There are still other piles on the table, but he props his forehead in his hands with a sigh of deep weariness.*

Enter, up R., LOVELL. *He pauses as he sees* RICHARD'S *attitude, and after a moment begins to go quietly away; but* RICHARD *has heard him.*]

RICHARD (*not moving*) Is that you, Francis?

LOVELL I didn't want to disturb you, sir, but it will soon be dark, and you have been at work since the morning.

RICHARD (*running his hands despairingly through the papers*) Money for the Navy, money for coast defences, money for continual levies, money for horsemen posted every twenty miles on all the main roads, money for intelligence, money to strengthen Calais—— I wish the fellow would make his invasion and be done with it, or we shall be bankrupt.

LOVELL It can't be much longer, sir. The spring is here.

RICHARD Yes. The spring. (*He says it slowly, thinking of* ANNE, *who has died in March after a long illness, and of the little promise this spring holds for him*) You came to say something.

LOVELL (*feeling that this is not the moment*) No, sir. Nothing important.

RICHARD (*aware of his change of mind*) You came to say something.

LOVELL It will keep till tomorrow.

RICHARD Then it was not pleasant?

LOVELL No, sir. I am afraid that it isn't. But it is something that you must be told about.

RICHARD (*who would never even have thought these words when he was* RICHARD OF GLOUCESTER) Treason, death, or desertion?

LOVELL None of them, sir. But there is a rumour; a libel. (*This is being very difficult for him*)

RICHARD Another?

LOVELL (*making heavy weather of it*) When Anne—when the Queen died there were stories——

RICHARD Yes; I know. I poisoned her, didn't I?

LOVELL (*relieved that* RICHARD *knows at least so much*) That was because of the eclipse of the sun that day. You know what they are. Now they have a new story.

RICHARD Have I killed someone else?

LOVELL No, sir; you are said to be going to marry the Princess.

RICHARD What Princess?

LOVELL Elizabeth.

RICHARD My niece Elizabeth? (*As* LOVELL *has come to the end of his words; rising abruptly in rage that is swamped in loathing and despair before he reaches the fireplace; after a pause*) Edward was right. Men are vile. (*Lifting his head but still with his back to* LOVELL) Agents, do you think? Or just those little people who have no drama in their own lives and so must make a bloody tale of others'?

LOVELL Agents, I think—working in fertile soil.

RICHARD Is my niece in the palace?

LOVELL She is with Cecily in the East Room, sorting old clothes with the nuns from St Leonard's.

RICHARD Ask her to come to me. Send the page.

[LOVELL *goes to the door, up L., and gives the order to the page outside it.*]

RICHARD (*turning to the room again*) Nothing but a public denial can deal with this. The day after tomorrow I shall meet the Mayor of London and the citizens in a public gathering, together with as many lords and bishops as can be summoned in the time. The great hall of St John's should hold them, I think. Letters must go to the mayors of all the principal towns, to detain anyone circulating such reports until they have confessed the source of their information. Perhaps that way we shall uncover the original fount.

LOVELL Shall I give that message to Kendal, sir?

RICHARD Yes. He can be getting on with the letters. I shall come down and see him myself when I have talked with Elizabeth.

[*As* LOVELL *opens the door* ELIZABETH *comes in. She bows with a slight smile to* LOVELL, *who receives her and goes.*]

ELIZABETH My lord. (*Coming down, to* RICHARD) Your Grace sent for me.

[*She is wearing mourning, and some of the spring glory has gone out of her youth, but none of her almost boyish forthrightness and simplicity; her sweet matter-of-factness.*]

RICHARD Yes. (*Looking for a gentle means of breaking it to her*) Elizabeth, you know that princes and personages are open targets for scandal, and that nine times out of ten it is wise to ignore the things that are flung at us.

ELIZABETH So my mother always said.

RICHARD (*remembering* ELIZABETH WOODVILLE'S *talent for avoiding unpleasant facts*) Yes. Unfortunately, a particularly horrible piece of invention is current in the city; so revolting and so dangerous that it cannot be ignored; and because indirectly it concerns you——

ELIZABETH I know. They say that you mean to marry me.

RICHARD (*staggered*) You have heard the story?

ELIZABETH Women have hair to be brushed, you know.

RICHARD (*relaxing for a moment*) Men shave. But my barber didn't tell me that one.

ELIZABETH You can tell a woman anything when you are brushing her hair. What are you going to do?

RICHARD I am going to give the lie to the rumour at a great public meeting at St John's in Clerkenwell. No mere scrap of paper can deal with something that concerns my honour so nearly; and yours. It must be a personal denial, face to face with the people, so that something of what I feel will be apparent to the meanest of them. Meanwhile it is obvious that you cannot stay here. I am going to send you to Sherrif Hutton.

ELIZABETH (*in great dismay*) To Yorkshire! Out of the world!

RICHARD (*with a half smile for this little Cockney*) Into the world. You will find it a much bigger world in the North. I could wish that it was my lot to go.

ELIZABETH But I don't know anyone there.

RICHARD Your cousin Warwick is at Sherrif Hutton. He is a dull boy, but amiable. Perhaps Cecily might brave the terrors of Yorkshire, if you worked on her sisterly devotion.

ELIZABETH Oh, that makes a difference. But must I leave London? Must I?

RICHARD Yes. Tomorrow morning.

ELIZABETH For how long?

RICHARD Until the invasion is over and we have time to arrange a marriage for you.

ELIZABETH Is it coming, the invasion?

RICHARD I hope so. A state of preparedness is very expensive.

ELIZABETH Are you anxious about it?

RICHARD About the fighting, no. But with this long defence the exchequer is empty. I have had to borrow money from my people, and I hate that.

ELIZABETH Can you pay it back?

RICHARD I have promised to.

ELIZABETH Then you will. I don't suppose the people mind. They know it is not for yourself. How can anyone fight for Henry Tudor! A horrid little man with a bald head and a splutter?

RICHARD (*amused at this inaccurate summing-up of* HENRY) If a man wants a parcel of land, or preferment, or a pardon, he is not apt to count the hairs on his benefactor's head. Besides, Henry's army will be largely French.

ELIZABETH Englishmen don't like foreigners tramping over their country.

RICHARD No. I am counting on that.

ELIZABETH (*her voice suddenly small*) I shall pray for your Grace.

RICHARD (*touched*) Thank you, my dear.

ELIZABETH And the moment the fighting is over you will send for me?

RICHARD On the field of victory my first action will be to send a courier to Yorkshire. I envy you, Elizabeth, that space, and quiet, and clean air in the North. I shall think of you often and grudge it to you, you undeserving Cockney. (*He smiles at her*)

ELIZABETH I wish it were not sinful.

RICHARD What?

ELIZABETH To marry you.

RICHARD (*staggered*) Elizabeth!

ELIZABETH Except for my father, I have not loved anyone as much as I have loved you. Even when I was little I used to watch you with him; so faithful and so quiet. Always at hand to cover up his mistakes. Putting England back in his lap every time it slipped.

RICHARD (*embarrassed*) I don't recognise the picture.

ELIZABETH I think that in all the world you are the only kind person I know. You, and Clement.

RICHARD (*realising that this is not a passionate declaration of love, a faint amusement stirring*) Who is Clement?

ELIZABETH (*genuinely different*) One of the squires. We have loved the same people too—Edward, and Anne, and my father. It would have been pleasant to spend the rest of our lives together.

RICHARD Presently you will fall in love, Elizabeth, and you will stop looking behind you.

ELIZABETH Do you know that the French plan to marry me to that Tudor person? That will join York and Lancaster very nicely, they say, and make him more acceptable.

RICHARD I promise you we shall not allow *that* to happen!

ELIZABETH I shouldn't allow it myself. (*Her mind coming back from academic considerations to the reality of the moment*) Shall I see you again before I go?

RICHARD No. I shall be busy in the morning.

ELIZABETH (*impressively taking the thin chain with its medal from her neck*) Will you take my little medal of St Catherine? (*She holds it out in a heap in her palm*)

RICHARD But that is precious to you.

ELIZABETH Please. You have people to give you armies, but no one to give you things like little medals any more.

RICHARD (*interpreting this incoherence correctly*) Yes. I will take it. Thank you, Elizabeth.

ELIZABETH (*sinking on one knee to kiss his hand*) Goodbye, your Grace. I shall always be glad that I knew you.

RICHARD What made you say that?

ELIZABETH (*at a loss*) I don't know. I had an odd feeling that I was not going to see you again.

RICHARD My dear child! Goodbye. (*As she is going*) Learn to like the North. It will reward you.

ELIZABETH (*at the door*) I shall try. The saints go with your Grace till we meet again. (*Rising from her deep obeisance; in her normal conversational tones*) And if you are kind to Henry Tudor, I shall be furious!

RICHARD (*smiling at her*) I assure you, there are limits to my goodheartedness.

[*He stands pouring the little heap of chain from one hand to the other, pleased with her gesture. Then, remembering why it was given, his hand goes over his face in a movement of unutterable weariness.*]

CURTAIN

SCENE 5

The interior of the KING'S *tent near Market Bosworth, in the early morning of August 22nd, 1485. It is not yet daylight, but in the grey half-light outside one can see, through the open door of the tent up-stage, the distant curve of the land against the sky. Inside the tent a single candle is burning. R., inside the door is a camp bed, and below it a folding table bearing the candle, a book, a rosary, and some toilet articles. Between the bed and the table is a silver basin on a stand, with a jug of water beside it on the ground. On the other side of the tent, L., is a long table on which the ready-burnished armour is set out—the famous and beautiful suit which the* KING *had worn at Tewkesbury.*

RICHARD *is lying on the cot, in hose and shirt, wide awake, a rumpled blanket over his knees; it has been a very warm night.*

Across the entrance to the tent, his servant, PAYNTER, *is lying asleep.*

Very far away a cock crows. The grey light outside is momentarily growing clearer. RICHARD *swings his feet to the ground, and sits on the edge of his cot with his head propped wearily in his hands.*

Someone at a little distance challenges a newcomer. One cannot hear the answer, but presently the challenge is repeated by a nearer guard, and one can hear the murmur of an answer. At the sound of approaching footsteps PAYNTER *leaps to his feet and stands protecting the tent entrance.*

LOVELL (*outside*) It is all right, Paynter.

RICHARD Come in, Francis; I am not asleep.

LOVELL (*coming in*) I thought I saw a light.

RICHARD Yes. You are early astir.

LOVELL (*who is in good spirits though he has had no sleep*) On the contrary, I am late abroad.

RICHARD Have you had no rest at all?

LOVELL I have been doling out arms to Brackenbury's crowd. They didn't arrive till midnight, and then they were scattered over half a county.

RICHARD What are they like?

LOVELL At a guess, I should say that a battle-axe would bounce off them.

RICHARD Tough?

LOVELL Beautiful! We have a grand army, Richard. What a lesson that Welshman is going to get. (*With a glance for the dawn outside*) It is going to be a wonderful day, too; blazing hot. I shall sweat myself down to the bones in armour on a day like this. (*Noticing* RICHARD's *face*) You look tired, sir.

RICHARD I did not sleep well.

LOVELL You will sleep tonight.

RICHARD Yes. (*He rises and pours water into the basin*)

LOVELL Your last worry over.

RICHARD (*to* PAYNTER, *who has come in at the sound of washing*) I don't need you, Paynter. (PAYNTER *retires to the tent door*)

LOVELL (*as* RICHARD *begins to dash the cold water on face and neck*) Paynter has made a lovely job of your armour. (*He admires the separate pieces set out on the table*) Are you leaving the crown on your helm? (*He refers to the thin gold circlet that adorns the steel headpiece*)

RICHARD Do you suggest that a King of England should go into battle disguised?

LOVELL No. But it is very conspicuous.

RICHARD I hope so. I want Henry to know me when we meet.

LOVELL You don't imagine that Henry is going to fight, do you?

RICHARD What then?

LOVELL Sit on a hillock and halloo on his troops, if I know anything about him.

RICHARD Then we must seek out the hillock. (*Against his will, standing still for a moment with the towel in his hand*) I dreamed last night that I saw that crown hanging in a hawthorn bush.

LOVELL (*after a moment's astonished pause, with deliberate lightness*) I once dreamed that I was a leopard with a pink frill round my neck.

RICHARD Yes. Yes, it is folly. (*He turns to look for the leather jerkin that he will wear under his armour.* LOVELL *picks it up and helps him to put it on, casting anxious glances at him the while*)

LOVELL (*helping with the coat*) Are you worried about something, sir?

RICHARD Yes.

LOVELL What are you afraid of?

RICHARD (*bitter at his own weakness*) The invisible. I keep wondering who is going to be the traitor this time.

LOVELL All your life you have met treachery, and it has not dismayed you before.

RICHARD No. I think my mind is sick.

LOVELL If you are in doubt, sir, we can wait until the rest come up. There are thousands more to come—Scrope, Dacre, Ogle, Greystoke, Conyers, Strickland, Musgrave, Plumpton, Constable, five thousand at least.

RICHARD We have more than enough now.

LOVELL There is no shame in being cautious.

RICHARD No. But there is shame in being afraid of shadows. If I am to spend the rest of my life being ruled by what may not happen, I might as well be dead.

LOVELL And what of England?

RICHARD (*who has sat down on the stool by the table, his jerkin still open, and picked up a comb for his hair; turning with a lightening of his face that is half a smile*) I think sometimes that it is presumptuous to consider that England needs any of us. She is greater and wiser than all of us put together. And no misrule of petty men or battling of giants can keep her from her destiny. At least I shall have English earth to lie in. Or would they let me lie?

A man who is both Tudor and Lancaster might have odd ideas about that. (*He picks up from among the toilet things* ELIZABETH's *token on its chain*)

LOVELL Tonight you will lie in six feet of down at the White Boar in Leicester.

RICHARD Elizabeth's token. (*He hangs it round his neck and buttons up his jerkin*) She is a sweet child. It occurs to me that Henry would never marry Elizabeth without declaring her legitimate.

LOVELL Of course not. He wants a claim on the throne.

RICHARD But that would automatically make those two boys legitimate. I wonder how Henry would deal with so awkward a situation.

LOVELL As any Tudor would deal with it.

RICHARD God forbid! Yes, it would be a pretty dilemma for Henry.

LOVELL He has a prettier one in front of him at this moment. I don't suppose he has any thought to spare for marriage.

RICHARD Have you noticed that Stanley has drawn up his men half-way between our camp and theirs?

LOVELL Is Stanley a traitor?

RICHARD I don't think he has made up his mind yet. He has a family to think of, and must not take chances.

LOVELL You have been too generous to men like Stanley.

RICHARD All my life I have believed that if you appeal to the good in men, the good will answer. I may have been wrong. I have been hard put to it lately to go on believing it. (*Picking up the book from the table*) If we fail today, do you know what my portion will be? Eternal infamy.

LOVELL (*puzzled*) Infamy?

RICHARD Men have found out how to perpetuate their lies. Can you imagine what Morton, writing for Henry, would make of me? (*He gets up from the table preparatory to leaving*)

LOVELL If Morton were not a priest, what I should make of him!

RICHARD (*smiling*) You would have my blessing. (*A distant trumpet sounds*) The camp is waking. Are you on the way to your own men?

LOVELL No, I am going to inspect Norfolk's artillery. It would be as well to know whether it is more likely to kill our troops or theirs.

RICHARD It would indeed. (*He turns to the table, where the crucifix belonging to the rosary is propped upright, kneels, speaks a whispered sentence of prayer, crosses himself, and rises)* We shall meet, then, at Sutton Fields. About eight o'clock. I shall speak to the whole army then. Paynter, I shall put on harness at the Bradshaws. Take it over there in about an hour. Go and say to Watkin that my charger is to be taken there too.

[PAYNTER *disappears.*]

LOVELL (*taking leave of* RICHARD *inside the tent door*) If I do not see you alone again, sir: for the sake of those who love you do not be rash.

RICHARD Would you love me as well if I sat on a hillock?

LOVELL No. But there is such a thing as honourable retreat.

RICHARD There is such a thing as surrender. No, Francis. If I die today, I die facing the enemy and King of England. And nothing they may write about me in books can ever alter that. Till eight o'clock.

[*Exit R. followed by* LOVELL *to the L.*]

[*The sky grows brighter as the sun nears its rising. A trumpet sounds far away. A second sounds, still far but nearer. A third still nearer. As a fourth begins its call a hundred yards from the tent, loud and clear and courageous,*

THE CURTAIN FALLS

NOTES

BUT for the treachery of one man (Stanley) Richard III would have won the battle of Bosworth; and the venomous hunch-backed monster who appears in the pages of Tudor historians would never have been invented. But Bosworth was lost; the dead body of the young King was flung, stripped and bleeding, over the back of a pony and carried from the field by the victors; and into the place of the Plantagenets came a Welsh nobody who by the aid of French money and native impudence had got himself a crown.

Since Henry Tudor achieved by conquest what he could not claim by birth (he was a great-grandson of an illegitimate son of John of Gaunt) it was desirable that the man he supplanted should be represented as unworthy to reign: a tyrant, a usurper, and if possible a murderer. Henry had several paid historians, but the most effective was Richard's greatest enemy, John Morton; whom Henry made

Archbishop of Canterbury. Morton either wrote or supplied the story now known as Sir Thomas More's, because it was found among More's papers. The story is detailed and dramatic, and although it is also very silly it achieved both credence and immortality; the first because Sir Thomas More's was a name to reverence, and the second because William Shakespeare used it as material for a play. And so the best of all the York princes became the villain of Tudor tradition.

As soon as the Tudors had gone, and it was once more safe to publish an opinion, the first doubt of this monstrous figure was expressed (by Buck, in the reign of James I). The caricature had been too gross; it offended the intelligence of thinking men. There was no written history of Richard's day with which to refute the Tudor historians, so the doubters had in their search for fact to go back to the records. The truth was to be found not in any man's account of contemporary events, partial and biassed as that must always be, but in the unconsidered mass of contemporary documents: Parliamentary Rolls, patents, proclamations, household accounts, and private letters. And out of these mute witnesses the truth was rebuilt. But alas! For a hundred and fifty years the Tudor myth had stood unchallenged, and to this day, in spite of Horace Walpole and all his colleagues in the work of vindication, nine persons out of ten not only think of Richard III as a hunch-backed murderer but are unaware that there is any evidence to the contrary.

To those who would inquire for themselves, it is suggested that as a beginning they should read not a defence of Richard, but the account of one of his detractors. James Gairdner, the historian, obstinately believed Richard to be a tyrant and a murderer; but being a writer honest, learned, and to the best of his ability impartial, it was not in him to suppress facts. The spectacle of Mr Gairdner trying to make his facts fit his theory will be found not only entertaining but more convincing than any defence of Richard could ever be.

Meanwhile here, in short, are the calumnies published about Richard III, and an outline of the answers to them:

(1) *That he was Hump-backed*

No contemporary mentions this except Morton; and none of the many portraits of Richard show such a deformity. Had Richard been obviously deformed, the many commentators on the extreme beauty of his brother Edward IV could hardly have failed to point the contrast.

(2) *That he had a Withered Arm*

This, too, is contributed only by Morton. A man whose prowess in battle was famous was not likely to be one-armed. If he had been, the oddness and gallantry of it would have made the defect famous.

(3) *That Richard, at the Age of Eighteen, Helped to Kill Edward of Lancaster (Henry IV's Son) in Cold Blood after the Battle of Tewkesbury*

Contemporary writers, of all complexions, are unanimous in saying that Edward was killed in the battle. Fabyan, writing for Henry VII, was the first to say that Edward survived the fight; he records that the youth was brought before Edward IV, hit in the face by the King, and despatched by the King's servants. Each of the following Tudor chroniclers added a piece to the story. Virgil, full of Italian imagination, added a Borgian scene wherein the youth, having been struck by the King, was finished off by Gloucester, Clarence, and Hastings. Hall repeated the story and added Dorset to the assassins. Holinshed reported that it was Gloucester who struck the first blow. So the story grew; and in its present form may be found in any history book.

(4) *That Richard Murdered the Invalid and Half-witted Henry VI in the Tower, to Rid his Brother Edward IV of an Encumbrance*

Richard, fresh from the military glory he had won at Tewkesbury, and due to go out next day on active service again, had only one night in London: the 21st of May. Knowing this, the Tudor historians gave the date of Henry's death as the 21st. Actually he died on the 23rd. Richard was then in Sandwich.

(5) *That Richard Murdered his Brother Clarence in the Tower*

Shakespeare is largely responsible for this calumny. Not even Tudor historians thought of that one. Clarence, impeached before Parliament and condemned to death for treason, met a mysterious end. 'Drowned in a butt of malmsey' was no doubt merely a cockney comment on a drunkard's end. Even Morton admits that Richard interceded with Edward for his brother.

(6) *That Richard Usurped the Throne*

When Edward IV died Richard was in the north of England. His first act was to attend a requiem mass for his brother at York and to call upon the nobility and gentry of the neighbourhood to swear allegiance to his young nephew. Not till then did he set out at a leisurely pace for London.

Before young Edward could be crowned, Bishop Stillington of Bath confessed that he had witnessed a marriage contract between Edward IV and Lady Eleanor Butler before the King's marriage to the Queen, and that Edward's children were therefore illegitimate. He brought his proofs before Parliament, and they expressed themselves as satisfied. (Knowing Edward's history, they were probably not unbearably surprised.) An Act of Parliament, known as Titulus Regius, recorded these events and gave Richard's title to the throne. Richard succeeded without opposition, and to the relief of everyone who had nothing to gain from a minority. His Coronation was the best attended on record.

When Henry Tudor came to power he ordered that this Act should be repealed without quoting the preamble, that it should be destroyed, and that no one should keep a copy of it on pain of fine or imprisonment during his pleasure.

The Tudor historians were now free to do their worst. They recorded that Richard based his claim to the throne on the fact that his two elder brothers, Edward and Clarence, were bastard; and that he caused his mother's shame to be preached in a sermon at Paul's Cross. (That he was living in his mother's house at the time did not daunt the Tudor fable-makers.) And on a secondary claim that a pre-contract on Edward's part with a courtesan called Elizabeth Lucy, invalidated his marriage. (Of which contract, they could point out, there was of course no tittle of evidence.)

This version of the story was current for a century and a quarter (and is still current). Then Sir George Buck discovered in a contemporary manuscript written at Croyland Abbey an account of the real tenor of the Act. But it was as long again before the question was settled for ever by the turning up of the undestroyed Roll of Parliament in the Tower records.

(7) *That Richard was a Tyrant*

This is so wide an accusation that only a small sample of facts can be adduced in answer:

He was popular on his accession, and greatly loved in the North where his home was.

His only Parliament was the most liberal and progressive since the time of Henry III.

Lord Hastings was not rushed from the council chamber and beheaded on a log before dinner, as Morton records; he was executed a week later after trial.

Lord Rivers, who was beheaded for treason, was not 'executed without the formality of a trial'; he was tried by his peers, and bore Richard so little grudge that he appointed him supervisor of his will.

He forgave Henry Tudor's mother her initial plotting, and so left her free to plot his downfall.

He forgave Henry Tudor's step-father, Lord Stanley, his share in the Hastings conspiracy, entrusted him with great responsibility, and so left him free to play the traitor at Bosworth.

Instead of sequestering the goods of traitors, it was his habit to provide generously for their dependants.

Jane Shore was imprisoned for her part in the Hastings conspiracy against Richard, but his Solicitor-General fell in love with her, and Richard released her and, more in sorrow than in anger, consented to the marriage. (The letter written by Richard on this occasion is still extant.)

(8) *That Richard Murdered his Nephews in the Tower*

There is no contemporary accusation of any such murder.

The boy's mother remained on friendly terms with Richard till his death, and her daughters took part in palace festivities. She wrote to her son by her first marriage, Dorset, to return from France and make his peace with Richard, and Dorset actually set out.

There was no motive. Had Richard caused the boys to be killed, there would still remain their five sisters and two boy cousins to provide possible rallying points for rebellion.

There was no need. The boys, since their illegitimacy had been proved, had lapsed into obscurity, and there is no evidence of any movement in their favour. On the contrary, at the time of the supposed murder, Richard was being given every evidence of his wide popularity.

Henry VII on his accession accused Richard in an Act of Attainder of tyranny, but *did not mention murder*. It is inconceivable that if Henry, who obtained possession of the Tower on his arrival in London, had found the boys to be missing, he would not have published the fact and accused Richard. The only possible conclusion is that the boys were not missing.

The Case Against Henry VII

Henry VII, in order to strengthen his hold on the crown, married the eldest of Edward IV's daughters, Elizabeth. By destroying the Parliamentary Roll with the reasons for Richard's succession, he destroyed the evidence of her illegitimacy. But by legitimising her, he automatically made the two boys, her brothers, heirs to the throne before her.

Now it was Henry's settled and considered policy to get rid of all possible Plantagenet heirs, except the one he married, by a process of legal murder, and he did so. He himself 'took care of' the boy princes' two cousins, Warwick and John of Gloucester; and his son, Henry VIII, made a clean sweep of the rest: Suffolk, Exeter, Surrey, Buckingham, and the Countess of Salisbury. The Tudors were taking no chances.

But it is not possible to bring a capital charge against a couple of children.

When Henry VII had been nearly a year on the throne, however, two things happened almost simultaneously. A report was published that Richard III had put the boys to death secretly; and the boys' mother was deprived of her lands and possessions and sent to the nunnery of Bermondsey. 'Whereat was much wondering.' Nine months later the boys' sister was at last crowned Queen.

Nearly twenty years after the first 'official' account of the young princes' end was given to the world. A man named Tyrrel, who had received many favours from Henry, was executed for being too friendly to the imprisoned Suffolk. After his death, his 'confession' that he had murdered the princes at Richard's instigation was made public. Its substance is recounted by Morton in More's History. The account is a mass of absurdities, inaccuracies, and contradictions. (An analysis of it will be found in Sir Clement Markham's *Richard III*.)

Note of Interest

On June 16th, 1486 (the first year of Henry VII's reign), Sir James Tyrrel received a general pardon. There was nothing unusual in that; it was the common practice to obtain such a thing from time to time; on entering new service, or otherwise coming to the end of or beginning a new phase. On July 16th, 1486, Sir James Tyrrel received a second general pardon. That was far from usual. What had Sir James done during that month?

And as a pendant, for further speculation: the boys' mother, who had been in Winchester with her daughter (the heir to the Tudor throne was born there in September), came back to London in the late autumn. In February she was shut up in a nunnery for the rest of her life. (The mother of ' the princes in the Tower ', who had lived free and happy under the rule of Richard III.)

GORDON DAVIOT

The Privateer

Published 1952   10s 6d

This was Gordon Daviot's first straight novel since that divergence into the theatre world which resulted in *Richard of Bordeaux* and other famous plays. It is a full-blooded, exciting and authenticated story of one of England's greatest adventurers.

Henry Morgan, gentleman and buccaneer, wrote his name from one end of the Caribbean to the other—not only across a thousand miles of sea but across three centuries, so that that name is as much a household word today as it was in the years of his triumph. And as long as men admire courage, and resource, and an impudent gaiety in the face of odds, that name will live.

"An historical novel of high quality based on an intelligent reading of the life of Henry Morgan."   T. W. HUTTON, *Birmingham Post*

"It is written in English with the sense of style one expects from the author of *Richard of Bordeaux*."   *John o'London's Weekly*

"I enjoyed this book mightily."
VERNON FANE, *The Sphere*

The novels of

JOSEPHINE TEY

The Man in the Queue

Reprinted 1953 *9s 6d*

First published over twenty-five years ago (under the author's other pen-name Gordon Daviot) *The Man in the Queue* escaped the eye of many a connoisseur. In this novel Detective-Inspector Alan Grant solves his first case.

" *The Man in the Queue* is an unknown, murdered in the pit queue on the last night of a London musical comedy. Inspector Alan Grant, my favourite detective of all time, painstakingly, fascinatingly identifies the body, then chases suspects up to the Highlands of Scotland and all round the town."

NANCY SPAIN, *Daily Express*

A Shilling for Candles

Reprinted 1953 *9s 6d*

Originally published in 1936 *A Shilling for Candles* started Josephine Tey on what was to be a brilliant though sadly short career as a writer of the highest class of detective fiction.

" Witty, ingenious, and makes one regret more than ever that there will be no more from the same pen." VERNON FANE, *The Sphere*

JOSEPHINE TEY

Miss Pym Disposes

Reprinting 1954   6s 6d

The scene is a young ladies' physical training college where Miss Pym, the author of a best-seller on psychology, discovers that the death of one of the students is not the accident it is supposed.

"A crime story of masterly elegance."
PAMELA HANSFORD JOHNSON, *John o'London*

The Franchise Affair

Cheap edition   5s

"This is the kind of mystery novel I, not by nature a crime-story addict, really enjoy; soundly made, well written and lighting the atmosphere of suspense with gaiety."
TULLIS CLARE, *Time and Tide*

"I applaud the telling of this tale, the working up of suspicion (at times Marion and her mother seem capable of anything), and the poisonous atmosphere of small-town gossip."
DANIEL GEORGE

Brat Farrar

Reprinted 1953   9s 6d

"Suspense is achieved by unexpected twists and extremely competent story-telling . . . credible and convincing."
MARGHANITA LASKI, *The Spectator*

"One of the most ingenious books that I have read for years. . . . A first-rate thriller . . . but it is also a novel worthy of the word."
The Church Times

JOSEPHINE TEY

To Love and be Wise

Reprinted 1953   9s 6d

"Miss Josephine Tey enjoys a category to herself. . . . The plot of *To Love and be Wise* centres round a fascinating impostor; but the nature of the deception is too good to give away. Admirers of *Brat Farrar* and *The Franchise Affair* will know what to expect and will not be disappointed."

RALPH PARTRIDGE, *The New Statesman*

The Daughter of Time

Reprinted 1953   10s 6d

"Most people will find *The Daughter of Time* as interesting and enjoyable a book as they will meet in a month of Sundays."

MARGHANITA LASKI, *The Observer*

"A detective story with a very considerable difference. Ingenious, stimulating and very enjoyable."   J. W. LAMBERT, *The Sunday Times*

The Singing Sands

Reprinted 1953   10s 6d

"There are not many 'detective story' writers whom I can read with so much pleasure, not only for the ingenuity of the detection but also for the writing itself."   HOWARD SPRING

"Really first class . . . a continual delight."

The Times Literary Supplement

"An adventure with company it is a privilege to meet."   *Sunday Times*